Complex Predicates in South Asian Languages

Complex Predicates in South Asian Languages

Manindra K. Verma
Editor

Manohar
1993

ISBN: 81-7304-043-5

First Published 1993

Published by
Ajay Kumar Jain
Manohar Publishers & Distributors
2/6, Ansari Road, Daryaganj
New Delhi - 110 002

Printed at
Elegant Printers
A-38/2, Maya Puri, Phase-I
New Delhi-110 064

PREFACE

The existence of multiple word verbal expressions has been noted for South Asian languages for quite some time, particularly by early European scholars. Work on individual languages, some more detailed than others, also has been undertaken by various scholars from time to time. However, not until the SALA Conference hosted by the University of Wisconsin-Madison in the summer of 1989 was any attempt made to bring together the data and descriptive facts from various South Asian languages to help provide a comparative picture as well as an overall theoretical perspective. The relatively recent theoretical interest in "complex predicates" as exemplified in such constructions as "light" verbs or "serial" verbs, etc. in genetically diverse languages of the world provided an impetus to hold such a conference designed to explore the nature of this structural phenomenon in the languages of South Asia where complex predicates of various types -- phrasally complex but functionally unitary or morphophonologically unitary but syntactically complex -- have been a readily identifiable feature that cuts across genetic and regional boundaries and contributes to the notion of South Asia as a linguistic area.

Numerous colleagues helped make this conference a big success. The idea of holding a conference on such a theme developed out of my discussions with K.P. Mohanan and Alice Davison, with a great deal of encouragement from the colleagues at the University of Illinois at Urbana. The Office of International Studies and the Anonymous Funds Committee of the University of Wisconsin were generous with their financial support. The Department of Linguistics at Wisconsin, and particularly Jacquelyn Drummy, provided a great deal of administrative support in the publication of the volume. Professor Peter Schreiber's editorial suggestions were invaluable. Laurie See's meticulous attention to detail in the preparation of the camera-ready copy of the manuscript by retyping just about every article for the uniformity of the font and ensuring painstaking adherence to editorial directives in regard to the format of the examples could be accomplished only with the academic interest she had in the project.

Finally, I must acknowledge that Mr. Ramesh Jain's enthusiasm and patience in publishing the volume is what would make any author or editor thank God for the existence of such publishing firms as Manohar. The somewhat belated appearance of the volume could be blamed on my numerous professional commitments if not also on my somewhat indifferent health during the preparation of the final manuscript.

Manindra K. Verma
University of Wisconsin

INTRODUCTION

Manindra K. Verma

The term ''complex predicate'' may be used as an umbrella term to designate a variety of forms/ expressions.* The core notion is exemplified by the merger of two or more morphological entities to form an expression with a single complex argument structure. The term is usually employed to refer to constructions whose constitutive pieces can appear separately in phrase structure. But it has also been used to refer to the merger of two or more morphological entities resulting in a morphonologically integrated (though syntactically not atomic) entity. An example of the former would be putative ''conjunct verb'' of Hindi, very comparable to the Noun + Light Verb construction in a language like Japanese; an example of the latter would be the morphological causative in Hindi and Japanese, or, for that matter the passive in Nepali. In fact, prima facie, there is no reason to leave out such constructions as the ''compound verb'' or the conjunctive participial verb of South Asian languages or the various kinds of serial verbs found in many languages of the world. An interesting question that this phenomenon raises and that needs to be addressed is whether such a merger take place at some level of argument structure in the lexicon itself or at some level of syntax. A proper analysis of complex predicates, thus, may furnish insight into the understanding of lexical-syntactic relations.

The term ''predicate'' itself is perhaps the cause of the various senses that the expression ''complex predicates'' has taken on. ''Predicate'' is a part of the vocabulary of logic as well as grammar, but the terms in these two disciplines have somewhat different denotations. In logic, a predicate refers essentially to a function that maps ordered n-tuples of arguments to truth values; more informally, we can think of logical predicates as expressing either relations between arguments or properties of arguments. In grammar, however, the term has various applications, none of which has fully mirrored the logical sense. The so-called ''complete predicate'' of traditional grammar (corresponding roughly to the VP in modern generative treatments) was the constituent that expressed the assertion made of or about the subject. The term was further extended to other constituents providing the major content of the predication, illustrated by terms like ''predicate adjective'' and so on. More recently, the term has also been extended to various constructions such as the objective complement which is regarded as a second predicate within the sentence; similarly, subjective complements (as in e.g., *John came home drunk.*) have also been regarded as secondary predicates. Even nouns have been described as predicates based on their argument structure, as in the *enemy's destruction of the city*.

There are further consequences of these obscurities in the use of the term ''predicates''. For example, the notions of functional word and categorial word may well not converge. Furthermore, in so far as the defining characteristics of the N+V type complex predicates is that the main semantic content of the predicate is provided not by the verb but by the nominal, it forces a rethinking of the notion ''predicate'' itself. For South Asian languages at least, the notion ''predicate'' may have to be

* This piece on Introduction to the notion of Complex Predicates has benefited substantively from the advice and phraseology provided by Peter schreiber.

expanded. At the very least, the notion "predicate" may have to be treated as independent of categoriality. For example, normally, only verbs and adjectives are treated as predicates, but for South Asian languages, the category Noun is also a potential candidate for Predicate function. This is very interesting in view of the fact that in natural languages (even in terms of feature combination or feature decomposition) there is supposed to be a sharp disjunction between Noun and Verb. Logically, then, one would expect that entities expressed by these categories will not share any grammatically significant behaviors. But, then, the N+V type complex predicates, where the N has the real predicate function, would seem inconsistent with our usual expectations.

There are other interesting questions, too. How does one identify a complex verb? Which concatenations are simple sequences and which ones are complex predicates? One could employ the test of certain grammatical properties, but which ones? And are these relevant grammatical properties all language specific or are they universal? Then, again, are all complex predicates equally complex or can they be graded in some sort of a relationship of 'cline' involving complete collapsing and partial collapsing. There can be further questions. How do the elements comprising complex predicates behave in regard to agreement or case marking or even specificity? We hope the article in this volume would provide food for thought in these regards if not definitive answers.

CONTENTS

CONTENTS

CAUSAL CHAINS AND COMPOUND VERBS

Elena Bashir
The University of Michigan

1. INTRODUCTION

Characterization of the distribution of the [C]ompound [V]erb continues to be one of the most interesting problems in the study of South Asian languages. COMPOUND VERB refers to a complex verb form consisting of a main verb in its root (or conjunctive participial) form plus a secondary VECTOR verb which bears tense and agreement morphology. These vectors belong to a small class, typically motion verbs like *go*, *come*, *sit* or basic transitives with a transparent motional component, e.g. *give*, *take*, *leave*, *put*.[1] Forms like Urdu and Hindi ***aa jaanaa*** 'arrive' (<'come go'), ***kar lenaa*** 'do' (<'do take'), ***kar denaa*** 'do' (<'do give') are prototypical examples of the CV.

The thesis advanced in this paper has its origins in an interaction among three sets of ideas: (i) my observations on the functioning of the (incipient) CV system in the NWIA language Kalasha; (ii) earlier work on the CV in Hindi and Urdu (most notably Hook 1974), and (iii) the model of an event schema as a causal chain developed by DeLancey in several articles on Tibetan (DeLancey 1981, 1982, 1984, 1985a, b, and 1986). Data from and analysis of Tamil are also adduced in support of the argument.

In this paper, I propose that one of the functions of the CV in Urdu and Hindi is to grammaticize categories which involve the KNOWLEDGE AND BELIEF STATE OF THE SPEAKER. These epistemological categories are involved in the evidentiality-inferentiality systems of languages like Tibetan and Kalasha, and, I propose, are also expressed by the CV/SV opposition in Hindi and Urdu.

The paper also argues that the patterns of occurrence of the CV as opposed to the SV in Hindi and Urdu, as well as in Kalasha, can be accounted for in substantial measure by reference to the model of an event schema as a causal chain. Many of the distributional patterns of the CV and the SV and the specific semantic effects of various CV vectors identified in earlier work are shown to follow from this explanation.[2]

2. COMPOUND VERBS IN KALASHA

In the NWIA language Kalasha, I have so far identified three verbs which function as vectors in a CV construction. These are ***parik*** 'go', ***thek*** 'put', and ***dek*** 'give'; they are illustrated in examples **[1]** - **[3]**.[3]

[1] ***baaba´-a cei uzuki´-par-au´*** (p. 220)
sister-OBL tea spill -go(PST-A)-3s
'Sister's tea spilled.'

[2] *su´da śurua´i-atha´-i* (p. 220)
baby fall-Cs-put(PST-A)-2s
'You let the baby fall.'

[3] *mai hat´ya ek krom kar´i-de* (p. 221)
I(OBL) for one work do(IMP2s)-give(IMP2s)
'Do a job for me!'

The vector ***parik*** 'go' combines with intransitives, ***thek*** 'put' with transitives, and ***dek*** 'give' occurs with both transitives and intransitives.[4]

The semantic function of ***parik´*** 'go' involves three components of meaning: finality, undesirable outcome, and the property of being (potentially) anticipated. In every example of 'go' compounds in my corpus except one, the outcome or event reported is a negatively valued one. Compounds with ***parik*** 'go' occur with concepts of burning (person, bread), slipping, drying up (of crops), breaking into pieces, getting crushed, boiling over, spilling, rolling away, falling down (wall), tearing (cloth), being extinguished, getting exhausted, falling out (hair), getting cold (tea). Sentences **[4]** and **[5]** are typical exemplars.

[4] *au´ du´i-ga´la atra´ ko ne paś´-is* (p. 242)
bread burn-go(PST-I)-3s there why not see(P/F-NS)2s
'The bread burned over there; why don't you watch (it)?'

[5] *paTĩgely´-a uk dyek ne haw´-au Su´Si-parin´-dai* (p. 243)
tomatoes-LOC water put not become(PST-A)-3s dry go(P/F-S)-3s
'The tomatoes didn't get watered; they are drying up.'

The second semantic component of these verbs is a sense of finality or completeness of the action; **[6]** illustrates this.

[6] *uTi´ki tyai uTi´ki tyai*[5] *sas lu´i thi ga´la* (p. 243)
jump beat(CP) jump beat(CP) become exhausted-(PST-I)-3s
'Jumping and jumping he got exhausted.'

The third component of meaning common to all of these usages is that they all are uttered from the point of view of a PREPARED MIND. I use this term with specific intent to contrast it with the term UNPREPARED MIND introduced by Slobin and Aksu (1982) in their discussion of the Turkish evidential particle ***miş***. A mind unprepared with reference to a particular event has no 'premonitory consciousness' of that event, and the event is not 'consonant with the current state of mind of the speaker' (p. 196). Conversely, the prepared mind is one into which the (possibility of) the event (to be) reported is already integrated, either by virtue of its being anticipated, feared, desired, ordered ..., or by virtue of its being a natural, foreseeable consequence of a circumstance or action already realized.

Now let us re-examine sentences **[4]** - **[6]** in the light of this concept. In **[4]** the expectation is that if one doesn't keep an eye on the bread while it is cooking, it is going to burn. Similarly in **[5]** if tomato plants are not watered, one can predict that they will dry up. Or, in **[6]**, as a result of jumping and jumping (trying to catch a sunbeam), the subject of this sentence becomes exhausted. Informants indicate that sentences like ***tu du´i paris´*** 'you will get burned' or **[7]** are uttered as warnings.

[7] *aya´ iślye´gi-par-is´* (p. 245)
here slip -go(P/F-NS)-2s
'You will slip here!'

A warning is an admonition to avoid an anticipated undesirable event -- precisely the semantics of the prepared mind that we are discussing.

In Kalasha, the categories of evidentiality/inferentiality are multiply grammaticized. In the past tenses, verbs are obligatorily specified for a contrast which I have called 'actual vs. inferential' (Bashir 1988). In the non-past tenses, the form ***hula***, which is the past inferential third person singular form of ***hik*** 'become', functions in a way very similar to ***miş*** in Turkish, that is to signal the 'unprepared mind'. Specific shades of meaning can range from simply new, unassimilated information to mild surprise, regret, or annoyance. Its function is illustrated in **[8]**.

[8] **[a]** **new information**
se peśaur jel-una a´-au hu´la (p. 74)
he P. jail-LOC be-(P/F)-3s ***hula***
'He is in jail in Peshawar.' (I just found this out.)

[b] **regret**
a galyati´ kai a´-am hu´la (p. 74)
I(NOM) mistake do(P PERF)-1s ***hula***
'I have made a mistake (and just realized it now).'

[c] **annoyance**
ko DuD´-iu hula (p. 74)
why sleep(P/F-NS)-3s ***hula***
'Why is (s)he sleeping?' (implied that person should not be sleeping at this time)

It is significant that compounds with ***parik´*** 'go' do not combine with ***hula***, which indicates newly acquired, as yet unintegrated information. (See **[9]**.)

[9] ***se iślyegi-par-iu´ (*hu´la)*** (p. 235)
he slip-go(P/F-NS)-3s
'He will fall.'

The meanings of these two elements are incompatible, ***hu´la*** signalling the unprepared mind and ***parik´*** the prepared mind.[6]

Now let us turn to the semantic function of compounds in ***thek*** 'put, keep'. There appear to be two senses that can develop from compounds in 'put'. The first is of emphasis on the activity itself, or on the completeness of an action, as in **[10]**, reading **[b]**.

[10] ***a kagas´ niveś´i-athe-s´*** (p. 246)
I letter write -put(PST-A)-1s
[a] 'I wrote the letter and put it down.'
[b] 'I HAVE (really, completely) written the letter.'

The second sense of the CV is more abstract. Consider the CV sentence in **[11a]**, for which the SV version is **[11b]**.

[11] **[a]** ***a palow´ brīk´i-athe-s´*** (p. 246)
I apples sell -put(PST-A)-1s
'I sold the apples (mistakenly).'

[b] ***a palow´ abrīk´-is*** (p. 246)
I apples sell(PST-A)-1s
'I sold the apples.'

Given the nature of the act of selling, that is of effecting a (permanent) separation between the agent and the object of selling, ***thek*** in such contexts could not possibly have its literal meaning of 'put, keep'. What it does express is a sense of REGRET, which is based on undesirable consequences learned of, or a situation which developed, AFTER the act of selling. For example, sentence **[11a]** might be uttered if the speaker later developed a desire to eat apples and then recalled that he had sold them. He realizes after the fact that selling the apples turned out to be a mistake.

The semantic contribution of ***parik´*** is to indicate an undesirable consequence impinging on a mind prepared by foresight, while ***thek*** indicates a consequence perceived as negative by hindsight.

parik	'go'	[prepared mind]	[negative consequence]
thek	'put'	[unprepared mind]	[negative consequence]

Thus in Kalasha the formal mechanism of the CV participates in the expression of that parameter -- actual vs. inferential, prepared vs. unprepared mind -- which is so saliently grammaticized in this language. Despite the fact that this opposition is already obligatorily expressed in basic verb morphology, it finds yet another reflection in the CV system.

3. THE CV AND THE PREPARED MIND IN HINDI AND TAMIL

3.1. **Hook's work on the CV in Hindi.** Hook (1976) summarizes his main conclusions about the function of the Hindi compound verb. (1) 'The compound verb expresses perfective aspect and is the marked member of a privative opposition perfective-imperfective.' (147) (2) 'One of the functions of the compound verb is to express the completion of one action relative to the completion of another ... If the structure of a discourse is such that the time of occurrence of one action is specifically contrasted with that of another action, then the verb expressing the earlier action must be compound and the verb expressing the later action must be simple.' (150) (3) 'If a verb is stative, then it is non-compound.' (152) (4) 'If there is no possibility of an action of event's being anticipated, it is expressed with a non-compound verb.' (153)

The last mentioned is perhaps Hook's most striking finding. It is illustrated in his 'Columbus discovered America' and 'mouse in the milk' examples, shown here as **[12a]** and **[b]**, in which the CV is not possible.

[12] [a] ***kalambas ne amriikaa kii khoj kii /*kar dii /*kar lii***
Columbus-ERG A. of discovery(fs) do(PST)-fs/do-give(PST)/*do-take(PST)
'Columbus discovered America.' (Hook 1974:240)

[b] ***kal duudh mẽ cuuhaa milaa*** (Hook 1976:153)
yesterday milk in mouse meet-DES
'Yesterday we found a mouse in the milk.'

In **[12a]** the CV can not occur; its use would suggest that Columbus knew about the existence of America before discovering it. In **[12b]**the CV (***mil gayaa***) would suggest that the speaker expected or feared finding a mouse in his milk. Hook states: 'In cases where the performance of an action is completely unforeseen by the speaker he may not use the compound verb,' (1974:248), whereas the CV presupposes that the action is already in some sense pre-existing in the mind of the speaker.

> Of all these conditions, the most intriguing ... the one by virtue of which the aspectual system of Hindi may very well depart from that of Slavic is that considered under the rubric 'lack of prior knowledge'. It is this condition (for simple manifestations of the verb) that suggests that the use of the compound verb depends on more than how the contour of the action is perceived by the speaker. It suggests he must also have presupposed or pre-entertained the existence of the entities his utterance describes. (1974:316)

Later (1976:154-5), Hook reaffirms the importance of this result:

> I find nothing in the conception of the compound verb as the marked expression of perfective aspect or as the expression of anteriority in a purwaapar contrast that will explain the restriction discussed here.

This 'no prior knowledge' condition is clearly related to the semantics of the unprepared mind encoded by Turkish ***miş*** or Kalasha ***hula***. It is this observation which is one of the starting points of this paper.

3.2. **The Tamil CV and the prepared mind.** Tamil also has a highly ramified system of CV's, which convey a variety of specific meanings including denoting resultativity, perfect, aspect, status, voice, and inferentiality (Fedson 1981:iv-v). In her discussion of the semantics of Tamil CV constructions, Fedson identifies several points at which the semantic parameter of evidentiality/inferentiality or prepared/unprepared mind interacts with the formal mechanism of the CV.

A CV construction consisting of main verb plus a finite form of ***aaku*** 'become' is, according to Fedson, subject to two constraints. (1) The situation reported must be 'not new'; that is 'when reporting the occurrence of a situation ***aaku*** conveys the nuance either that (a) something occurred as one might expect, given the circumstances, or that (b) something occurred which one hoped would occur.' (2) It must be 'not undesirable' to the speaker.

I quote Fedson's discussion of the 'not new constraint' at some length here because of its remarkable similarity to the descriptions of the 'prepared mind' for Turkish and to Hook's characterization of the 'no prior knowledge' environment which requires the non-compound verb in Hindi.[7]

> ... a totally new discovery, the possibility of which was not ever suspected (e.g. the discovery of a new moon of Jupiter's), cannot be reported using ***aaku***. If the milkman who normally comes at four o'clock, shows up at eight in the morning (unexpectedly), one can report his coming only with ***iru*** not with ***aaku*** or ***viTu***. If, however, a genetic mechanism which triggers the growth of neoplastic as opposed to normal, cell growth were to be discovered, even if such a discovery were not SPECIFICALLY EXPECTED it is something which one MIGHT EXPECT and as such, can be reported using ***aaku***. If a missing person (whom one knew was missing) were found, as an event which one HOPED might occur, rather than EXPECTED to occur, it can be reported with ***aaku***. In such uses, ***aaku*** conveys the nuance that something has happened 'at last'. Routine situations can be reported using the construction, on the one hand, and on the other, momentous situations, which were not specifically expected, but which are not totally new or unexpected, given the general knowledge of the speaker. (63-4)

4. DELANCEY'S CAUSAL CHAIN MODEL

4.1. **Event as vector**. DeLancey's cognitively based model analyzes a situation (i.e. event or state) as a set of vectors having two endpoints which can be interpreted at the most general level as ORIGIN and TERMINATION (DeLancey 1985:47). This can be schematized as follows.

ORIGIN ----------->	EVENT ----------->	TERMINATION
Temporal onset	Action/Event	Temporal conclusion
Cause		Resultant State
(Act of volition)		
Agent		Patient
Source		Goal
- - - - - - - - - -	- - - - - - - - - -	- - - - - - - - - -
Relevant antecedent state (e.g. expectation, premonition, fear, conceptualization of potential)		

This generalized schema underlies varying specific manifestations, depending on whether one focuses on the entities (nominal arguments) involved in a situation, or on the logically or temporally sequential stages of a situation. Thus the ORIGIN and TERMINATION endpoints of the vector can be associated with the concepts AGENT and PATIENT, with SOURCE and GOAL, or with CAUSE and RESULT.[8]

In this analysis I exploit the generality of the causal chain model to extend the interpretation of the ORIGIN end to include the notion of RELEVANT ANTECEDENT SITUATION. Relevant antecedent situations with respect to a given event may be either objective events or mental states of the observer/speaker. These include but are not limited to acts of volition, expectations, premonitions, fears, presuppositions, or simply a prior conceptualization of the potential of an event's occurrence. The analysis advanced in this paper depends on treating the knowledge/belief state of the speaker as a relevant antecedent situation in a causal chain.

4.2. **Interaction of event vector and observer.** A situation may impinge upon a speaker/observer's awareness at any point along its causal vector -- at its origin, at the point of actual occurrence, or at the terminal end of the vector. Thus a speaker/observer may, for example, become aware of an event only by observing its resultant state -- the termination of the causal chain. Or, a speaker/observer may be aware of (the potential of) an event from the stage of its cause or antecedent situation. This is the case if a situation is anticipated, feared, foreshadowed by preceding events or circumstances, predicted, or actively caused by the speaker/observer. Or yet again, a speaker/observer may become aware of the event as it is actually happening, that is in the middle stage of the causal chain.

These differences in the point at which an event impinges upon an observer/speaker's awareness are grammaticized in many languages. In (various dialects of) Tibetan, all three impingement point possibilities are morphologically distinguished.[9] Consider example **[13]**.

[13] [a] *gza-spen-ba la tsod-´du yod* (DeLancey 1986:206)
Saturday LOC meeting exist
'We have a meeting on Saturday.'

[b] *gza-spen-ba la tsog-´du ´dug*
Saturday LOC meeting exist
'There's a meeting on Saturday.'

Sentence **[13a]**, according to DeLancey, would be appropriate if the speaker is involved in some way in planning the meeting, whereas **[13b]** could be uttered by someone who had learned of the meeting only by reading a notice about it. 'The use of ***yod*** indicates an assertion made on the basis of direct knowledge of the entire vector, while ***´dug*** indicates direct knowledge of the result but not of the cause.' (ibid.) That is, the choice between ***yod*** or ***´dug*** depends on the impingement point of the causal vector with the speaker.

The Turkish form ***miş*** encodes a range of specific meanings, ranging from hearsay and inferentiality to surprise and irony. The common core of meaning of all these uses involves 'the externality of the process to awareness' (Slobin and Aksu 1982:192). In terms of the model followed here, the speaker's awareness impinges only at the result end of the causal vector. For example, a person might utter **[14]**

[14] ***usu-muş-um*** (Slobin and Aksu 1982:192)
sleep-***miş***-1s
'I must have fallen asleep.'

upon awakening slumped over his books. I shall continue to refer to the case of an event's impinging on an observer only at its result phase with Slobin and Aksu's term 'unprepared mind'.

The Kalasha form ***hula*** (cf. **[8]** above) also grammaticizes the impingement of speaker awareness at the result end of the vector. A similar set of meanings is associated with the Korean particle *-**kun***, which encodes consciously known but unassimilated information (Lee 1985). And in many other languages[10] the perfect acquires an inferential sense -- a consequence of the fact that the perfect encodes a state impinging on the observer at its result end.

This paper argues that one of the central functions of the CV/SV opposition in Urdu and Hindi also is to grammaticize intersection points of observer-speaker and event.

5. THE CAUSAL CHAIN MODEL AND CV-FORMATION

One idea basic to this paper is that at the most general level the CV in Urdu and Hindi as well as Kalasha encodes an action as MARKED for conceptualization as a vector including MORE THAN ONE PHASE of the causal chain. Thus the CV allows a verbal conception to be differentiated into STAGES of ORIGIN, EVENT, and RESULT. Any single stage may be singled out for focus, and the links between them may be affirmed or denied separately. The SV, on the other hand, encodes the verbal notion as an undifferentiated, single-stage conception.[11]

5.1. **Presupposition and the CV**. The three most common CV sequences in Urdu and Hindi are intransitive main verb plus ***jaanaa*** 'go', and ***denaa*** 'give' or ***lenaa*** 'take' with a transitive main verb. With these CV sequences, the stages distinguished are POTENTIAL (cf. ORIGIN) and REALIZATION (cf. TERMINATION).[12] With the CV, the potential is prefigured (presupposed), and the realization asserted. Both of these stages are simultaneously accessible to the speaker-observer's awareness. With the SV, however, both potential and realization (or non-realization) are presupposed or asserted together. Depending on which of the possible presuppositions an utterance responds to (cf. **[15]**), the nature of the action may be presupposed (old information) and some other sentence element asserted (new information), or simply the fact of some unspecified event taking place may be presupposed, and both its specific nature and other sentence elements asserted.

SV: (POTENTIAL + REALIZATION) Presupposed/Asserted
CV: (POTENTIAL) Presupposed + (REALIZATION) Asserted

Consider the sentences in **[15]**, one with the SV and the other with the CV.

[15] [a] ***ek laRkaa aayaa hai***
one boy has come(SV)
'A boy has come.'

[b] ***laRkaa aa gayaa hai***
boy has come(CV)
'The boy has come/arrived.'

Sentence **[15a]** could be a response to either of the two questions (i) or (ii). (i) ***kaun aayaa haĩ***? 'Who has come?', or (ii) ***kyaa huaa***? 'What happened?' The corresponding presuppositions are (i) 'Someone came,' or (ii) 'Something happened.' **[15b]**, on the other hand, answers the question ***kyaa laRkaa aayaa*** (***aa gayaa***) ***hai yaa nahĩĩ***? 'Has the boy come (yet) or not?' which carries the presupposition[13] (iii) 'The boy may come.'[14]

The presupposition of a potential can give rise to either a positive or negative expectation; one can expect either E(vent) or not-E to occur. Note that the conceptualization of not-E implies the prior conceptualization of E. If E is realized, we have the pragmatic effect of confirmation of an anticipated event; if not-E is realized, the effect of surprise is produced. On the other hand, if not-E is expected, but E occurs, the effect is also one of surprise.

Several writers have noted that the Hindi and Urdu vector ***jaanaa*** 'go' appears to contribute mutually contradictory meanings. Porizka (1969:43) points out that while some authors consider 'suddenness' or 'hastiness' to be a part of the meaning conveyed by ***jaanaa***, as in the following example:

[16] ***acaanak hamaare paRosii kaa baccaa chat se gir gayaa*** (Porizka 1969:44)[15]
suddenly our neighbor's child roof from fell
'Suddenly our neighbor's child fell from the roof.'

others emphasize the meaning of expected action illustrated in **[15b]** above.[16]

Hook (1974) discusses other data relevant to the point being made here. In the indicative, CV's normally do not occur in the negative. There is a class of non-indicative uses, however -- future imperatives, expressions of fear, and ***jab tak*** 'until' clauses in which the CV co-occurs regularly with a negative element.[17] Example **[17]** illustrates these three cases:

[17] [a] *(rassii)* ***choR na diijiegaa*** (Hook 1974:209)[18]
rope release NEG give(F IMP)
'Please do not let go (of the rope).'

[b] ***meraa dil kããp rahaa thaa ki kahı̃ı̃ swaamii*** (Hook 1974:212)[19]
my heart tremble(PST PROG) COMP lest S.
sacmuc aatmaghaat na kar lẽ
really suicide NEG do-take(SUBJUNCTIVE)
'I was worried to death that Swami might really commit suicide.'

[c] ***jab tak (ki) meraa xat aap ko mil na jaae***
until (that) my letter you DAT meet NEG go(SUBJ-CV)
aap śikaago na jaaẽ
you Chicago NEG go(SUBJ)
'Don't go to Chicago until you receive my letter.'

In his discussion of these contexts in which CV's co-occur with negative elements, Hook observes that 'the corresponding sentence without negation does not express the positive occurrence of an actual event but rather the eventual, contingent or CONJECTURED occurrence of some IMAGINED [emphasis mine] event.' (1974:209) From the point of view of this analysis, the key words are IMAGINED and CONJECTURED; these contexts all involve situations in which the speaker has already integrated the (possibility of the) event into his conceptual structure -- that is, in which he has presupposed the (existence of) the potential of the event. They all involve, in other words, the PREPARED MIND. In the case of fearing, the expectation/hope is the non-occurrence of the event. As Hook also noted (1974): '... it is an eventual, unreal, imagined event whose negation is desired, not reported on.'

If, as proposed in the present analysis, the CV grammaticizes the separation of a presupposed POTENTIAL and an asserted REALIZATION, this regular appearance of NEG with the CV in non-indicative contexts ceases to be puzzling. In non-indicative situations, the event is as yet UNrealized, and NEG encodes the speaker's wish that the event not be realized (or, with ***jab tak*** 'until', the period during which it is unrealized). Thus it is not in conflict with the assertion of an (already) realized event as it is in the indicative.[20]

5.1.1. Definiteness. Since, with the CV, the existence of the potential of an event is presupposed, the existence of the entities (NP arguments) involved in the event must also be presupposed. The distribution of SV and CV is thus related to the referential status of associated NP arguments. Indefinite NP subjects tend to take the SV:

[18] [a] ***kyaa aap ko is hafte mẽ koii xat milaa (?mil gayaa)***[21]
what you DAT this week in any letter met(SV) (?met(CV))
'Have you received any letters this week?'

[b] ***hamaarii klaas mẽ ek nayaa laRkaa aayaa (?aa gayaa) hai***[22]
our class in one new boy has come(SV) (?CV)
'A new boy has come into our class.'

Indefinite NP objects also prefer SV forms:

[19] ***kyaa aap ne koii gaaRii becii (?bec dii)***
what you ERG any car sold(SV) (?sold(CV))
'Have you sold any cars?'

A definite NP direct object will tend to induce a CV.

[20] ***kyaa aap ne gaaRii bec dii (?becii)***
what you ERG car sold(CV)
'Have you sold the/your car?'

Conversely, a CV in a simple sentence like **[21]** with an unmarked NP subject will produce a definite reading for the NP subject.

[21] ***(kyaa) xat mil gayaa hai?***
(what) letter has met(CV)
'Have you received the (*a/*any) letter?'

The relationship between the concept of definiteness as applied to NP's and as extended to verbs can be stated as follows. With NP's, previously identified NP's are definite (i.e. old information), with verbs, actions previously identified (i.e. the potential of which is presupposed) are 'definite' (and take the CV).[23] First mention of a nominal participant requires an indefinite NP; first mention of an action/event in a discourse requires an 'indefinite' verb form (simple verb).

5.1.2. Focus. Another consequence of the fact that the CV is marked for the separation of a presupposed potential and an asserted realization is the interaction of CV and SV forms with sentence focus. FOCUS refers to the part of an utterance which conveys new as opposed to old information. Recall that the CV splits an action into two phases -- potential and realization. It is the potential which is old information (presupposed) but its realization which is new (asserted).

At this point it is necessary to distinguish between normal (or unmarked) sentence focus, which I will call rhematic focus following Kim 1988, and contrastive (or marked) focus, the function of which is to direct attention AWAY FROM AN EXPECTED ELEMENT and toward an unexpected one.[24]

5.1.2.1. Rhematic focus. Hook (1979:234) notes that the CV tends to appear when the action itself is in focus,[25] as in **[20]** above. When some element other than the verb itself is in focus, the SV appears. In Urdu and Hindi, a non-verbal focal element normally occupies the position immediately preceding the verb. Thus with **[22]**,

[22] *wah [bas se]*FOC *aayaa*
he bus by came(SV)
'He came BY BUS.'

in which the PP ***bas se*** 'by bus' is in focus, we get the SV. WH-question words, as inherently focused elements, fall in the preverbal position, and prefer the SV.

[23] *yah laRkaa kahãã se* FOC *aayaa*?
this boy where from came
'Where did this boy come from?'

Conversely, a SV will tend to attract a focal element. The SV sentence **[24]** was considered odd without an adverbial in the focus position.

[24] *wah *(abhii) uThaa hai*
he *(just now) has got up
'He has got up *(just now).'

The incompatibility of ***hii*** 'only', in its limiting function noted by Hook (1974:230), with the CV is a special case of focus on sentence elements other than the verb selecting the SV. See **[25]**.

[25] *raam ne meraa hii kaam kiyaa* /**kar diyaa* (Hook 1974:230)
Ram ERG my only work did(SV)/*did(CV)
'Ram did only MY work.'

There is some indication that *nahĩĩ* /*na* 'NEG' may be an inherently focused element; it receives primary stress and occurs in preverbal position. If this is correct, it contributes another explanatory factor for the rarity of CV's in negated indicative sentences. (cf. **[26]**)

[26] *mãĩ ne us ko paise nahĩĩ diye* (**de diye*) (Hook 1974:100)
I ERG him DAT money not gave(SV) (*CV)
'I did not give him the money.'

5.1.2.2. Contrastive focus. If the CV, in which the realization of the event is inherently focused (new) information, DOES co-occur with another focused element, the effect of contrastive focus is generated. Compare sentence **[27]**,

[27] *wah bas se* FOC *aa gayaa* FOC (*raaste mẽ gaaRii xaraab ho gaii thii*)
he bus by came(CV) (road in car bad became(CV))
'He did come -- by bus!' (His car broke down on the way.)

in which we have both the focused instrumental adverbial ***bas se*** 'by bus' and the CV ***aa gayaa***, with **[22]** above. Sentence **[27]**, with contrastive focus on ***bas se*** 'by bus' would occur if the person in question had been expected to arrive by some means of transportation specifically other than a bus, whereas in **[22]** no such specific expectation about the means of transportation is violated.

It has been frequently noted that compound verbs do not co-occur with WH-question words in an interrogative meaning. Thus in the sentences in **[28]**

[28] [a] *us ne tumhẽ kyaa* FOC *bec diyaa* FOC
he ERG you-DAT what sold(CV)
'What did he sell you!' (He sold you a pup!)[26]

[b] *aisii kyaa baat* FOC *ho gaii* FOC
such what thing became(CV)
'What has happened that's so bad!?' What happened?
(Nothing that bad has really happened.)

the meanings are of rhetorical questions with an implied denial (or denigration) of the event expressed by the verb.

Those rare instances in which the CV does occur in a negated indicative sentence, e.g. **[29a,b]**,

[29] [a] *ra. sir jhukaae cintaa mẽ Dubaa khaRaa thaa.* (Hook 1974:226)[27]
R. head bowed thought in drowned standing was
jaalpaa ne us kii daSaa jaan kar bhii cizõ ko kyõ Thukraa nahĩĩ diyaa
J. ERG him of condition knowing even things DAT why give up NEG gave
'R. stood with his head down brooding. Jalpaa knew his financial situation and yet why hadn't she given up these things.'

[b] *us ne mujhe duudh nahĩĩ bec diyaa* (Burton-Page 1957:473)
he ERG me-DAT milk NEG sold(CV)
'He hasn't sold me the milk (yet, but I'm expecting him soon).'

can be seen as instances of contrastive focus. **[29a]** points up the failure of the natural expectation that 'Jalpaa would give up these things,' and **[29b]** the failure of the milk-seller to come according to expectations.

5.1.3. Factivity. Factive predicates are those which imply a presupposition by the speaker that the proposition expressed in an embedded complement sentence is true.[28] Factivity can be related to definiteness in the following way. If we construct the analogy -- existence:entity :: truth:proposition, we can extend it as follows: existential presupposition:entity :: presupposition of truth:proposition. Then the property of definiteness for NP's becomes analogous to the property of factivity for complement-taking predicates.

Hook (MS) presents two very interesting examples of CV distribution, which he relates to the concept of factivity. These are reproduced here as **[30a]** and **[b]**.

[30] [a] *mãĩ ne aaj siikhaa (*mãĩ aaj siikh gayaa) ki Tokiyo ciin mẽ hai*
I ERG today learned(SV) (*learned (CV)) that Tokyo China in is
'I learned today that Tokyo is in China (but it seems that's a mistake.)'

[b] *mãĩ aaj siikh gayaa ki Tokiyo jaapaan mẽ hai.*[29]
I today learned(CV) that Tokyo Japan in is
'Today I learned that Tokyo is in Japan.' (I had it wrong before.)

Reflecting on these examples, we see that it is not whether the assertion in the complement sentence is true that is crucial, but the speaker/observer's belief about its truth. Rejection of the starred version of **[30a]** requires that the speaker realize that Tokyo is not in China, that is to say realize his own mistake (by hindsight). A speaker could say the starred version of **[30a]** if he really believed that Tokyo is in China, even though in fact it is not.

Since in the above two examples speaker and agent are identical, the pragmatic effect generated is of a mistake realized by hindsight. If we separate the functions of speaker and agent, as in **[31]**,

[31] ***kyaa tum ne yah siikhaa*** **(*siikh liyaa*)** - ***ki Tokiyo ciin mẽ hai***
what you ERG this learned(SV) (*learned(CV)) that Tokyo China in is
'Did you learn that Tokyo is in China!?' (You are wrong; it really isn't.)[30]

the effect of hindsight disappears. In **[31]**, simultaneously, the speaker knows that Tokyo is not in China while the learner apparently believes that it is.

The semantics of factivity in these examples can be seen as a consequence of the causal-chain explanation of CV distribution.[31]

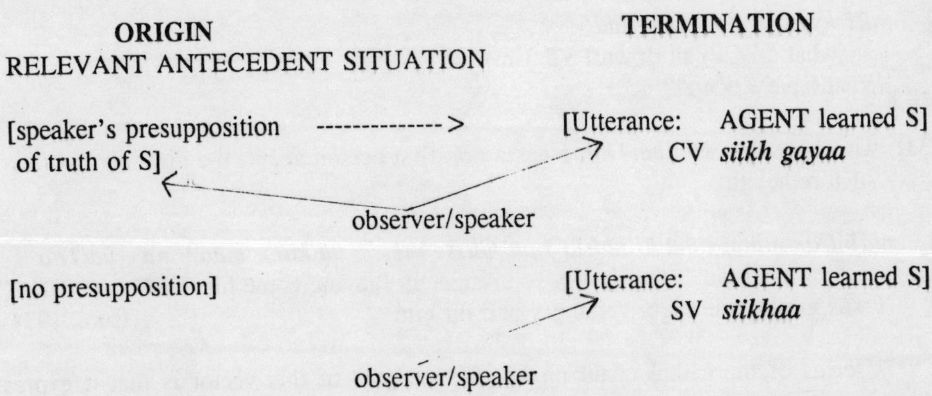

In the case when the speaker does not presuppose the truth of the complement S -- that is, he either knows that it is false or has no specific idea about its truth value -- he may use ***siikhaa***, the SV form of ***siikhnaa*** 'learn'. Use of the CV form ***siikh gayaa*** requires the presupposition.

That the category of factivity overlaps cognitively with the categories of inferentiality and of the prepared/unprepared mind seems clear. In addition to the indications we have seen above from the Hindi and Urdu CV system, it is certainly no coincidence, for example, that the English non-factive predicates *seems*, *appears*, *happens*, *chances*, *turns out*, *to be supposed to be* are precisely those which are used in English to encode both inferentiality and newly acquired and as yet unassimilated information.

5.2. **Non-simultaneous apprehension of event and result**. With other CV sequences, a different consequence of the construction's separation of an event into ORIGIN and RESULT stages is emphasized. While with ***jaanaa*** 'go', ***denaa*** 'give', and ***lenaa*** 'take' the split is between the prefiguring and the realization of an event, with the vector ***baiThnaa*** 'sit' the split is between the apprehension of an event and the apprehension of its result.

Many discussions of the vector ***baiThnaa*** 'sit' stress its multiple, apparently conflicting meanings. For example, Hacker (1961:513) says:

> If ***baiThnaa*** is used, the compound may also sometimes be understood, in accordance with the situation, to denote a wrong or improper action, but in this case this character of the action is either regretted, or understood to be done in a certain state of confusion, or denounced as impertinent and, perhaps, as somehow aggressive.

In example **[32]**, with a first person agent, ***baiThnaa*** conveys surprise and dismay felt after the fact.[32]

[32] ***mãĩ kyaa kar baiThaa***
I what do(CP) sit down(PST 3sm)
'What have I DONE!?'

In **[33]**, where the CV with ***baiThnaa*** has a non-first person agent, the meaning is of rashness and lack of forethought.

[33] ***mãĩ Dar rahaa thaa ki kahĩĩ tum Gusse mẽ aa kar maar na baiTho***
I was afraid that lest you anger in having come hit NEG sit(SUBJ-CV)
'I was afraid you might get angry and hit him.' (Hook 1974:35)[33]

In terms of the causal chain model, the analysis of this vector is that it expresses a situation in which awareness of both the cause and the result ends of the vector occurs but is separated -- either temporally or by virtue of occurring in different individuals. With a first person speaker (the situation in which speaker and agent are identical), an agent performs an action without being aware of the link of the action to its result. The link of the action to (some aspect of) its result is realized only later; and the specific pragmatic effect is one of surprise, dismay, or regret. Thus the apparent contradiction between performing a volitional act and feeling surprise at it is explained. With a non-first person speaker, the awareness of the (inappropriate) result resides in the observer, while the awareness of the motivation (origin) is in the agent.

With ***baiThnaa*** the causal chain is MARKED for the absence of linkage between cause and result. This is the same semantics we saw associated with the Kalasha vector ***thek*** 'put'. Schematized, the situation is like this:

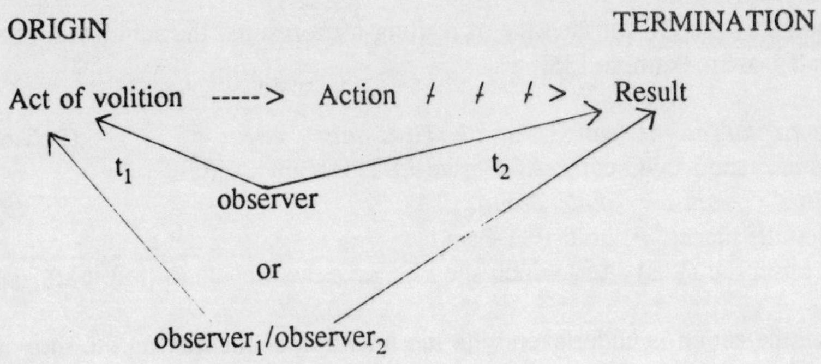

This analysis explains several observed facts of the syntax of ***baiThnaa***. As pointed out by Kachru, CV's in ***baiThnaa*** do not undergo passive. Thus, ****raaj se sab kuch kah baiThaa gayaa*** '*Everything was blurted out by Raj in a rash manner' (Kachru 1980:121). If passive is a result/patient-oriented construction, in which the link of an action with its result rather than with its agent is salient, the failure of linkage of the result end to the origin end of the vector signified by ***baiThnaa*** explains the non-appearance of passive.

It also explains the fact that while ***baiThnaa*** usually implies completion (Hook 1974:179), in some cases it does not (as in **[34a]**).

[34] [a] ***raam Gusse mẽ aa kar mujhe fon kar baiThaa*** (Hook 1974:180)
R. anger in having come me-DAT phone do-sat
lekin mãĩ ghar par nahĩĩ thaa
but I home at NEG was
'Getting mad, Ram rang me up, but I wasn't home.'

[b] ***mãĩ ne das baje aap ko fon kar liyaa (*lekin aap nahĩĩ mile)***
I ERG 10 o'clock you DAT phone did(CV) (*but you NEG met)
'I called you up at ten o'clock (*but I couldn't get you).' (Hook 1974:166)

The markedness of this construction for separation of event origin and result accounts for this possibility. This is to be contrasted with **[34b]**, in which a CV with the vector ***lenaa*** 'take' cannot be followed by a denial of the completion of the event. Recall that with ***jaanaa*** 'go', ***lenaa*** 'take', and ***denaa*** 'give' the observer's apprehension of both the ORIGIN and RESULT ends of the causal vector is simultaneous.

In Tamil, the vector ***vai*** 'put' participates in two types of causal chains. Its most general characterization, according to Fedson, is that 'the action is viewed not in itself but in its result-producing capacity.' (1981:263) Whether the construction conveys intentional or unintentional production of these results depends on whether the sentence reports the ACTOR'S performance of an action WITH AN EYE TO ITS RESULT [emphasis mine] or the SPEAKER'S view of an action as HAVING LED TO a given (unintended) result. If a sentence concerns the ACTOR performing the action denoted by the CP for the sake of its long-term results, the action is INTENTIONAL (cf. 'prepared mind'), as in example **[35]**.

[35] *avan enta kaTai-y-il caikkiL-ai koTu-tt-aan enRu* (Fedson 1981:263)
he which shop-LOC cycle-ACC give-PST-3sm QUOT(CP)
kavanittu vaittu koN-T-aan
observe(CP) place(CP) hold-PST-3sm
'... he observed (Res) (Act) which shop he gave the bicycle to (left it at).' [A.1969:69][34]

In this sentence the action is undertaken with the intention of identifying the shop in the future. If, on the other hand, a SPEAKER is viewing an action as having (unexpectedly) produced certain results, the use of ***vai*** 'put' conveys that the result was *unintentional* (cf. 'unprepared mind'). An example of this development is given here as **[36]**.

[36] *niinkaL pala-peer mun-nilay-il kuRRa-vaaLi-aay* (Fedson 1981:266)
you-HON many-3pe front-state-LOC accused -ADV
kaTT-unTu niR-kum nilai-y-ai eeRpaTutti vai-tt-een-ee
be bound(CP) stand-nfut state-ACC create(CP) place-PST-1s-EMPHR
'(lit.) Alas, I created (Res) the state of your standing bound in front of many people as the accused.' [K.M.S. 1965:67]

The context for this example is that the speaker, viewing her own action in HINDSIGHT feels that she has unintentionally been the cause of the king's disgrace.[35]

Note that Fedson's distinction between sentences reporting on an agent performing an action in order to CAUSE a result and those reporting a speaker viewing the RESULT end of the causal chain parallels the difference between the semantics of ***jaanaa*** 'go', ***denaa*** 'give', and ***lenaa*** 'take' and that of ***baiThnaa*** 'sit'.[36]

In Kannada, according to Bhat (1979), the vector ***biDu*** 'to release' has two distinct meanings.

> While occurring after transitive verbs that have a human being as their Agent, it indicates that the events referred to are carried out intentionally through great effort, whereas while occurring after transitive verbs that have a human being as their Object, or after intransitive verbs, it indicates that the event or action took place rather accidentally. (p. 303)

These three cases are illustrated in **[37]**.

[37] [a] *raaju aa pustakavannu oodi biTTa* (p. 303)
Raju that book(ACC) read released
'Raju read that book with effort.'

[b] *aa naayi raajuvannu kacci biTTitu*
that dog Raju(ACC) bit released
'That dog accidentally bit Raju.'

[c] *raaju biddu biTTa*
Raju fell released
'Raju accidentally fell down.'

In **[a]** the action is viewed from the point of view of its human agent, yielding the 'with great effort' meaning. In **[b]** the action is accidental not from the point of view of the agent (the dog), but from the point of view of its effect on the human patient (Raju). In these Kannada examples, the operative principle seems to be that the observer's awareness intersects the causal chain at the location of the salient participant (in the sense of an animacy or empathy hierarchy).

5.3. **Observer awareness of result only**. The verb ***nikalnaa*** 'come out' with its vector meaning of 'turn out to be' carries the meanings associated with the impingement of an event ONLY at the result end of its causal vector -- the semantics of the 'unprepared mind'.[37] Hook (1974:131-33) identifies several classes of meanings, ALL of which point to this conclusion: ***nikalnaa*** occurs with verbs of speaking involving unpredictable or involuntary utterances, with verbs denoting 'sudden and startling appearance of sound or light', with verbs denoting outbursts of feeling, and carrying the meaning 'with great ease' (i.e. lack of planning or foresight).

[38] *mãĩ śaraab ke naśe mẽ unhẽ na jaane kyaa kyaa kah niklaa* [Hook 1974:132]
'God knows what I said to them while I was drunk.'

Sentence **[38]** shows precisely the same meanings -- unconscious action, lack of control, non volitionality -- which have been shown to develop with inferential forms and first person experiencers in Lhasa Tibetan (DeLancey 1985a) and in Kalasha (Bashir 1988, Chapter 2); example **[39a]** is from Tibetan and **[39b]** from Kalasha.

[39] [a] *ŋa-s brjed-bźag* (DeLancey 1985a:68)
I-ERG forget-PERF/INFERENTIAL
'I've forgotten.'

[b] *atra´ thai a´-am ãga´ ne thi pha´to ga´la-him*
there put(P PERF)-1s aware not become(CP) then go(PST-I)-1s
'I put it there. Then without remembering (it) I left.' (Bashir 1988:71)

The context in **[39b]** is that the speaker took off his watch and put it on a rock to wash his face. Then he got up and left without remembering to put it back on.

Particularly revealing is the contrast between examples **[38]** and **[40]**. In contrast to the meaning conveyed by ***nikal-*** (< 'come out') is that carried by ***nikaal-*** 'to cause to come out' --

that of 'successfully overcoming some difficulty, resistance or unlikelihood' (Hook 1974:143) as in **[40]**,

[40] *unhõ ne madad de kar apne riśtedaarõ ko is zindagi se* ***ubhaar nikaalaa***
'By giving his relatives help he raised them up from this kind of life.' [Hook 1974:143]

where the addition of the CAUSATIVE morpheme *-aa* changes the point of impingement of the action from the result end to the origin end of the causal vector, and the semantics from that of the unprepared to that of the prepared mind.

An interesting usage of the vector ***rakh-*** 'put, keep', which Hook (1974:138-9) finds characteristic of the speech of Dehra Dun in the northwest sector of the Hindi area, is reminiscent of the semantics ([+negative] [+unprepared mind]) of the 'put' vector ***thek*** in Kalasha. Of Hook's eight examples, all eight report negatively valued events, and five of them (his a, b, d, e, f) arguably report events that were unanticipated by the speaker. I reproduce Hook's examples (a) and (d) here as **[41]**.

[41] [a] ***gaaRii mẽ gaRbaR ho-rakhii hai*** (Hook 1974:138)
car in trouble(fs) become-put-P PERF(fs)
'Something's gone wrong with the car.'

[b] ***mãĩ apne makaan kaa raastaa bhuul rakhaa hũũ*** (Hook 1974:139)
I own house of road forget put am
'I have forgotten the way home.'

Recall that in languages in which inferentiality is grammaticized, the verb 'forget' is one of the most likely to allow inferential forms with first person agents (cf. **[39a,b]**). Example **[41b]** provides strong evidence for associating the vector ***rakhnaa*** in this dialect of Hindi with the semantics of the unprepared mind -- the result only impingement case.

6. CONCLUSION

Defining the contribution of the compound verb in terms of the causal chain model unifies many of the significant findings on the CV contributed by several researchers.

Given the generality of the causal chain schema, the effect of the CV in differentiating an event into stages will be manifested simultaneously at multiple levels of the grammar and of the language-use situation, giving rise to an overlapping multiplicity of specific semantic effects. The distribution of the CV with respect to (1) prepared vs. unprepared mind semantics, (2) stativity, (3) factivity, (4) referential status, (5) sentence focus, (6) negative in indicatives, and (7) markedness for separation of potential and realization have been shown to follow from the causal chain characterization of the CV.

It is now possible to construct a rudimentary typology correlating compound verb semantics with awareness impingement points using the causal chain model. The forms and vector verbs that have been discussed in this paper can be classified as follows.

I. ORIGIN ------> EVENT -----> RESULT

Observer

jaanaa, *denaa*, *lenaa* (Hindi, Urdu)
parik (Kalasha)
aaku (Tamil)
vai (Tamil-agent orientation)
biDu (Kannada-with human agent)
nikaalnaa (Urdu, Hindi)

II. ORIGIN ------> EVENT RESULT

1 2

Observer/
Time

baiThnaa (Urdu, Hindi)
thek (Kalasha)
vai (Tamil-result orientation)
biDu (Kannada-with human patient, or with intransitives)

III. ORIGIN EVENT RESULT

Observer

hula (Kalasha)
miş (Turkish)
kun (Korean)
iru (Tamil)
nikalnaa (Urdu, Hindi)
rakhnaa (Dehra Dun Hindi)
to turn out that (English)
to seem (English)

IV. ORIGIN (--->) EVENT (--->) RESULT

Observer SV (Hindi, Urdu)

or

Observer

In these diagrams, the arrow, --->, represents the marked presence of a connection between stages of the causal chain; an arrow within parentheses, (--->), signifies that the presence or absence of links between the phases of the causal chain is unmarked, i.e. irrelevant to the particular conceptualization; and the absence of an arrow, ( ), indicates the marked absence of a connection. Note that the marked absence of something implies its relevance to the conception.

In the type I situation, both the origin and the result stage impinge together on the observer's awareness. In type II, both ORIGIN and RESULT are apprehended, but separately. With first person agents the separation is in time: the agent/observer does not realize the RESULT of his (volitional) act until some time later. With non-first person agents, awareness of the origin/action resides in one observer, and awareness of the RESULT in another. Type III represents awareness of the RESULT only end of the causal chain, with the marked absence of awareness of ORIGIN. Type IV, on the other hand, represents a situation in which only a single stage is relevant to the conception -- neither the presence nor the absence of other stages is encoded.

NOTES

1. The term VECTOR originates with Pray (1970:189), who selected it because it 'emphasizes the positional and directional components' of these stems. In the present analysis the concept of vector applies to the representation of an event as a causal chain, rather than to the motional components of the secondary verbs.

2. Abbreviations appearing in this paper are:

A	actual		
Cs	causative	m	masculine
DAT	dative	NS	non-specific
ERG	ergative	OBL	oblique
f	feminine	p	plural
I	inferential	P/F	present/future
IMP	imperative	PST	past
NOM	nominative	PERF	perfect
1,2,3	first, second	S	specific
	third persons	s	singular
LOC	locative	SUBJ	subjunctive

Transcription conventions: Vowel length is indicated by repetition of the vowel symbol, nasalization by a tilde (˜) above the vowel symbol. Retroflex consonants are capitalized. Syllable stress is marked (in Kalasha) by <´> following the stressed syllable.

I am grateful to Shaheen Cole and Afroz Taj of the University of Michigan in Ann Arbor, Baber Khan of the University of Illinois, Asif Agha of the University of Chicago, and Tahseen Siddiqi of the University of Wisconsin for sharing and discussing their native speaker intuitions on a long list of Urdu sentences on which I asked their opinions. Whatever mistakes in understanding or interpretation of their contributions I may have made is, of course, my responsibility.

3. Kalasha examples are from Bashir 1988.

4. It appears that ***dek*** 'give' may only occur with imperatives. So far my only examples of this vector are with imperatives.

5. The form ***uTi´ki tyai*** (lit. 'jump-beat') looks like another candidate for investigation for possible compound verb status. I have no other examples of this type with 'beat', however, and this could be a conjunct verb formation analogous to the Panjabi ***chaal maarNaa*** (lit. 'jump-beat') 'to jump'.

6. Compounds in ***parik´*** also do not combine with the subjunctivizing element ***haw´-au***. This fact is also consistent with ***parik´*** 'go' as indicating a prepared mind, and with the sense of finality conveyed by ***parik´***. If an event is already anticipated, already present in clear contour in the mind, then the tentativeness, the hypotheticality carried by the subjunctive ***haw´-au*** is incompatible with that mind-set.

7. The 'Columbus discovered America' situation.

8. See DeLancey 1982:172.

9. These possibilities are discussed and illustrated in detail in DeLancey 1985a and b, and 1986.

10. For example Persian (Windfuhr 1982), Wakhi (Grjunberg and Steblin-Kamensky 1976), and Georgian (DeLancey 1982:175). See Comrie 1976:110 for discussion of this often observed correlation.

11. This conclusion has been arrived at via reflection on the Kalasha data vis-a-vis the causal chain model. It is in agreement with but independent of the formulation in Hook (1979:231):

> An action may be thought of as consisting of a number of stages or phases. First is the stage of inaction, of intention and preparation; then comes the stage of effort; then the consummation of action leading to an achievement, change or transition to something new. In most general terms, using a compound verb allows the mind to travel across the phases of an action. Using the simple verb illuminates a single stage.

12. This line of thinking is prefigured in the work of Porizka (1967-9), who emphasizes the REALIZATION of the action as an identifiable stage. 'In the speaker's mental apprehension, the action is represented in its full REALIZATION inclusive of its FINAL RESULTANT STAGE; the CONNECTION BETWEEN THE ACTION AND OTHER FACTORS [here, especially the object of the action] is presented as KNOWN.' (1969:26) [emphasis mine]

13. the presupposition of a potential.

14. The SV version ***kyaa laRkaa aayaa*** ... suggests that the boy is expected but not at any specific time, while ***kyaa laRkaa aa gayaa*** ... suggests that the speaker expected him to arrive by the time of the utterance.

15. Quoted from Prabhaakar, Vishnu. 1950. *Acchi paRosii*, p. 9.

16. Porizka maintains out that neither hastiness and surprise nor expectedness is an inherent part of the meaning contributed by ***jaanaa***. CV's with ***jaanaa***, he says, are simply marked with respect to the realization of the action.

17. The occurrence of the CV in ***jab tak*** 'until, unless' clauses is also conditioned by the referential status of the subject NP; viz. **[a]**, in which an indefinite NP subject takes the SV.

[a] ***aap kisii ke ghar na jaaie jab tak ki aap ko***
you anyone GEN house NEG go(IMP) unless that you DAT
wahãã se daavat naamaa na mile
there from invitation NEG meet(SUBJ-SV)
'Don't go to anyone's house unless you receive an invitation from there.'

Compare **[a]** with **[17c]**.

18. Quoted by Hook from *Rangbhumii* by Premchand as cited in Gaeffke 1967.

19. From *Karmabhuumii* by Premchand as quoted in Gaeffke 1967.

20. Given that these CV vectors assert realization, and NEG asserts non-realization, one could also say, impressionistically, that NEG and the vectors ***jaanaa*** 'go', ***denaa*** 'give', and ***lenaa*** 'take' are in a kind of complementary distribution, thus accounting for their failure to co-occur.

21. Use of the CV is not impossible in this string, but would convey the meaning in which the existence of the NP's in question is presupposed, i.e., 'Out of a specific set of letters expected to be received, have you received any one of them?' The meaning intended in **[18a]** is of a non-specific NP. A similar comment applies to **[19]**.

22. With the CV ***aa gayaa hai*** the sense is that the boy's arrival is counter to expectations and that he is (probably) unwelcome.

23. This might account for Hacker's attribution of definiteness (Bestimmtheit) to the compound verb. 'The most general law concerning the semantic function of the "explicator" operation is that these impart the mode of DEFINITENESS (Bestimmtheit) to the expression of the action.' (1961:491).

24. This description of the function of contrastive focus is due to Stephen R. Poteet 1989.

25. 'The compound verb emphasizes the action as such. Elements in the sentence that qualify the action in such a way as to draw attention away from it often prefer the SV.' (1979:234)

26. This is Burton-Page's much discussed example (1957:473).

27. From *Gaban*:69 by Premchand as cited in Gaeffke 1967.

28. Kiparsky and Kiparsky 1971.

29. Asif Agha, in discussing these examples, prefers the CV versions with ***lenaa***, i.e. ***mãĩ ne aaj siikh liyaa ki ...***

30. I am grateful to Asif Agha for discussion of this set of examples. This further example is due to him.

31. The contrast CV > factive/SV > non-factive probably holds only for those verbs whose SV forms are ambiguous with regard to factivity; ***siikhnaa*** 'learn' and ***samajhnaa*** 'understand' are two such verbs. With unambiguously (inherently) factive verbs, e.g. ***pachtaanaa*** 'to regret', ***hairaan honaa*** 'to be surprised', ***afsos karnaa*** 'to regret', the semantic effect of the CV form is different.

32. I am grateful to Peter Hook for this example.

33. Hook's example is from *A Premchand Reader* by Zide, Masica, Bahl, and Chandola. Honolulu: East-West Center Press, 1962.

34. (Res) and (Act) refer to Fedson's categories (result orientation) and (actor orientation).

35. Fedson also has similar examples with 2nd and 3rd person actors, in which the speaker and actor are not the same person.

36. The CV system in Tamil interacts with the parameter of inferentiality/evidentiality in yet another way. There exists a specifically inferential construction consisting of main verb CP plus ***iru*** 'be', about which Fedson says:

> The inferential construction indicates that the speaker infers from direct evidence or from other sources, that a certain situation held prior to the time of reference ... ***iru*** in the inferential does commit the speaker to the validity of what he is saying, but at the same time disavows first-hand knowledge ... (1981:48)

According to Fedson this is a common usage in all registers of Tamil. I reproduce one of her examples here as **[a]**.

[a] ***piLLai-kku paZam puLitt- iru-kkiR-atu at-an-aal***
child-DAT fruit be sour(CP) be-P-3sn that-INST
taan at-ai caapiTa-v-illai / caapiT-aamal irunt-iru-kkir-atu
EMPH it-ACC eat(INF)-NEG eat-(NEG CP) be(CP)be-P- 3sn
(= Fedson's #83, p. 49, transcription retained)
'The fruit has evidently been too sour for the child, that's why he didn't eat/has evidently not eaten it.'

This construction is distinct from a specifically reportive (cf. 'hearsay') morpheme *-aam* (= neuter future < ***aa /aaku*** 'become'), which indicates that an utterance is reported as second-hand information, and which does not commit the speaker to the truth of the statement.

37. The meanings conveyed by ***uThnaa*** 'get up' overlap to some extent with those of ***baiThnaa*** but are not identical. The causal chain representation of ***uThnaa*** remains to be determined.

REFERENCES

Bashir, Elena. 1988. Topics in Kalasha syntax: An areal and typological perspective. Ann Arbor, Michigan: University of Michigan dissertation. [University Microfilms.]

Bhat, D. N. S. 1979. Vectors in Kannada. International Journal of Dravidian Linguistics 8:2.300-309.

Burton-Page, J. 1957. Compound and conjunct verbs in Hindi. BSOAS 19.469-78.

Chafe, Wallace, and Johanna Nichols (eds.) 1986. Evidentiality: The linguistic coding of epistemology. Norwood: Ablex.

Comrie, Bernard. 1976. Aspect. Cambridge: Cambridge University Press.

DeLancey, Scott. 1981. An interpretation of split-ergativity and related patterns. Lg. 57.626-57.

DeLancey, Scott. 1982. Aspect, transitivity and viewpoint. In Hopper (ed.) 1982.

DeLancey, Scott. 1985a. Categories of non-volitional actor in Lhasa Tibetan. In Zide et al. 1985.

DeLancey, Scott. 1985b. Lhasa Tibetan evidentials and the semantics of causation. Proceedings of the Eleventh Annual Meeting of the Berkeley Linguistics Society. Berkeley, California: Berkeley Linguistics Society.

DeLancey, Scott. 1985c. On active typology and the nature of agentivity. In Plank (ed.) 1985.

DeLancey, Scott. 1986. Evidentiality and volitionality in Tibetan. In Chafe and Nichols (eds.) 1986.

Fedson, Vijayarani Jotimuttu. 1981. The Tamil serial or compound verb. Chicago: University of Chicago dissertation.

Gaeffke, Peter. 1967. Untersuchungen zur Syntax des Hindi. The Hague: Mouton and Co.

Gundel, Jeanette K. 1977. Role of topic and comment in linguistic theory. Bloomington: Indiana University Linguistics Club.

Hacker, Paul. 1958. Zur Funktion einiger Hilfsverben im Modernen Hindi. Mainz: Akademie der Wissenschaften und der Literatur.

Hacker, Paul. 1961. On the problem of a method for treating the compound and conjunct verbs in Hindi. BSOAS 24.484-516.

Hammond, Michael, Edith Moravcsik, and Jessica Wirth. 1988. Studies in syntactic typology. Amsterdam/Philadelphia: Benjamins.

Hook, Peter Edwin. 1974. The compound verb in Hindi. (The Michigan Series in South and Southeast Asian Languages and Linguistics, 1.) Ann Arbor: The University of Michigan Center for South and Southeast Asian Studies.

Hook, Peter Edwin. 1976. The Hindi compound verb: What it is and what it does. Readings in Hindi-Urdu linguistics, ed. by K. S. Singh. Delhi: National Publishing House.

Hook, Peter Edwin. 1981. Hindi structures: Intermediate level. (Michigan Papers on South and Southeast Asia, 16.) Ann Arbor: The University of Michigan Center for South and Southeast Asian Studies.

Hook, Peter Edwin. Two more non-aspectual functions of the Hindi compound verb: Factivity and narrative cohesion. Ann Arbor: University of Michigan, MS.

Hopper, Paul J. (ed.) 1982. Tense-aspect: Between semantics and pragmatics. Amsterdam/Philadelphia: Benjamins.

Kachru, Yamuna. 1979. Pragmatics and verb serialization in Hindi-Urdu. Studies in the Linguistic Sciences 9:2.157-69.

Kachru, Yamuna, and Rajeshwari Pandharipande 1980. Toward a typology of compound verbs in South Asian languages. Studies in the Linguistic Sciences 10:1.113-24.

Kim, Alan Hyun-Oak. 1988. Preverbal focusing and type XXIII languages. In Hammond et al. (eds.) 1988.

Kiparsky, Paul, and Carol Kiparsky. 1971. Fact. In Steinberg and Jakobovits (eds.) 1971.

Lee, Ho Sang. 1985. Consciously known but unassimilated information: A pragmatic analysis of the epistemic modal - ***kun*** in Korean. Proceedings of the First Annual Meeting of the Pacific Linguistics Conference. Eugene, Oregon: University of Oregon Department of Linguistics.

Mourelatos, Alexander P. D. 1981. Events, processes and states. In Tedeschi and Zaenen (eds.) 1981.

Plank, Frans (ed.) 1985. Relational typology. Berlin: Mouton.

Porizka, Vincenc. 1967. On the perfective verbal aspect in Hindi. Archiv Orientalni 35.64-88, 208-31.

Porizka, Vincenc. 1968. On the perfective verbal aspect in Hindi. Archiv Orientalni 36.233-51.

Porizka, Vincenc. 1969. On the perfective verbal aspect in Hindi. Archiv Orientalni 37.19-47, 345-64.

Poteet, Stephen R. 1989. On the postverbal position of the direct object in Mandarin Chinese. Paper presented at the 25th Annual Regional Meeting of the Chicago Linguistic Society.

Pray, Bruce R. 1970. Topics in Hindi-Urdu grammar. Berkeley: University of California Center for South and Southeast Asia Studies.

Slobin, Dan I., and Aynana A. Aksu. 1982. Tense, aspect, and modality in the use of the Turkish evidential. In Hopper (ed.) 1982.

Steinberg, Danny D., and Leon A. Jakobovits. 1971. Semantics: An interdisciplinary reader in philosophy, linguistics and psychology. Cambridge: Cambridge University Press.

Tedeschi, Philip, and Annie Zaenen (eds.) 1981. Tense and aspect. (Syntax and semantics, 14.) New York: Academic Press.

Windfuhr, Gernot L. 1982. The verbal category of inference in Persian. Acta Iranica, Deuxieme Serie, Hommages et Opera Minora. Monumentum Georg Morgenstierne. II. Leiden: E. J. Brill.

Zide, Arlene R. K., David Magier, and Eric Schiller (eds.) 1985. Proceedings of the Conference on Participant Roles: South Asia and Adjacent Areas, an ancillary meeting to the CLS Regional Meeting, 25 April 1984. Bloomington: Indiana University Linguistics Club.

CONSCIOUS CHOICE AND SOME LIGHT VERBS IN URDU

Miriam Butt
Stanford University

1 Introduction

Complex predicates in South Asian languages are notable for their versatility, frequency of usage and for the many factors that play a role in their construction. A complex predicate consists of two parts: a HOST and a LIGHT VERB.[1] Each light verb has a corresponding FULL VERB. Masica (1976:141) characterizes the shift from the full version of a verb to the light version as 'lexical emptying'. One of the many issues that remains to be explored when examining complex predicate constructions is what semantic information the light verb does retain and how this affects the overt manifestation of an expression in terms of case-marking and valency.

An approach that generates a better understanding of the mechanics of complex predicates is to think of the semantic information that is found in them in terms of SEMANTIC STRUCTURE and SEMANTIC SUBSTANCE. In Urdu the light verb can be thought of as contributing SEMANTIC STRUCTURE, i.e. the kind of information that determines syntactic aspects such as case marking on grammatical functions (subject), to an expression. The host, on the other hand, contributes the SEMANTIC SUBSTANCE, i.e. most of the meaning that the complex predicate has. This is because the host retains all of its original semantic substance when it combines with a light verb while the light verb is emptied of most of its original semantic substance. The light verb does retain semantic structure, which then influences the structure of the complex predicate by overriding the semantic structure of the host verb. An example of how this works will be given in this paper.

Although in Urdu the host may be either a noun, adjective, or verb, I will confine myself to examining verb-verb type constructions in this paper.[2] In particular, I will examine light verbs like *ḍaalnaa* (to put) and *parnaa* (to fall). These light verbs play a part in determining whether or not the actor in an expression is seen to have conscious control over the action performed. ***Daalnaa*** seems to attribute conscious choice to the actor while ***parnaa*** does not. **[1]**[3] for example, where ***daalnaa*** is attached to the host *piinaa* (to drink)[4], conveys that the actor intended to do the specified action, while **[2]**, where ***parnaa*** is attached to ***girnaa*** (to fall), favors a reading in which there is a complete lack of control over the action.

[1]	*us-ne*	*davaii*	*pii*	*daalii*
	he-Erg	medicine-Nom	drink	put
	'He downed the medicine.'			

[2]	*šiila*	*gir*	*parii*
	Sheila-Nom	fall	fell
	'Sheila fell.'		

Certain correlations between the case assigned to the subject of a complex predicate, conscious choice, the structure of the light verb, and the resulting structure of the complex predicate are found when investigating light verbs like ***ḍaalnaa*** and ***parnaa***. An examination of these correlations illuminates some of the mechanics of complex predicate constructions and also provides support for the idea that separating out different kinds of semantic information in the manner described above provides better insights about the interaction of semantics and syntax in general.

2 Conscious Choice

2.1 The Full Verbs

In order to be able to correctly understand the light verbs ***ḍaalnaa*** and ***parnaa***, we need to examine them in their full forms first. The full verb ***ḍaalnaa*** (to put), an example of which is given in **[3]**, can be represented as in **[4]**. Its subject (the put-er) always takes the ergative. The thing being put (put-ee), which is the object, can take either the accusative or the unmarked (nominative) case. The choice of the accusative rather than the unmarked nominative for the object depends on whether or not the object is some definite entity and whether or not it is human.[5]

[3]	***šiila-ne***	***rotii-ko***	***dabe-mẽ***	***ḍaalaa***
	Sheila-Erg	bread-Acc	box-in	put
	'Sheila put the bread in the box.'			

The representation in **[4]** has three parts: the SEMANTIC STRUCTURE and ARGUMENT STRUCTURE of the full verb ***ḍaalnaa***, and the case markings it induces in the OVERT EXPRESSION (i.e. the sentence). The semantic structure carries information necessary for the selection of syntactic features like case markers. As will be demonstrated further on in the paper, whether or not the actor (in this case PUT-ER) of the action is capable of conscious choice determines the case the actor is marked with. Therefore, a feature like [+conscious] must be included in the semantic structure of a verb. The argument structure depicts the valency of the predicate and the relative prominence of its arguments.[6] For the sake of convenience and simplicity I use terms like PUT-ER to represent the semantic structure of a verb. A use of traditional theta role terminology here would complicate the issue in terms of theoretical implications. Centrally relevant to this paper is not which theta roles the arguments of a verb should be assigned, but the notion of conscious choice.

[4]	*ḍaalnaa* (to put)	[put-er[+conscious]	put-ee	location]	Semantic Structure
		‖	‖	‖	
		[ARG1	ARG2	ARG3]	Argument Structure
		‖	‖	‖	
		[Erg	Acc/∅	Loc]	Overt Expression

In Urdu there is a correlation between the ergative case marker and conscious choice on the part of the subject of an expression. This is illustrated by examples **[5]** and **[6]**. When the ergative case is used in **[6]**, the actor is attributed with the intention of screaming. This in turn implies that a conscious decision was made to scream by the actor. In **[5]**, on the other hand, no conscious choice is attributed to the actor: the action of screaming is seen to be entirely involuntary. Again, it is this correlation between the ergative case and conscious choice that motivates the [+conscious] feature in the semantic structure of *ḍaalnaa*.

[5] *voo* *ciikhaa*
he-Nom screamed
'He screamed (despite himself).'

[6] *us-ne* *ciikhaa*
he-Erg screamed
'He screamed (on purpose).'

The structure of the full verb *parnaa* (to fall) is given in **[8]**. An example of its use is shown in **[7]**.[7] The ∅ in the structure representations signifies the nominative, unmarked case. *Parnaa* (to fall) is an intransitive verb while *ḍaalnaa* (to put) is transitive.

Since *parnaa* does not attribute conscious choice to the actor in an expression, the relevant feature in its semantic structure is represented as [−conscious]. However, the situation in Urdu is a little more complex than the correlation of ergative and conscious choice vs. nominative and lack of conscious choice. This will become evident later on.

[7] *šiila* *zamiin-par* *parii*
Sheila floor-on fell
'Sheila fell onto the floor.'

[8]	*parnaa* (to fall)	[faller[−conscious]	location]	Semantic Structure
		‖	‖	
		[ARG1	ARG2]	Argument Structure
		‖	‖	
		[∅	Loc]	Overt Expression

2.2 The Light Verbs

Examples **[9]** - **[20]** illustrate the effect the light verbs *parnaa* and *ḍaalnaa* have on the semantics of an expression and the role they play in the selection of case on the subject. The argument structure (valency) of the host verb and the case its subject takes are demonstrated to be irrelevant.

[9] and **[10]** show that *roonaa* (to cry) is an intransitive verb with a nominative subject. In **[12]** the *ḍaalnaa* gives the act of crying a deliberate, completed aspect while in **[11]** *parnaa* contributes suddenness and surprise (lack of control) to the action. In **[12]** the subject takes the ergative case while in **[11]** it is unmarked (nominative).

[9] ***voo rooyaa***
he-Nom wept
'He wept.'

[10] ****us-ne rooyaa***
he-Erg wept
'He wept.'

[11] ***voo roo paraa***
he-Nom weep fell
'He fell to weeping (burst into tears).'

[12] ***us-ne roo ḍaalaa***
he-Erg weep put
'He wept copiously (heavily, mightily).'

[13] - **[16]** give the effects of ***ḍaalnaa*** and ***parnaa*** when combined with a transitive host that takes an ergative subject. The reading in **[15]** is one in which the singer sang a song he intended to sing and completed singing it with a certain amount of force. **[16]**, on the other hand, depicts somebody suddenly, unconsciously bursting out into a song. The effect of ***ḍaalnaa*** and ***parnaa*** on the case of the subject is evident: ***ḍaalnaa*** assigns the ergative case while ***parnaa*** assigns the nominative.

[13] ***usne gaanaa gaayaa***
he-Erg song sang
'He sang a song.'

[14] ****voo gaanaa gaayaa***
he-Nom song sang
'He sang a song.'

[15] ***us-ne gaanaa gaa ḍaalaa***
he-Erg song sing put
'He sang a song (completed a song he had set out to sing).'

[16] ***voo gaanaa gaa paraa***
he-Nom song sing fell
'He fell to singing (burst out into song).'

As we have seen, *ciikhnaa* (to scream) is an intransitive verb that can take either an ergative or a nominative subject. When the subject is ergative, as in **[18]**, the action becomes more intentional than when the subject is nominative as in **[17]**. **[19]** and **[20]** therefore are not surprising.

[17] ***voo ciikhaa***
he-Nom screamed
'He screamed (despite himself).'

[18] ***us-ne ciikhaa***
he-Erg screamed
'He screamed (on purpose).'

[19] ***voo ciikh paraa***
he-Nom scream fell
'He began screaming suddenly (despite himself).'

[20] ***us-ne ciikh ḍaalaa***
he-Erg scream put
'He screamed violently (on purpose).'

In order to demonstrate the correlations under investigation more clearly, it would be nice to be able to present another set of data, one in which the host is a transitive verb that takes a nominative subject. However, I am not sure that such a creature exists in Urdu.

The correlations that have emerged so far nevertheless seem to be quite clear. The light verb ***ḍaalnaa*** contributes a reading of conscious choice to an action and assigns the ergative case to the subject of the complex predicate. The light verb ***parnaa***, on the other hand, implies a lack of conscious choice and assigns the nominative, unmarked case to the subject.

2.3 Similar Light Verbs

There are other verbs that work like ***ḍaalnaa*** and ***parnaa***. ***Maarnaa*** (to hit) is a ***ḍaalnaa*** type verb. Its full verb use is given in **[21]** and an example of it as a light verb is illustrated by **[22]**. It is evident that ***marnaa*** as a light verb does assign the ergative case and does attribute conscious choice to the performer of the action.

[21] ***šiila-ne aadmii-ko maaraa***
Sheila-Erg man-Acc hit
'Sheila hit the man.'

[22] ***us-ne khat likh maaraa***
he-Erg letter-Nom write hit
'He dashed off a letter.'

[23] and **[24]** demonstrate how ***baithnaa*** (to sit), a ***parnaa*** type verb, works. ***Uthnaa*** (to get up), as is shown in **[25]** and **[26]**, functions similarly. Both of these light verbs assign the nominative case and a lack of conscious control to the actor.

[23] ***šiila zamiin-par baithii***
Sheila-Nom floor-on sat
'Sheila sat on the floor.'

[24] ***voo roo baithii***
she-Nom weep sat
'She wept (caused by an external event).'

[25] ***šiila zamiin-se uthii***
Sheila-Nom floor-from got up
'Sheila got up off the floor.'

[26] ***voo gaa uthii***
she-Nom sing got up
'She burst out singing.'

2.4 Mechanics

There are two kinds of verbs that relate to consciousness of choice: those that function like ***ḍaalnaa*** (to put) and those that function like ***parnaa*** (to fall). ***Ḍaalnaa*** type verbs mark their subject with the ergative in the full form and mark the subject of a complex predicate with the ergative. ***Parnaa*** type verbs have unmarked subjects in the full form and will cause the subject of a complex predicate to be unmarked as well. The valency and transitivity/intransitivity of the host verb is irrelevant. ***Ḍaalnaa*** type verbs contribute consciousness of choice to an action on the part of the actor while ***parnaa*** type verbs denote a lack of conscious choice.

Given what has been discovered about ***parnaa*** and ***ḍaalnaa*** so far, their light verb representations should look as in **[27]** and **[28]** respectively. The 'semantic emptying' effect is expressed in terms of loss of arguments and the amount of semantic information that is retained by the one argument, which in both cases represents the actor of the predicate.[8]

[27] ***parnaa*** (to fall) [[−conscious]] Semantic Structure
‖
[ARG1] Argument Structure
‖
[∅] Overt Expression

[28] *ḍaalnaa* (to put) [[+conscious]] Semantic Structure
||
[ARG1] Argument Structure
||
[Erg] Overt Expression

Examples of how *parnaa* and *ḍaalnaa* are combined with host verbs are represented by **[30]** and **[32]**. **[29]** and **[31]** give the corresponding expressions. The host verb contributes semantic information expressed by valency and the roles attributed to the various arguments. The light verb determines additional semantic information like conscious choice that is relevant to the selection of case on ARG1.

[29] ***voo gaanaa gaa paraa***
he-Nom song sing fell
'He fell to singing (burst out into song).'

[30] ***gaanaa* (to sing)** [singer[+conscious] singee] ***parnaa*** (to fall) [[−conscious]] SS
[ARG1 ARG2] [ARG1] AS
[Erg Acc/∅] [∅] OE

***gaa parnaa* (to begin singing)** [singer[−conscious] singee] Semantic Structure
[ARG1 ARG2] Argument Structure
[∅ Acc/∅] Overt Expression

[31] ***us-ne roo ḍaalaa***
he-Erg weep put
'He wept copiously (heavily, mightily).'

[32] ***roonaa* (to weep)** [weeper] ***ḍaalnaa* (to put)** [[+conscious]] SS
[ARG1] [ARG1] AS
[∅] [Erg] OE

***roo ḍaalnaa* (to weep heavily)** [weeper[+conscious]] Semantic Structure
[ARG1] Argument Structure
[Erg] Overt Expression

The generalizations illustrated by these examples are as follows:

1) The valency of the complex predicate is the same as the valency of the host verb (see **[30]**).

2) Case marking on the complex predicate subject is determined by the light verb, due to the fact that it contributes such subtle semantic information as conscious choice or the lack thereof on the part of the actor in an expression.

From these generalizations it is evident that the light verb provides the semantic structure for the complex predicate while the host verb contributes the semantic substance: the host verb does not lose any of its arguments so that, unlike the light verb, its original semantic information is not interfered with.

3 Availability and Exercise of Conscious Choice

3.1 Some Evidence

There is, however, more to the conscious choice vs. lack of conscious choice contributions of light verbs than has met the eye up to now. This becomes clear when the expressions examined so far are tinkered with a bit more. For example, if ***ḍaalnaa*** (to put) type verbs really express control over an action by virtue of the fact that the actor is making conscious choices, then they should be incompatible with any additions to the expression that suggest otherwise. So, if the phrase ***galtii-se*** (by mistake) is added to expressions that have a ***ḍaalnaa*** type light verb, the expression should become bad. Similarly, if the phrase ***dʰiyaan-se*** (with care) is added to expressions containing ***parnaa*** (to fall) type light verbs, those expressions should become bad. **[33]** - **[36]** show that ***ḍaalnaa*** type verbs do indeed work the way they should. In **[34]** the medicine can be drunk by mistake; however, in **[36]** where ***ḍaalnaa*** attributes conscious choice to the agent, the action cannot be taken to be accidental: the assertion sounds strange.

This set of examples also illustrates another aspect that has been glossed over so far. Up to now an ergative case marker on the subject has been automatically equated to the feature [+conscious]. However, **[34]** shows that the ergative marker may be present even when conscious choice is not necessarily attributed to the actor. It therefore seems appropriate to make a distinction between conscious choice when it is AVAILABLE and when it is EXPRESSED. In other words, the lexical representation of ***piinaa*** (to drink) should be marked something like [+cc available] (conscious choice available) and both the light verb ***ḍaalnaa*** and the complex predicate in **[35]** should be marked with [+cc expressed] (conscious choice available and expressed). So in **[33]** - **[35]** conscious choice could be attributed to the drinker since it is available. In cases like **[34]**, where conscious choice on the part of the speaker seems inappropriate, it can therefore simply be ignored. However, in cases like **[36]**, where the presence of ***ḍaalnaa*** has made the expression of conscious choice explicit, it cannot be ignored and therefore the sentence sounds strange.

[33] *us-ne* *davaii* *pii*
he-Erg medicine-Nom drank
'He drank the medicine.'

[34] *us-ne* *galtii-se* *davaii* *pii*
he-Erg mistake-Inst medicine-Nom drank
'He drank the medicine by mistake.'

[35] *us-ne* *davaii* *pii ḍaalii*
he-Erg medicine-Nom drink put
'He downed the medicine.'

[36] *#us-ne* *galtii-se* *davaii* *pii ḍaalii*
he-Erg mistake-Inst medicine-Nom drink put
#'He downed the medicine by mistake.'

When the same strategy is applied to ***parnaa*** type verbs, a similar pattern, shown in **[37]** - **[40]**, emerges. In **[38]** it is possible to jump carefully. However, as soon as ***parnaa*** becomes a part of the construction, the conscious choice implied by the phrase 'with care' is unacceptable semantically. **[38]** also shows that the nominative case on the subject is not necessarily restricted to expressing a lack of conscious choice. Rather, a reading of conscious choice vs. a lack of conscious choice seems to depend on the particular main verb, i.e. what particular feature it carries in terms of conscious choice. This is further illustrated below.

In terms of features then, ***parnaa*** should carry [−cc available] (no conscious choice reading available). ***Kuudnaa*** in **[38]** should be marked with [+cc available]. The combination of the two, the complex predicate in **[39]** and **[40]**, has a conscious choice reading suppressed by ***parnaa*** and would therefore be labeled [−cc expressed] (conscious choice available but not expressed), which is semantically incompatible with the phrase 'with care' in **[40]**.

[37] *mãĩ* *kuudii*
I-Nom jumped
'I jumped.'

[38] *mãĩ* *d^hiyaan-se* *kuudii*
I-Nom attention-Inst jumped
'I jumped carefully.'

[39] *mãĩ* *kuud parii*
I-Nom jump fell
'I jumped (unintentionally).'

[40] *#mãĩ dʰiyaan-se kuud parii*
I-Nom attention-Inst jump fell
#'I jumped carefully.'

When ***parnaa*** type verbs are combined with hosts like ***calnaa*** (to walk), a lack of consciousness of choice on the part of the actor is not necessarily implied. So neither **[42]** nor **[44]** are semantically odd because ***parnaa*** is not contributing a sense of a lack of conscious control to the expression in this situation.

[41] *mãĩ calii*
I-Nom walked
'I walked (went).'

[42] *mãĩ dʰiyaan-se calii*
I-Nom attention-Inst walk
'I walked carefully.'

[43] *mãĩ cal parii*
I-Nom walk fell
'I started walking.'

[44] *mãĩ dʰiyaan-se cal parii*
I-Nom attention-Inst walk fell
'I started walking carefully.'

The thing about *calnaa* is that it can appear in two forms. When its subjects are animate, it carries an implication of conscious choice with it. When its subjects are inanimate, however, it necessarily implies a lack of control on the part of the subject.[9] An example of this is given in **[45]**, where the car cannot be said to have made a conscious decision to start up.

[45] *gaarii cal parii*
car-Nom walk fell
'The car began running (started up).'

So, *parnaa* type verbs contribute a reading that implies a lack of conscious choice on the part of the actor when the host verb is not [+cc expressed]. Verbs like *calnaa* that have two versions, one in which conscious choice is expressed and one in which it is not available must be treated as exceptions. In these cases *parnaa* can function as a light verb, however, when it combines with the [+cc expressed] version of the host verb, it cannot contribute a lack of conscious choice reading. Exactly why verbs like *calnaa* should behave differently in being able to override the light verb in terms of conscious choice needs to be explored some more.

3.2 The Complete Picture

After examining some further evidence contributed by the examples in **[46]** - **[49]**, a fairly complete description of how things work can be given. In **[46]** the host verb ***piinaa*** (to drink), as we have already seen, carries the feature 'drinker[+cc available]'. ***Parnaa*** carries the feature [−cc available]. When the two are combined, it results in 'drinker[−cc expressed]' and therefore the actor in **[46]** cannot be seen as having any conscious control over the action.

In **[47]** ***girnaa*** (to fall) is marked with 'faller[−cc available]' since one does not usually fall intentionally (when one does, it is regarded as a special case). The complex predicate results in being marked as 'faller[−cc available]' as well. Since neither the host nor the light verb have a possibility of expressing conscious choice, the complex predicate cannot result in being marked 'faller[−cc expressed]'.[10]

[46] ***voo davaii pii paraa***
he-Erg medicine-Nom drink fell
'He started drinking the medicine (suddenly, without much forethought).'

[47] ***mãĩ gir parii***
I-Nom fall fell
'I fell.'

[48] ****mãĩ gir ḍaalii***
I-Nom fall put
'*I fell.'

[49] ****mãĩ cal ḍaalii***
I-Nom walk put
'*I walked.'

[48] and **[49]** represent incompatible combinations of conscious choice features. In **[48]** 'faller[−cc available]' is combined with the [+cc expressed] of ***ḍaalnaa***. In **[49]** 'walker[+cc expressed]' combines with [+cc expressed]. This ought to work, but it does not. Again, there seems to be something different about verbs like ***calnaa***.

Some examples of how combinations like the ones described above would look in their full-fledged forms are given in **[50]** - **[52]**.

```
[50]  roonaa (to weep) [weeper[+cc available]]  daalnaa (to put) [[+cc expressed]]  SS
                        ||                                          ||
                       [ARG1]                                      [ARG1]            AS
                        ||                                          ||
                       [∅]                                         [Erg]             OE

      roo daalnaa (to weep heavily)   [weeper[+cc expressed]]   Semantic Structure
                                       ||
                                      [ARG1]                    Argument Structure
                                       ||
                                      [Erg]                     Overt Expression

[51]  gaanaa      [singer[+cc available]  singee]   parnaa     [[−cc available]]  SS
      (to sing)    ||                      ||       (to fall)   ||
                  [ARG1]                  [ARG2]               [ARG1]             AS
                   ||                      ||                   ||
                  [Erg                    Acc/∅]               [∅]                OE

      gaa parnaa (to begin singing) [singer[−cc expressed] singee]  Semantic Structure
                                     ||                     ||
                                    [ARG1]                 [ARG2]   Argument Structure
                                     ||                     ||
                                    [∅]                    Acc/∅]   Overt Expression

[52]  girnaa (to fall) [faller[−cc available]]   parnaa (to fall) [[−cc available]]  SS
                        ||                                         ||
                       [ARG1]                                     [ARG1]             AS
                        ||                                         ||
                       [∅]                                        [∅]                OE

      gir parnaa (to fall)  [faller[−cc available]]        Semantic Structure
                             ||
                            [ARG1]                         Argument Structure
                             ||
                            [∅]                            Overt Expression
```

On the whole, a simple set of rules can be formulated for what kinds of host verbs can combine with which kinds of light verbs by examining what conscious choice feature they carry.

I) **Host verb [+cc available]**: (*piinaa* (to drink), ***gaanaa*** (to sing), etc.)

   a) Light verb is [+cc expressed] (*ḍaalnaa*). This results in the complex predicate being [+cc expressed]. Its subject is in the ergative.

   b) Light verb is [−cc available] (***parnaa***). This results in the complex predicate being [−cc expressed]. Its subject is in the nominative.

II) **Host verb [−cc available]**: (*girnaa* (to fall))

a) Light verb is [+cc expressed]. Complex predicate is ill-formed. **Not possible.**

b) Light verb is [−cc available]. Complex predicate is [−cc available]. Subject is in the nominative.

The one host verb examined in this paper that is [+cc expressed] does not display the correlations between case and conscious choice that is evident in the other verbs. Verbs like ***calnaa*** (to walk) need to be investigated in their own right more thoroughly before it is possible to determine exactly how they fit into the scheme presented here.

4 Conclusion

By examining a specific correlation between semantic information such as conscious choice that is contributed by light verbs and the selection of case for the subject of the complex predicate, this paper has tried to explore and understand the mechanics of complex predicates in terms of semantic structure and semantic substance. It has been shown that the host verb contributes semantic substance to the complex predicate while the light verb provides the semantic structure. This can be expressed more specifically by the following generalizations:

1) The valency of the complex predicate is the same as the valency of the host verb.

2) Case marking on the complex predicate subject is determined by the light verb, due to the fact that it contributes such subtle semantic information as [−cc available] and [+cc expressed] to an expression.

It has also become evident that host verbs can be classified as belonging to different categories when examined from the point of view of features such as conscious choice in this paper. It should be worthwhile to investigate other light verbs and semantic aspects in a manner similar to the one employed in this paper. A greater insight might develop as to what kind of syntactically pertinent semantic information must be included when coming up with a representation for a verb. This could result in generalizations that would contribute more towards an overall understanding of how syntax and semantics interact.

NOTES

1. The term is used in the sense of Jespersen (1954) and Cattell (1984). A given verb is considered LIGHT when it loses part of its semantic content so that, when used in conjunction with a HOST, its FULL meaning is not contributed to the construction. Auxiliaries function similarly, but they have lost all of the original content of the corresponding FULL VERB.

2. It becomes evident, after only a brief inspection of the three different kinds of complex predicate constructions, that very different things go on in terms of case assignment, valency, and agreement displayed by the light verb. There is not enough space to demonstrate these differencs in this paper, but it is quite clear that the mechanics of each of the constructions needs to be explored carefully in its own right.

3. The following abbreviations for case markers are used in examples throughout the paper: **Erg** for ergative; **Nom** for nominative; **Acc** for accusative; **Dat** for dative; **Inst** for instrumental.

4. I am further restricting myself to the examination of verb-verb type complex predicates in which the host verb appears in the BARE, uninflected form. There are other kinds of complex predicate constructions in which the host manifests itself in what Bender (1967) calls the INFINITIVE OBJECT form. An example would be: ***Sheila girne lagii*** 'Sheila began to fall', where the ***girnaa*** 'to fall' is inflected just like nouns ending in ***-aa*** when they appear as obliques. The mechanics surrounding this construction seem to be different from the ones under investigation here and need to be explored in depth.

5. For a brief discussion of the factors that determine the accusative/nominative alternation in direct objects see Comrie (1981:126).

6. Rather than defining relative prominence in terms of theta-role hierarchies, as is usual, my relative prominence orderings are based on the canonical word order the arguments appear in. Whether or not this is warranted remains to be seen.

7. This example sounds funny at first to speakers of Urdu/Hindi. This is because ***parnaa*** is very seldom actually used as a full verb. When it is used as a full verb, the meaning 'to be lying down' seems to be accessed first. It would be very instructive to investigate the history and other uses of this verb in order to arrive at a better understanding of it.

8. Intuitively, ***maarnaa*** 'to hit', ***baithnaa*** 'to sit', and ***uthnaa*** 'to get up' seem to retain more of their semantic content than ***ḍaalnaa*** and ***parnaa***. This difference can be characterized by attaching more semantic information to the ARG1 of ***maarnaa***, ***baithnaa***, and ***uthnaa*** than for ***parnaa*** or ***ḍaalnaa***. So ARG1 would carry 'hitter[+conscious]' or 'sitter[−conscious]' in the semantic structure.

9. A few more verbs like this exist in Urdu. One example is ***boolnaa*** (to talk).

10. Recall that [−cc expressed] conveys the information that conscious choice was available but not expressed.

REFERENCES

Bender, Ernest. 1967. Urdu grammar and reader. Philadelphia: University of Pennsylvania Press.

Comrie, Bernard. 1981. Language universals and linguistic typology. Chicago: The University of Chicago Press.

Glassman, Eugene H. 1977. Spoken Urdu. Lahore: Nirali Kitaben.

Hook, Peter Edwin. 1974. The compound verb in Hindi. Ann Arbor, Michigan: University of Michigan Center for South and Southeast Asian Studies.

Masica, Colin P. 1976. Defining a linguistic area: South Asia. Chicago: The University of Chicago Press.

A UNION ANALYSIS OF A TELUGU COMPLEX PREDICATE CONSTRUCTION

William D. Davies
University of Iowa

0. Introduction

As is well-known, many South Asian languages contain complex predicate constructions, in which the verbal element of a sentence is made up of two verbal elements or a nominal expression and a finite verb. The Dravidian language Telugu contains complex verbal constructions such as the following:[1]

[1]	***siita***	***ramu-ni***	***babu-ni***	***koṭṭ-am-an-in-di***
	Sita	Ram-ACC	Babu-ACC	beat-IMP-say-PST-3sf

'Sita asked Ram to beat Babu.'

The verbal element in **[1]** consists of a base verb stem followed by the 1st plural imperative suffix (glossed "IMP") followed by an inflected form of the verb ***anu*** 'to say'. Its arguments obligatorily include an addressor in the nominative (***siita***) and an addressee in the accusative (***ramuni***), with other arguments determined by the valence of the base verb. The construction, which I will refer to as the ***anu***-construction, denotes a request by one participant for action by another, thus the class of base verbs is largely restricted to volitional predicates.

In this paper I propose a Union analysis of this construciton, in which both ***koṭṭu*** 'beat' and ***anu*** 'say' are predicates at some level of structure, although the construction comprises a single clause. The analysis employs the monoclausal analysis of Union proposed by Davies and Rosen (1988).[2] **[1]** would have the representation in **[2]**.

[2]

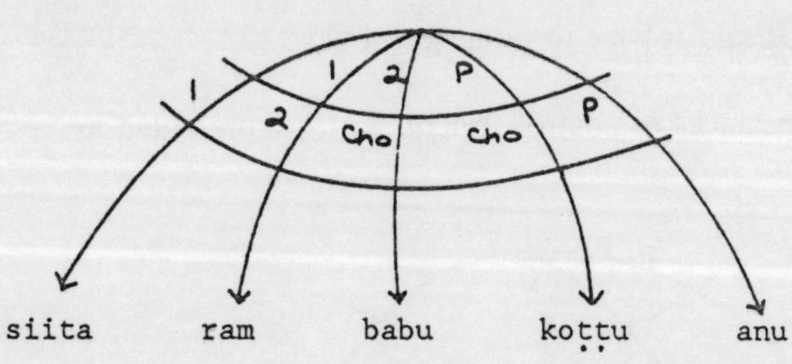

Details of the analysis are described below, and evidence for the analysis is examined in section **2.**

The valence of the ***anu***-construction depends on both the base predicate and ***anu***. This fact can be captured in terms of the Union analysis and Davies and Dubinsky's (1991) system for representing grammatical valence. This aspect of the analysis is examined in section **3.**

The Union analysis and the valence formalism can be extended to further cases of complex predicates. In section **4** I suggest that certain complex predicate constructions including "light" verbs may be open to a Union analysis. For instance, I show that facts of the Malayalam benefactive construction (Mohanan 1983), which consists of a base predicate and the "light" verb 'give', follow naturally in an analysis incorporating these two constructs.

1. The Union Analysis

The sentence in **[1]** contrasts with **[3]**, a propositionally equivalent construction with a similar range of arguments; however, in **[3]** the verb designating the requested action is a separate constituent, taking the complementizer ***ani***[3] and acting as complement to ***aḍugu*** 'to ask' or ***anu*** 'to say'. As in the ***anu***-construction, the addressor is in the nominative and the addressee in the accusative.

[3] ***siita babu-ni kott-am-ani ramu-ni aḍig-in-di / an-in-di***
Sita Babu-ACC beat-IMP-COMP Ram-ACC ask-PST-3sf/ say-PST-3sf

'Sita {asked/said to} Ram to beat Babu.'

The sentences in **[4]** - **[5]** show the same correspondence as **[1]** and **[3]**.

[4] ***siita nannu pustakaalu te-mm-an-in-di***
Sita I.ACC books bring-IMP-say-PST-3sf

'Sita asked me to bring the books.'

[5] ***siita pustakaalu te-mm-ani nannu aḍig-in-di / an-in-di***
Sita books bring-IMP-COMP I.ACC ask-PST-3sf/ say-PST-3sf

'Sita {asked/said to} me to bring the books.'

I take **[3]** and **[5]** to be instances of control structures, **[3]** represented as:[4]

[6]

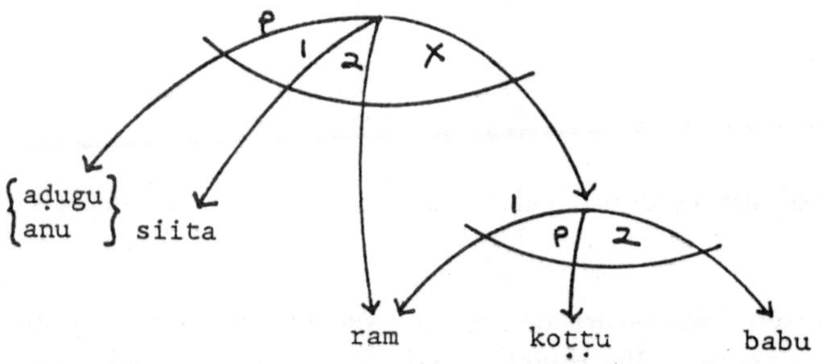

In **[3]** ***ram*** bears thematic relations to both the matrix and embedded predicates and thus bears a grammatical relation (GR) in the initial stratum of each clause. Absence of ***ram*** or a third person masculine pronoun in the nominative in **[3]** signals the control construction. As final direct objects take accusative case and ***ram*** is marked accusative in **[3]**, it is assigned the 2-relation in **[6]**.

In contrast to **[6]**, I propose the ***anu***-construction has the Union structure in **[2]**, repeated here.

[2]

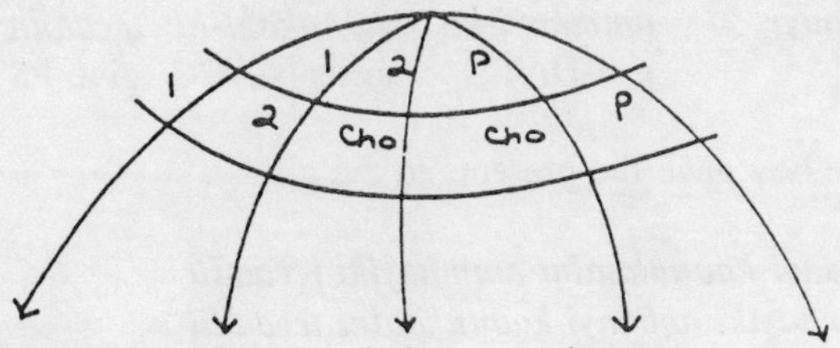

The important aspects of the structure in **[2]** are (i) that all nominal and verbal elements are dependents of a single clause node and (ii) that within the single clause there are two verbal elements that stand in the Predicate relationship to the clause (i.e. bear the P-relation), here ***koṭṭu*** 'beat' and ***anu*** 'say'. Thus, the structure in **[2]** has characteristics of sentences with a single predicate (that of having all elements members of a single clause) and characteristics of sentences with complement clauses (that of having multiple predicates). This structure is therefore able to capture both the similarities and differences exhibited by **[1]** and **[3]**. Some of these properties are discussed in the following section, which provides motivation for the structure in **[2]**.

The details of **[2]** are that the first stratum of structure includes the verb ***koṭṭu*** and its arguments, ***ram***, the agent and subject, and ***babu***, the theme and direct object. In the second stratum, the verb ***anu*** and its arguments, ***siita***, the agent and subject, and ***ram***, the goal and direct object, are licensed. The stratum in which a particular element bears the P-relation is called the *P-sector* of that element. Thus, in **[2]** the initial stratum is ***koṭṭu***'s P-sector and the second stratum is ***anu***'s P-sector. Following the Stratal Uniqueness Law (Perlmutter and Postal 1977 as extended by Davies and Rosen 1988), each stratum may contain only one 1, one 2, one 3, and one P; thus, ***koṭṭu*** and ***babu*** are demoted to chômeur in the Union stratum (the first stratum in which ***anu*** bears the P-relation. Assuming that animate 2-chômeurs as well as final 2s are obligatorily marked accusative, the accusative case of ***ram*** and ***babu*** in **[1]** are accounted for by the structure in **[2]**.[5]

2. Evidence for the Union Structure

Apart from the fact that the ***anu***-construction contains a single complex verbal element, word order and adverb scope facts provide evidence that all elements of the construction are dependents of a single clause node.

Basic Telugu word order is SOV. However, constituent order in a clause can be relatively free provided the verb stays in final position, as in **[7]**.

[7]	a.	*abbaayi*	*ammaayi-ki*	*kaanukaal-ni*	*iccaaḍu*
		boy	girl-DAT	presents-ACC	give.PST.3sm

'The boy gave the presents to the girl.'

b. ***abbaayi kaanukaalni ammaayiki iccaaḍu***
c. ***ammaayiki abbaayi kaanukaalni iccaaḍu***
d. ***ammaayiki kaanukaalni abbaayi iccaaḍu***
...

The indirect object, ***ammaayi*** 'girl', and direct object, ***kaanukaalu*** 'presents', can occur in either order with respect to each other, **[7a.- b.]**. Also the subject, ***abbaayi*** 'boy', can follow one or more of the arguments in the clause, **[7c.- d.]**.

However, word order respects clause boundaries:

[8]	a.	*siita*	*[abbaayi*	*babu-ni*	*kottadani]*	*anukuntindi*
		Sita	boy	Babu-ACC	beat.COMP	think.NONPST.3sf

'Sita thinks that the boy beat Babu.'

b. ***[abbaayi babu-ni siita kottadani] anukuntindi***

In **[8a.]**, the matrix subject, ***siita***, precedes all embedded arguments, illustrating the canonical word order. In **[8b.]**, ***siita*** follows both embedded arguments, and the sentence is ungrammatical. Informally we can account for this by including in the grammar of Telugu a constraint against ordering matrix arguments following two or more embedded dependents.

The ***anu***-construction, exhibits considerable freedom of word order.

[9]	a.	*siita*	*abbaayi-ni*	*babu-ki*	*pustakamu*	*ivvamanindi*
		Sita	boy-ACC	Babu-DAT	book	give.IMP.say.PST.3sf

'Sita asked the boy to give the book to Babu.'

b. ***babuki siita abbaayini pustakamu ivvamanindi***
c. ***babuki pustakamu siita abbaayini ivvamanindi***

Crucially, in **[9c.]**, ***siita***, the subject of the clause, can follow the arguments ***babu*** and ***pustakamu*** 'book'. The freedom of word order in the ***anu***-construction thus parallels the word order possibilities of simple clauses (compare **[9c.]** and **[7d.]**).

Further evidence for monoclausality as well as multiple P-sectors comes from the interpretation of adverbs. In monoclausal structures the adverbial ***budhavaaram*** 'Wednesday' can occur in any pre-verbal position in the clause.

[10]	a.	*ammaayi*	*abbaayi-ki*	*pustakamu*	*budhavaaram*	*iccindi*
		girl	boy-DAT	book	Wednesday	give.PST.3sf

'The girl gave the book to the boy on Wednesday.'

b. ***ammaayi abbaayiki budhavaaram pustakamu iccindi***
c. ***ammaayi budhavaaram abbaayiki pustakamu iccindi***
d. ***budhavaaram ammaayi abbaayiki pustakamu iccindi***

Regardless of the position of ***budhavaaram***, the events described are understood to have occurred "on Wednesday", i.e., the adverb has scope over the entire clause.

Granting for now that an adverb modifies the clause of which it is a dependent, its placement in different positions in biclausal constructions naturally results in different interpretations.

[11]	a.	*budhavaaram*	*babu*	*[pustakaalu temmani]*	*ramu-ni*	*aḍigaaḍu*
		Wednesday	Babu	books bring.COMP	Ram-ACC	ask.PST.3sm

'On Wednesday Babu ASKED Ram to bring the books.'

	b.	*babu*	*[pustakaalu*	*budhavaaram*	*temmani]*	*ramuni*	*aḍigaaḍu*
				Wednesday			

'Babu asked Ram to BRING the books on Wednesday.

In **[11a.]**, ***budhavaaram*** is sentence-initial, a dependent of the highest clause node, and modifies the matrix predicate, ***aḍugu*** 'to ask' (as indicated by small capitals in the translation). When

budhavaaram occurs between the embedded direct object and the embedded predicate, ***teccu*** 'to bring', and is thus a constituent of the embedded clause **[11b.]**, the adverb has scope only over the predicate of the embedded clause, and the interpretation is that the bringing took place (or is to take place on) Wednesday. These sentences are unambiguous.

Interestingly, when ***budhavaaram*** occurs between ***babu*** and ***pustakaalu***, the sentence is ambiguous, ***budhavaaram*** having scope over either the matrix or embedded verb.

[12]	***babu***	***budhavaaram***	***pustakaalu***	***temmani***	***ramu-ni***	***aḍigaadu***
	Babu	Wednesday	books	bring.COMP	Ram-ACC	ask.PST.3sm

'On Wednesday Babu ASKED Ram to bring the books.'
'Babu asked Ram to BRING the books on Wednesday.'

The ambiguity in **[12]** is unsurprising: given the relative freedom of word order and the fact that ***budhavaaram*** occurs at the boundary of the matrix and embedded clauses in **[12]**, surface structure does not directly indicate what clause the adverbial is a constituent of. When it is a constituent of the matrix clause, we get the first interpretation; when a constituent of the embedded clause, the second interpretation.

In the ***anu***-construction, we find that all placements of the adverbial result in ambiguity.

[13]	a.	***budhavaaram***	***babu***	***ramu-ni***	***pustakaalu***	***temmannaadu***
		Wednesday	Babu	Ram-ACC	books	bring.IMP.say.PST.3sm

'On Wednesday Babu ASKED Ram to bring the books.'
'Babu asked Ram to BRING the books on Wednesday.'

b. ***babu ramuni pustakaalu budhavaaram temmannaadu***
c. ***babu budhavaaram ramuni pustakaalu temmannaadu***
d. ***budhavaaram babu ramuni pustakaalu temmannaadu***

The fact that the temporal element can occur in any position in the clause without affecting the scope of the adverbial parallels the facts in **[10]**. In **[10]**, a simplex clause, placement of the temporal element had no effect on meaning. Thus, the ***anu***-construction again shows properties of a single clause, as is directly represented in the structure in **[2]**.

Obviously, the facts here differ importantly from single predicate structures in that the adverbial can be interpreted as modifying either of the predicates in the ***anu***-construction. The Union analysis can account for this fairly straightforwardly. Given the two P-sectors, we can say that the adverbial has scope over the predicate in whose P-sector it first heads an arc. Thus, when ***budhavaaram*** first heads an arc in the P-sector of ***teccu*** 'to bring', it has scope over that predicate, while when it first heads an arc in the P-sector of ***anu*** 'to say', it has scope over that predicate and its arguments. This is shown in the RNs in **[14]** and **[15]**, respectively.

[14]

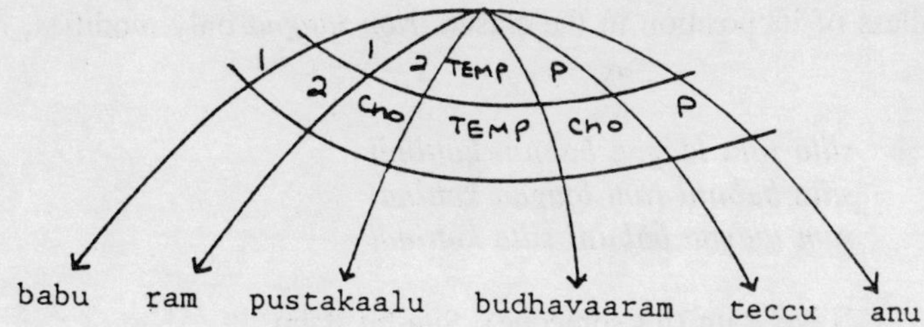

[15]

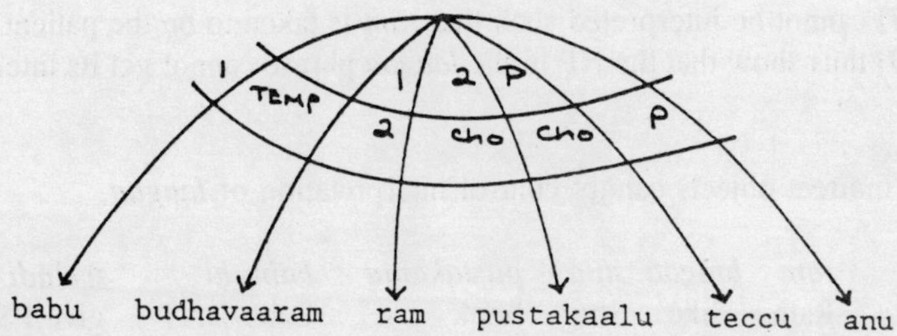

In **[14]**, ***budhavaaram*** heads a Temp(oral)-arc in the initial stratum, ***teccu***'s P-initial stratum. In **[15]**, it first heads a Temp-arc in ***anu***'s P-initial stratum. Reference to P-initial strata for adverbial scope determination will generalize to cases of adverbial scope in the monoclausal and biclausal cases examined above.

Additional evidence for the multiple P-sector analysis comes from phenomena sensitive to subjects. The Union structure in **[2]** asserts that the ***anu***-construction contains more than one subject, albeit in different P-sectors. A grammatical property sensitive to subjects should identify more than one subject in these constructions. Such evidence is available from interpretation of the adverbial ***laagaa*** 'like'.

The adverbial ***laagaa*** 'like' occurs in a construction [NP + ***laagaa***], in which the associated NP receives its semantic interpretation from some other nominal in the clause, or put differently, the adverbial phrase serves as a modifier of a particular nominal in the clause. **[16]** illustrates.

[16]	***ram***	***laaga***	***siita***	***babu-ni***	***koṭṭindi***
	Ram	like	Sita	Babu-ACC	beat.PST.3sf

'Like Ram (hit someone), Sita hit Babu.'

In **[16]**, ***ram***, the NP in the adverbial phrase, is interpreted as an agent, and the adverbial asserts that Sita's action is similar to some present or past action of Ram's. Of interest here is that the

laagaa construction gets its interpretation from a subject and only a subject. As the variants in **[17]** show, regardless of its position in the clasue, ***ram laagaa*** only modifies, or is controlled by, ***siita***.

[17] **a.** ***siita ram laagaa babuni koṭṭindi***
b. ***siita babuni ram laagaa koṭṭindi***
c. ***ram laagaa babuni siita koṭṭindi***

'Like Ram (hit someone), Sita hit Babu.'
* 'Sita hit Babu like (someone hit) Ram.'

The clauses in **[17]** cannot be interpreted such that ***ram*** is taken to be the patient of some act of hitting. **[16]** - **[17]** thus show that the NP in the ***laagaa*** phrase cannot get its interpretation from a direct object.

Likewise, indirect objects cannot control interpretation of ***laagaa***.

[18]	**a.**	***ram***	***laagaa***	***siita***	***pustakamu***	***babu-ki***	***iccindi***
		Ram	like	Sita	book	Babu-DAT	give.PST.3sf

b. ***siita pustakamu babuki ram laagaa iccindi***

'Like Ram (gave to someone), Sita gave the book to Babu.'
* 'Sita gave the book to Babu like (someone gave to Ram).'

Regardless of word order, in **[18]** ***ram*** cannot be interpreted as a recipient; it does not get its semantic role from the indirect object. As in **[16]** - **[17]**, ***ram*** must be interpreted as having the same semantic relationship to an understood predicate as ***siita***, the subject.

In **[16]** - **[18]** the NP in the ***laagaa***-construction is interpreted as an agent, and the subjects of these clauses are agentive. However, as the following show, a thematic analysis interpreting the ***laagaa*** NP with an agentive function is not possible.

[19]	***ram***	***laagaa***	***ammaayi***	***baadhapaḍindi***
	Ram	like	girl	suffer.PST.3sf

'Like Ram (suffered), the girl suffered.'

In **[19]**, ***ram*** is interpreted as an experiencer or patient of the state of suffering. This is the thematic relation that ***ammaayi*** 'girl', the subject, bears to the predicate ***baadhapadu*** 'to suffer'. Likewise, the ***laagaa***-construction can get its interpretation from the subject of a passive clause, as in **[20]**.

[20] *ram laagaa devili-ki ammabaḍḍaaḍu*
Ram like devil-DAT sell.INF.PASS.PST.3sm

'Like Ram (was sold), Babu was sold to the devil.'

In **[20]**, ***babu*** is a patient but crucially also the final subject of the clause.

In the ***anu***-construction the facts are different. Consider the clauses in **[21]**.

[21] a. *ram laagaa siita babu-ni pustakaalu temmanindi*
Ram like Sita Babu-ACC books bring.IMP.say.PST.3sf

'Like Ram (asked X), Sita asked Babu to bring the books.'

b. *siita babuni ram laagaa pustakaalu temmanindi*
like

'Sita asked Babu to bring the books like Ram (brought X).'

The clauses in **[21]** show that in the ***anu***-construction there is more than one possible controller of ***laagaa***; however, interpretation is sensitive to word order.[6] In **[21a.]**, the adverbial occurs clause initially and the interpretation of ***ram*** depends on the final subject, ***siita***; given the subject-condition on ***laagaa*** interpretation, this result is expected. In **[21b.]**, the adverbial follows the final direct object, ***babu***, and the adverbial NP is interpreted as having the same semantic role as ***babu*** bears to the embedded predicate ***teccu*** 'to bring'. **[21b.]** is easily accounted for under the Union analysis of the ***anu***-construction: since ***babu*** is the subject of the inner P-sector, this nominal is a legitimate controller. The clauses in **[22]** provide additional evidence.[7]

[22] a. *ram laagaa siita nannu abbaayi-too maṭlaḍamanindi*
Ram like Sita I.ACC boy-COM speak.IMP.say.PST.3sf

'Like Ram (asked X), Sita asked me to speak to the boy.'

b. *siita nannu ram laagaa abbaayitoo maṭlaḍamanindi*

'Sita asked me to speak to the boy like Ram (spoke).'

3. Valence

It is notable that in the ***anu***-construction the number of nominal elements in the clause is predictable from the valence of the base predicate and the valence of ***anu***. As shown in **[3]** and **[5]**, in a biclausal control structure, ***anu*** takes an agentive subject, a goal direct object, and a proposition of which the goal argument is the final subject. Naturally, in that construction the predicate of the embedded clause determines the number of arguments in the embedded clause. In the ***anu***-construction, the valence requirments of ***anu*** remain the same: an agentive subject, a goal direct object, and a propositional element. Thus the synonymy of **[1,3]** and **[4,5]** can be accounted for easily.

In recent work, Davies and Dubinsky (1991) have proposed that valence requirements of predicates can be represented by valence sets specifying the P-initial GRs that must accompany predicates. Thus, ***anu*** 'to say' would specify an initial set of subject, direct object, and proposition, and this proposition could either take the form of a clausal element or a Predicate chômeur. This is represented schematically in **[23]**, which utilizes an arc notation to be read [Grammatical Relation(head,tail) < stratal coordinate >).

[23] $$[P(\textit{anu},b)<c_i>) \rightarrow \left\{ \begin{array}{l} [1(a,b)<c_i>) \\ [2(c,b)<c_i>) \\ [X(d,b)<c_i>) \\ \left\{ \begin{array}{l} (1(c,b)<c_{i-1}>) \\ (1(c,d)<c_f>) \end{array} \right\} \end{array} \right\}$$

Although the formalism is rather obscure, and not central to our primary concern here, **[23]** asserts that in a structure in which ***anu*** first bears the Predicate relation to clause *b* (i.e. stratum c_i), there must also be a subject (1), a direct object (2), and a propositional argument (X). Additionally, the direct object (nominal *c*) introduced by ***anu*** is also the final subject of the preceding P-sector or the embedded clause. When *X* is a clausal relation, nominal *c* must be the embedded final 1, as depicted in the diagram in **[6]**; when *X* is a chômeur, nominal *c* must bear the 1-relation in the first P-sector, as depicted in the diagram in **[2]**. Although not reflected in [23], thematic role assignments would be made by ***anu*** to those elements it introduces in its initial coordinate, c_i. The specific valences of ***anu*** and the base predicate of the propositional argument thus determine the valence of the entire construction.

4. "Light" Verbs and Union

The foregoing discussion was intended to show the viability of a Union analysis for a Dravidian complex predicate construction. Union analyses have been proposed for other complex predicate constructions in South Asian languages as well, notably causatives and other semi-causatives of the type just described. This particular Telugu construction is not a "light" verb construction (in the sense of a semantically "bleached" or empty verb). However, I would like to suggest that complex predicate constructions based on light verbs may be open to Union analyses as well.

Such analyses have been suggested outside of the South Asian area. For example, Rosen (1987) has shown that a Union analysis of Italian auxiliary constructions captures a number of important syntactic generalizations in that language. Additionally, in recent work

Dubinsky (1989) has successfully applied the Union approach to "light" verb constructions in Japanese. Dubinsky has proposed that the sentence in **[24a.]** has the structure in **[24b.]**.

[24] **a.** ***Taroo wa tenisubu ni nyukai-sita***
Taro TOP tennis.club DAT join-do.PERF

'Taro joined a tennis club.'

b.

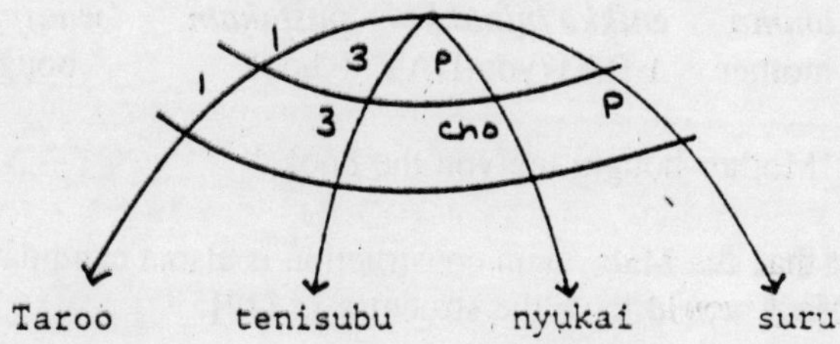

The semantic and syntactic facts fall out from the valence of ***suru*** 'do' and the fact that in its light verb manifestation it has no thematic roles to assign. Dubinsky shows that complex syntactic restrictions on the nature of the inner predicate (a 'verbal noun') fall out from his Union analysis.

Tamil has a light verb construction very similar to the Japanese case. Again a Union analysis might prove profitable. As an example consider the following alternation.

[25] **a.** ***ammaa makanukku eccerittaarkal***
mother son.DAT warn.PAST.3HON

'Mother warned her son.'

b. ***ammaa makanukku eccerikkai ceytaarkal***
mother son.DAT warning do.PAST.3HON

'Mother warned her son.'

In **[25a.]**, the verbal form of ***eccer-*** 'warn' is used; there is an agentive subject and a goal indirect object.[8] In **[25b.]**, the main predicate is ***cey-*** 'do' and we have the nominal form ***eccerikkai*** 'warning'. However, the two constructions are essentially synonymous. The light verb ***cey*** adds no semantic information and imposes no special restrictions. It may be entirely appropriate to apply the analysis proposed by Dubinsky for the parallel Japanese construction to this case.

Mohanan (1983) discusses an intriguing benefactive construction in Malayalam he refers to as *give*-compounding that takes a base predicate combined with the verb 'give', either ***tar̄*** or ***kotukk***. The construction takes a base predicate and its arguments, suffixes the appropriate form of *give*, and, if necessary, adds a goal argument as beneficiary. This is illustrated in **[26]**.[9]

[26] **a.** ***amma*** ***kuttikkə*** ***pustakam*** ***waaŋŋikkotuttu***
mother child.DAT book bought.gave

'Mother bought the child the book.'

b. ***amma*** ***enikkə /ninakkə*** ***pustakam*** ***waaŋŋittannu***
mother I-DAT/you-DAT book bought-gave

'Mother bought me/you the book.'

I would like to suggest that the Malayalam construction is also a candidate for a Union analysis. Under this analysis **[26a.]** would have the structure in **[27]**.

[27]

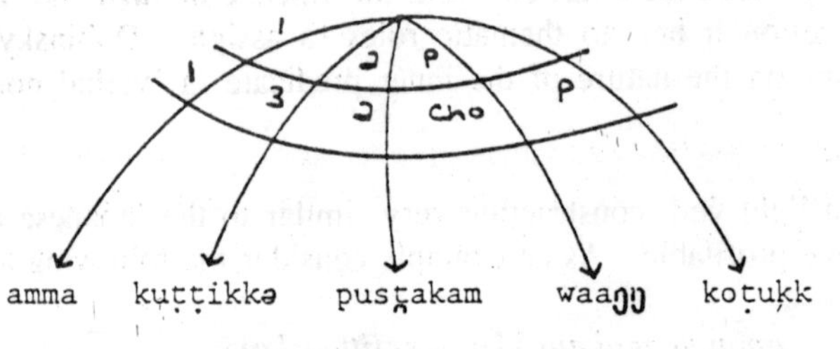

In this construction, as a light verb, *give* inherits all the arguments from the inner P-sector that it can. However, in the absence of a goal argument in the inner P-sector (here represented as an indirect object, 3), it must add this argument in its P-initial stratum. It must also assign an appropriate thematic role to that argument. Nothing additional need be stated in the lexical entry for 'give' other than the fact that it need not head a clause initial P-arc, only a P-initial P-arc. This is reflected in **[28]**, where the initial stratum for the arc headed by ***koṭukk*** is designated c_i rather than c_1.

[28] [P(***koṭukk***,b)<c_i>) → { (1(a,b)<c_i>)
(2(d,b)<c_i>)
(3(e,b)<c_i>) }

A principle difference between "light" verb constructions and other Unions is their semantically bleached (or in some cases thematically empty) nature. It seems that "light" verbs retain certain syntactic requirements such as number of arguments and case oddities, and in some instances assignment of thematic roles. However, in the majority of cases it seems that thematic assignments are the purview of the inner or base predicate. Regardless, it seems likely that a Union analysis, which has shed light on a number of issues with respect to complex predicate constructions cross-linguistically, may prove a valuable tool in investigating complex predicate constructions involving "light" verbs.

NOTES

1. The following abbreviations are used in the morphemic glosses: ACC - accusative, CAUS - causative, COM - comitative, COMP - complementizer, DAT - dative, IMP - imperative, INF - infinitive, INSTR - instrumental, NOM - nominative, NONPST - nonpast tense, PASS - passive, PST - past tense, f - feminine, m - masculine, n - neuter, and s - singular.

2. For differences between the monoclausal analysis and the biclausal approach (as in Aissen and Perlmutter 1976, Gibson and Raposo 1986, and many others), see Davies and Rosen 1988.

3. The complementizer ***ani*** is the past participle of ***anu*** 'to say' and is commonly referred to as the 'quotative particle'. It appears that it has become grammaticized and no longer patterns as a past participle.

4. It is not clear what grammatical relation the embedded clause bears to the matrix in the control structure in **[6]**. Since this is unimportant to present concerns, I ignore the issue and use the relational sign *X*.

5. Cross-linguistically, it is not unusual for 2s and 2-chômeurs to take the same morphological case marking. The notion *acting 2* (Perlmutter and Postal 1984) captures this class of elements.

6. Takahashi (1981) reports that for the speaker with whom she works word order was not relevant and that in causatives either controller (causer or causee) could control ***laagaa*** when the adverbial appeared in initial position. She reports no data in which the adverbial phrase is not in clause-initial position.

7. Additional evidence for there being two P-sectors is available from control constructions in which the inner subject controls a null subject in an embedded clause and antecedence of reflexive ***tana***, which requires a third person subject antecedent. For economy of space, supporting data will not be provided here.

8. Other cases, including the accusative and human locative are possible on the goal argument in both **[25a.]** and **[25b.]**.

9. The particular form of *give* depends on whether the beneficiary is 1st, 2nd, or 3rd person.

REFERENCES

Aissen, Judith, and David Perlmutter. 1976. Clause reduction in Spanish. Proceedings of the Second Annual Meeting of the Berkeley Linguistics Society, 1-30.

Davies, William D., and Stanley Dubinsky. 1991. On representing and constraining lexical government of syntactic structures. Linguistics 29.

Davies, William D., and Carol Rosen. 1988. Unions as multi-predicate clauses. Lg. 64.52-88.

Dubinsky, Stanley. 1989. Compound 'suru' verbs and evidence for unaccusativity in Japanese. Papers from the 25th Annual Regional Meeting of the Chicago Linguistic Society, 98-111.

Gibson, Jeanne D., and Eduardo P. Raposo. 1986. Clause union, the stratal uniqueness law, and the chômeur relation. Natural Language and Linguistic Theory 4.295-331.

Mohanan, K. P. 1983. Move NP or lexical rules? Evidence from Malayalam causativization. Papers in lexical-functional grammar, ed. by L. Levin, M. Rappaport, and A. Zaenen. Bloomington, IN: Indiana University Linguistics Club.

Perlmutter, David M., and Paul M. Postal. 1977. Toward a universal characterization of passivization. Proceedings of the Third Annual Meeting of the Berkely Linguistics Society, 394-417.

Perlmutter, David M., and Paul M. Postal. 1984. Impersonal passives and some relational laws. Studies in Relational Grammar 2, ed. by David M. Perlmutter and Carol Rosen, 126-70. Chicago: University of Chicago Press.

Rosen, Carol. 1987. Star means bad: a syntactic divertimento for Italianists. Italica 64.443-76.

Takahashi, Gail. 1981. Clause union in Telugu. San Diego, CA: University of California, MS.

COMPLEX VERB-VERB PREDICATES IN TAMIL

Vijayarani Jotimuttu Fedson
University of Chicago

I shall attempt an overview of the first of the two types of complex constructions which involve verb concatenation, one verb-verb, and the other noun-verb, each unit making but a single predication. My goal will be primarily descriptive, as a contribution to what I shall term sound "linguagraphy", the linguistic equivalent of ethnography, for I have seen too much model-building and theorizing based on inaccurate or very sketchy data where Tamil is concerned. The theoretical assumptions I employ for heuristic purposes can be inferred quite easily. I ignore discourse-functional and stylistic parameters of the use of complex predicates in this sketch.

Verb-verb complex predicates of the kind referred to as serial or compound verbs, are common in Tamil. In the minimal unit, v1v2, a given verb v2 which can occur independently as a predicating verb, occurs in collocation with another verb v1 not to make a second predication, but to modify or add to the meaning of v1 which makes the predication, or to make a complex predication jointly with v1. The meaning it contributes is not identical with its meaning as an independent verb. In certain instances, a v2 in a sentence can equally felicitously signify either a second predication or its compound verb meaning. The morphological form that v1 takes is either that of the conjunctive participle (which bears the morphological past-tense morpheme) in which tense and voice are neutralized, or that of the infinitive. These v1v2 complexes are tightly bound semantically and syntactically. Modals and negatives are also complex verb-verb predicates, but I do not consider them as coming under the category of serial or compound verbs, because in a given modal or negative v1v2 sequence, the auxiliary v2 contributes the same full meaning to the complex as it does when and if it can be used independently as a predicating verb.

In my 1981 University of Chicago dissertation, *The Tamil Serial or Compound Verb*, I have identified and discussed over fifty verbs which occur as v2s in compound verb constructions. I sorted these into six groups as follows: compound verbs which 1) form stative predicates which denote identifiable states resulting from dynamic events, 2) denote perfect meaning which I class with tense, 3) denote meaning related to the category of status in Aronson's (1977) revision of Jakobson (1957), 4) denote aspectual meaning including perfective, imperfective, and progressive aspects, and additionally what I termed "gradive" and "continuous" aspects, 5) denote meaning related to the category of voice, and 6) a new category I proposed called "manner of action", calqued on Aktionsart. In some of these I showed that specific reference is made to the participants in the speech event, so that some of these compounds are "shifters" in Jakobson's schema. I would imagine that the term for this phenomenon that is currently in the mode is "viewpoint". I shall touch briefly upon a few examples from each of these groups.

I. **Stative Predicates.** These compounds involve existential and locative verbs like ***iru*** 'be, exist, be located', ***uL*** 'exist, be, have', and ***kiTa*** 'lie' which as v2s do not predicate being or location or having, but a complex state resulting from the earlier occurrence of a dynamic event denoted by v1. These resulting states contrast with primary states. The following is an example with ***kiTa*** 'lie' which conveys in addition to signifying a resulting state, a notion of neglect, of a lack of control or concern.

[1] ***maram en- R- a -peer-ukku onR-iraNTu puLi muLaittu-k kiTa-nt-ana.***
tree quote-pa-adp name-dat one two tamarind sprout cp LIE -pa-3pe

'So as to be called (named) trees one or two tamarind (trees) had sprouted up (by themselves, with no one caring for them).'

With ***iru*** 'be, exist' in the past tense in the above example the gloss would be the same, except that the nuance of neglect would be missing. With ***uL*** 'exist, have', no morphological tense marking is possible, so the gloss would be a present perfect 'have sprouted', again with no additional nuance. As statives, a more accurate gloss would be 'tamarind trees were asprout', but the same dual readings of stative and perfect are possible for the sentence as in English. Note that the not taking place of a dynamic event also results in an identifiable state which can be expressed with this construction, using the negative conjunctive participle and the verb ***iru***.

II. **Perfect Constructions.** The existential verbs ***iru*** and ***uL*** and two others, ***viTu*** 'leave' and ***aaku*** 'become' indicate perfect meaning used serially. In this use only the past tense form of ***viTu*** is involved and ***aaku*** occurs only in the past tense 3rd singular neuter form. To use Comrie's (1976) classification, ***iru*** signifies the experiential perfect and the perfect of result, ***uL*** the experiential perfect and the perfect of result, ***viTu*** the perfects of result, persistent situation, and recent past, and ***aaku*** the perfects of result, persistent situation and recent past with additional nuances. I use Comrie's description because English is the metalanguage here, and in translating the English perfect *have* one has to choose from among four Tamil forms, a fact missed so far by Tamil and non-Tamil writers on this subject.

I give below examples with ***iru***, ***viTu***, and ***aaku***; the latter two were not recognized as perfects in Tamil before 1981. Note that ***viTu*** 'leave' is used as v2 in all tenses to indicate perfective aspect in addition to its use in the past tense to indicate perfect meaning. A given occurrence of ***viTu*** in the past tense form can therefore signify either perfect tense or perfective aspect depending on discourse context. This kind of overlap of the perfect and perfective is seen in Russian as well.

[2] ***avaL tuunki viT- T-aaL.*** / vs. ***viTu- kiR-aaL.***
she sleep cp LEAVE-pa-3sf. / LEAVE- pr- 3sf

'She slept (pfv). She has slept.' / vs. 'She sleeps (pfv).'

Where the three verbs overlap in the perfect of result, the difference between them lies in differing presuppositions. This can be seen in questions.

[3]	*enna*	*muTivu*	*ceytu*	*iru-kkiR-aay*? /
	what	conclusion	do cp	BE -pr- 2s
				viT- T-aay?
				LEAVE-pa-2s
				aa-y- iR-Ru?
				BECOME-pa-3sn

'What conclusion have you come to? / Nothing much I'm sure.'

With ***iru*** the presupposition is that s/he was going to come to some conclusion. The question asks for information in a straightforward way. With ***viTu*** and ***aaku*** no such presupposition exists on the part of the speaker. The question is rhetorical; it does not ask for information from the addressee, but contradicts, denies, or belittles an overt claim or covert implication that the addressee had come to a conclusion, or made a decision.

[4]	*nii*	*muTivu*	*ceytu*	*iru-kkiR-aay-aa*?
	you	conclusion	do cp	BE- pr- 2s-query
				viT- T-aay-aa?
				LEAVE-pa-2s-query
				aay- iR- R- aa?
				BECOME-pa-3sn-query

'Have you come to a conclusion?'

With ***iru*** here, there is no presupposition that s/he was going to come to a conclusion. Rather, the question seeks corroboration from the addressee as to whether the addressee had done so because the speaker has just become aware that s/he might have come to some conclusion, or made a decision. With ***viTu*** and ***aaku***, however, there is a presupposition that s/he was going to come to a conclusion and the speaker wishes to know whether the anticipated event has taken place. In both instances ***iru*** is neutral and transparent. There is a further interesting nuance in the construction with ***aaku***.

aaku conveys additional nuances when it is used TO REPORT NEW INFORMATION, new events. It cannot report something totally new. There is some kind of givenness, which does not have to be explicit, but be a possibility, about the reported predicate. It signifies that something happened as was possible, or as one might expect or as one hoped would occur, given the circumstances, and also that what took place was not undesirable to the speaker. ***aaku*** contrasts with the verb ***poo*** 'go' used as v2 which conveys the notion that the event denoted by v1 was undesirable, and proceeded without control, where v1 is a member of a certain set of inchoative verbs which have to be listed. I do not wish to categorize ***poo*** as a v2 indicating perfect tense. It indicates perfect tense in context. In other instances, in all tenses, it occurs as a v2 denoting change of state. I discuss it below under the category of voice for reasons I shall give later.

[5] ***veLLari muRRi aay- iR-Ru. / pooy-iR-Ru.***
cucumber mature cp BECOME-pa-3sn / GO- pa-3sn

'The cucumber has matured. (just right) / too much. has gone to seed. / went to seed.'

The two forms ***aaku*** and ***poo*** have to refer to two different cucumbers, if the same speaker is uttering both sentences, for in the former case, the reference is to a cucumber which has matured to just the right degree, and in the latter, to a cucumber which has become over-mature, where the action denoted by v1 has gone unchecked, undesirably. On the other hand, if the same cucumber is being referred to, two different speakers are involved: in the first case the speaker must be a person who wanted seed-cucumber, where the right degree of maturity would indicate going to seed. In the second case the speaker must be one who wanted a cucumber to eat, which had not gone to seed, so the seed-cucumber to him has matured too much, past the eating stage. This, as stated earlier, applies when ***aaku*** reports new, but not totally unexpected or undreamt-of-as-possible information.

When REFERRING TO events which have already taken place and which are known to speaker and addressee, i.e. referring to patently given information, these two constraints do not apply with the use of ***aaku*** as v2. Hence, referring to an accident which is old information, one can say:

[6] ***avan-0 kaal uTaint- aa-y- iR-Ru. ini kai uTai-y-um- oo?***
he-0 leg break cp BECOME-pa-3sn. now arm break- fut 3n-dubit

'His leg has fractured. Now will his arm break, I wonder?'

Note that TO REPORT that the leg has fractured ***aaku*** would be infelicitous normally. It would suggest that one had hoped it might happen and that it was not undesirable.

III. **Indication of Status.** A further use of ***iru*** 'be' as v2 is to indicate that the predication that is being made with v1 is intended as an inference on the part of the speaker. The present tense form of ***iru*** is used. The perfect tense signifies that the dynamic event indicated by v1 is viewed as having relevance at a later time, as being of moment later; that is why its having taken place is asserted. It is, in Jespersen's (1933) terms, "prospective" and it is deductive. The inferential is the obverse of this: from certain indications at a later time an inference is made that an event took place earlier. It is retrospective and inductive.

[7] ***vaNTi inta pakkam pooy iru-kkiR-atu.***
vehicle this side go cp BE- pr- 3sn

'The vehicle has (evidently) gone this way.'

IV. **Aspectual Compound Verbs.** ***viTu*** 'leave' and ***koL*** 'hold, contain' occur as v2s to indicate perfective and non-perfective or non-durative and neutral aspect as in the following: It is best to present the contrast in this way rather than as perfective and specifically imperfective.

[8] ***raaman paTatt- ai maRaittu viTu- v- aan. / -k koL- v- aan.***
Raman picture-acc hide cp LEAVE-fut-3sm / HOLD-fut-3sm

'Raman will hide (pfv) the picture.' / (neut) (actor focus)

These two forms occur in all tenses. Perfective aspect with ***viTu*** 'leave'does not indicate COMPLETED action, but rather the viewing of the event as a whole, not divisible temporally into phases, as a point rather than as a continuum. There is, additionally, with ***viTu*** "event focus", an emphasis on the action or event rather than on the actor as with ***koL***. The example with ***koL*** conveys an extra nuance of what I term "actor focus" which emphasizes the active involvement of the agent, a heightened degree of agency, a spotlighting of the agent as role-player.

A further meaning contributed by ***viTu*** as v2 which comes under the category of aspect is its denotation of semelfactivity, i.e. indicating the doing of something once, after which the action might or might not continue, WITHOUT FURTHER INPUT FROM THE ACTOR. This particular use will, of course, be seen only with those v1s which are semantically suitable. Some examples are: ***uruTTu*** 'roll' vs. ***uruTTi viTu*** 'set rolling'; ***iZu*** 'pull' vs. ***iZuttu viTu*** 'give a pull, yank'; ***toTakku*** 'start, begin something' vs. ***toTakki viTu*** 'start something off'. Whereas ***viTu*** can be contracted phonetically when used to convey aspectual meaning, it cannot be contracted in this use. Semelfactive ***viTu*** can be followed immediately by perfective ***viTu*** as in ***izuttu viTTu viTu*** 'give a pull' (pfv).

The form ***koL*** in collocation with ***iru*** and ***kiTa*** forms the complex sequences ***koNTiru*** and ***koNTukiTa*** which indicate progressive aspect in all three tenses. To my thinking, it is the locative meaning of ***iru*** 'be located' which is involved here, and the locative meaning 'lie, be in a lying position' of ***kiTa***. It should be noted that the other existential verb ***uL*** 'be, exist, have' which does not have a locative meaning does not occur in a progressive complex with ***koNTu***. In this complex as well, ***kiTa*** contributes the nuance of lack of control or care that we saw in its use as a stative-forming v2. The progressive in Tamil is a very focussed progressive, rather than a looser "imperfective" and less frequently used than the English progressive. ***koNTu*** occurs in two other complexes with ***vaa*** 'come' and ***poo*** 'go' to indicate what I have called "continuous" aspect, which is distinct from progressive aspect. It may be glossed broadly as 'keep verbing, continue to verb', in which the continuation of the dynamic action denoted by v1 is signified. Whereas ***koNTuvaa*** is neutral in meaning, ***koNTu poo*** conveys the sense that the action denoted by v1 continued without check or control. In these multiple v2 complexes, I see ***koNTu*** as contributing the abstract meaning "durative", ***iru*** as indicating existence in a metaphoric sense, ***vaa*** as signifying movement toward a deictic centre, and ***poo*** as conveying movement away from a deictic centre or movement at a distance from a deictic centre, with no specified direction. I shall pass over the other aspectual v2s with the following exception. ***vaa*** 'come' used as v2 with the infinitive of a verb v1 signifies what I have termed "gradive" aspect. It is a durative aspect in which a dynamic event is seen as linear, unrolling in degrees or stages to its completion. This is found in all three tenses.

[9]	*avaL*	*avan-ai*	*nampa*	*va-nt-aaL.*
	she	he-acc	believe cp	COME-pa-3sf

'She came to believe him. She gradually ended up believing him.'

V. **Compound Verbs Which Concern Voice.** I shall go over just a few of the v2s in this group which concerns partcipant role. ***viTu*** 'leave' and ***koL*** 'hold' enter into another opposition here, that of orientation or version. ***viTu*** signifies that the dynamic event is other-oriented, and ***koL*** that it is actor or agent-oriented.

[10]	*cankili-y-ai -p*	*pooTTu*	*viT- T-aan.*	/	*k koN- T- aan.*
	chain- acc	put on cp	LEAVE-pa-3sm	/	HOLD-pa-3sm

'He put the chain on someone.' / 'He put the chain on himself.'

With no other NP to indicate the recipient, ***viTu*** and ***koL*** by themselves are enough to indicate whether the recipient is the actor or an other. Note, however, that both forms can occur with direct objects which are coreferential with the actor or with an other.

[11]	*avaL*	*tan-n- ai-k*	/	*avan-ai-k*	*kaNNaaTi-y-il*	*paar-tt-aaL.*
	she	coref3-acc	/	he-acc	mirror- loc	see- pa-3sf
						/ *paarttu* *viT- T-aaL.*
						see cp LEAVE-pa-3sf
						/ *paarttu-k* *koN- T-aaL.*
						see cp HOLD-pa-3sf

'She saw/looked at (her)self/him in the mirror.' / (pfv event focus) / (actor focus)

Example **[11]** illustrates the use of the simple verb and the two compound constructions with the third person coreferential form ***tan*** (the oblique form of ***taan*** the nominative) which is usually mislabelled the reflexive. It is not a reflexive pronoun, for among other things, it can occur in the NOMINATIVE, and it is DISCOURSE-REFERENTIAL, not merely clause or sentence referential. The pronoun ***tan*** can occur as direct object coreferential with the actor subject with actor-orienting v2 ***koL***, and also as direct object coreferential with the subject with other-orienting ***viTu***. When in discourse there is a cross orientation, so to speak, between the direct object and the compound verb which indicates version, the orientation of the direct object overrides or neutralizes the orientational signification of ***viTu*** and ***koL***. Another way of describing this is to state that ***viTu*** and ***koL*** indicate version or orientation when it is not specified elsewhere. The third variant which I have glossed simply "actor focus", without an additional gloss "impfv", again illustrates the fact that ***koL*** is the unmarked member in aspectual contrast. ***viTu*** is marked, and always signifies non-durative, perfective aspect. ***koL*** is non-perfective or neutral. It is crucial to bear in mind that any predicating verb v1 can occur by itself, being non-specific aspectually; i.e., that it can be durative or non-durative in its signification, depending on discourse context. Returning to the category of voice, where orientation or version is concerned, I would like to analyze ***koL*** as specifically signalling actor focus and ***viTu*** as showing event focus or non-actor focus. I have not decided the best way to put it. ***viTu***, when it occurs to mark orientation cannot be reduced phonetically. Other-oriented ***viTu*** can be followed by perfective ***viTu***. Semelfactive and other oriented ***viTu*** cannot follow each other. This constraint also awaits better formulation. ***koL*** can also be reduced phonetically in all its occurrences as v2, which includes the progressive and continuous complexes. It never follows itself; this, to me, signifies that it does not convey different meanings as v2, unlike ***viTu***. And while non-perfective ***koL*** cannot follow perfective ***viTu***, but can follow semelfactive and other-oriented ***viTu***, perfective ***viTu*** can follow ***koL*** as well as all the other durative forms -- the progressives and the continuous complexes. This makes sense semantically.

In this area of signification, the use of ***koL*** is obligatory in some contexts. Where actions are carried out on the actor's own body, ***koL*** is required if the whole body or self is involved. If, however, the action is carried out on a part of the actor's own body, ***koL*** is optional. Note that the 3rd person coreferential pronoun ***taan*** in its genitive (oblique base) form ***tan*** is also optional, not required, before possessed nouns, whether alienable or inalienable, as in the following examples:

(tan) kaal- ai -c coRi- nt-aan. / coRintu koN- T-aan.
3coref leg/foot-acc scratch-pa-3sm / scratch cp HOLD-pa-3sm

'He scratched his leg/foot.' / (actor focus)

Another set of v2s related to voice is the pair ***koTu*** 'give' and ***taa*** 'give'. In a compound verb construction with transitive or intransitive verbs these v2s convey the broad meaning 'perform action denoted by v1 in an accomodating, responsive manner'. To refer to either complex as a "benefactive" as has been done in the past characterizes its use only with transitive verbs. Even with transitive verbs, the term "benefactive" is problematic for Tamil, for there exists a phrase ***aTi vaanki-k koTu*** 'beating get give' which means 'see that one gets the beating one deserves', where the motive is not benevolent.

[12] ***at- aRk- um uur acaintu koTukka-v- illai.***
that-dat incl village move (intr) cp GIVE inf- neg

'The village did not budge even at that (a threat).'

In the above example with an intransitive verb which does not suggest a beneficiary, the dative case marks a peripheral noun phrase which is not necessary for the predication to be complete. With a transitive verb as well, the dative-marked beneficiary of the action is optional in discourse context. Some interesting restrictions apply. Where the recipient of the action is also the beneficiary, the accusative, not the dative, is used, suggesting that the role of patient (recipient) is more important to mark overtly than the role of beneficiary. ***taa*** is the marked member of this pair, denoting a 2nd person beneficiary; ***koTu*** is unmarked and can occur with all three persons. Other-oriented ***viTu*** and ***koTu*** are in complementary distribution with some verbs.

I shall now touch upon the compounds which indicate passive voice. (Yes, Virginia, there is a passive voice in Tamil.) This involves the infinitive of v1 in tandem with the verb ***paTu*** 'suffer, experience' or ***peRu*** 'bear' as v2s. The latter is usually limited to a high, formal register. I give two examples, one formal, the second not.

[13] ***paaTa-p paTT- a- varkaL aru-v-ar.***
sing inf SUFFER-adjp- 3pe six- 3pe

'Those sung (about) are/were six.'

[14] ***talai pinna- p paTa-v-illai.*** vs. / ***pinna-v- illai***
head braid inf SUFFER inf neg / braid inf neg

'(Her) hair has/had not been braided.' vs. / did not braid.

I return now to the verb ***poo*** which I touched upon earlier. ***poo*** used as v2 views the dynamic event denoted by an intransitive v1 as an occurrence, a happening. It is used largely with intransitive verbs which denote a change of state, so that the complex can be glossed 'become or turn out as v1'. The contrast with ***aaku*** was noted. With a set of verbs which can denote entry into or departure from a deictic centre, as in example **[5]**, ***aaku*** indicates entry into such a state and that the dynamic event was not undesirable, while ***poo*** suggests departure from a deictic state and that the event was undesirable. With other verbs, a dynamic event is viewed as simply happening, and if there is a role-player, the role-player is viewed as EXPERIENCING the event, not as actively playing a part. Dative-subject experiencer constructions in Tamil generally deal with states of mind or body of the experiencer. ***poo*** extends the category of experiencer to include a participant in the narrated event VIEWED as experiencing, being caught up in, rather than actively partcipating in an objectively verifiable event. ***poo*** is also used with the negative conjunctive participle of transitive and intransitive verbs to signify the non-performing of an action, or the non-taking place of an event. With a transitive verb, the construction might indicate that the non-performing of the action was unintentional or happenstance; 'happen or turn out not to verb' is a suitable gloss. There is an attenuation of the notion of a fully involved causing or acting agent. Taken together, the use of ***koL*** as actor-focusser, emphasizing involvement of the actor, the presence of dative-subject experiencer constructions, and the existence of experiencer ***poo*** constructions point to a strong emphasis on or sensitivity in Tamil to the extent of actor participation or lack of it. The scale of agency (degree of involvement of a role-playing participant) goes from an inactive acted upon patient through a non-active experiencer of states of mind or body, a non-fully-acting experiencer of actions and events, to an actor (a participant who carries out an intransitive action), a heightened actor (with ***koL***), on to an agent (a participant who carries out a transitive action on a patient) and a heightened agent (with ***koL***). The roles of patient and agent are mutually implying and each role acknowledges causes and effects; the roles of experiencer and of an experiencing actor caught up in an action emphasize the state, event or action as experienced, and the role of actor focusses on the event or action by itself. The following examples should make the semantics of ***poo*** clear.

[15] ***avan tuunk-in-aan. / tuunki-p poo-n-aan.***
he sleep-pa-3sm / sleep cp GO-pa-3sm

'He slept.' (active) / 'He fell asleep.' (non-active)

[16] ***avan-ukku-t tuukkam va- nt-atu. / vantu poo-y-iR-Ru***
he- dat sleep come-pa-3sn / come cp GO- pa-3sn

'Sleep came to him. (He felt sleepy.)' / 'Sleep occurred to him.'
(Sleep is active.) (Sleep is inactive.)

[17] ***avan-ukku-t tuukkam vara-v-illai. / vara-aamal poo-y-iR-Ru.***
he- dat sleep come inf-neg / come neg cp GO -pa-3sn

'Sleep did not come to him.' (active) / 'Sleep turned out not occur to him.' (inactive)

[18] ***avan katav-ai aTaikka-v-illai. / aTaikk-aamal poo-n-aan.***
he door-acc shut inf neg / shut neg cp GO-pa-3sm

'He did not shut the door.' (full participation) / 'It turned out that he did not shut the door.'

Still in the category of voice, causative constructions also use the infinitive form of v1 with the second verb ***cey*** 'do, make', ***paNNu*** 'make', ***vai*** 'place, set down' or ***aTi*** 'beat'. I can best present these by stating that ***vai*** indicates that the causer is viewed as having an immediate or direct effect on the causee, whereas ***cey*** and ***paNNu*** denote that the causer is viewed as having a non-immediate or remote effect on the causee, or they focus on the causer and caused event. This does not suggest geographic remoteness. This difference in meaning is seen further in the fact that ***cey*** can occur after a passive, whereas ***vai*** cannot, and that ***cey*** can also occur after a negative conjunctive participle, where ***vai*** cannot, with the meaning 'cause not to verb'.

[19] ***avan avaL-ai aZuka vai- tt-aan. / -c cey- t- aan.***
he she-acc cry inf PLACE-pa-3sm / MAKE-pa-3sm

'He made her cry.' / 'He caused her to cry.'

[20] ***aracan pala koovil-kaL kaTTa-p paTa-c cey- t-aan. / *vai***
king many temple-pl build inf SUFFER MAKE-pa-3sm

'The king caused /*made many temples to be built.'

cey and ***vai*** can follow themselves or each other in multiple embedded causative constructions, the only constraint being cognitive, i.e. ease of interpretation. ***aTi***, which is limited in use, signifies that the dynamic event was inimical to the causee and occurs usually with intransitive verbs.

[21] ***avan-ai naan tookk- aTi- tt-een.***
he-acc I be defeated inf BEAT-pa-3sm

'I defeated him (caused him to be defeated).'

VI. **"Manner of Action" Complexes.** I now come to the last group of complex verb-verb predicates in which the v2s all describe the manner in which the v1 is carried out or takes place. This is a viewing of the dynamic event in a particular way, and is adverbial in the broadest sense. I should add that in Tamil the stock of adverbs, which are denominal derivatives, is limited. I shall touch upon just a few of these v2s.

The verb *taLLu* 'push' as v2 suggests that the action denoted by v1 was executed speedily and exuberantly.

[22] *uur nilan-kaL viLaintu taLLi iru-nt-ana.*
village land-pl produce cp PUSH BE-pa-3pn

'The village lands had yielded exuberantly.'

vai 'place, set down' conveys the idea that the dynamic event is viewed as producing or leading to consequences or lasting effects which may or may not have been intended by the actor.

[23] *tappi-p pooy...manuSan-ka matti-y-il-ee vantu piRantu vacc- iru-kk-u.*
by mistake man-pl midst-loc-advp come cp be born cp PLACE cp BE-pr-3sn

'By mistake she has come and been born (with consequences) in the midst of men (incarnated as a human).'

T. Janakiraman. <u>uyirt</u> <u>teen</u>. 1974:257

A verb which had not been recognized till recently as a v2 is ***eTu*** 'take, pick up', which suggests that the event referred to by v1 is viewed as an ordeal that the direct object of the complex is taken or put through.

[24] *inta keeLvi avar- ai amp-aaka tuLaittu eTuttu viT- T-atu.*
this query 3 ehon-acc arrow- adv pierce cp TAKE cp LEAVE-pa-3sn

'This query pierced him/her (honorific) like an arrow.'

I have not taken up many of the verbs which occur in these different categories of complex predicates. I have not cited any of those that I have analyzed as shifters.

Many v1v2 units are frozen and lexicalized. Some examples are: ***colli-k koTu*** 'say GIVE' for 'teach'; ***purintu koL*** 'be understood HOLD' for the active verb 'understand'; ***kotikka vai*** 'intransitive boil PLACE' for transitive 'boil'; ***piTittu viTu*** 'take hold LEAVE' for 'massage'. There are many other idiomatic units which also need listing which are not possible to go into now.

I see in all these verb-verb concatenations a general process of greater semantic focussing. The compound verb either changes the kind of predication being made, e.g. an inferred statement as opposed to a straight assertion, or it adds more detail or colour to the broader meaning sketched out by the plain verb v1. Note that the use of the v1v2 complex is obligatory when categories like perfect tense, stative versus active kinesis, and status are involved. It is generally not obligatory to indicate the category of aspect. The simple verb in Tamil is unmarked aspectually as we noted earlier, and spans the durative-nondurative range, so that perfective, imperfective, and progressive do not always have to be specified. There are some exceptions to this.

By and large, specific features chosen from among the bundle of features which constitute the meaning of a given v2 as an independent verb are seen to apply in its v2 use. The use of the locative and existential to indicate being in an identifiable state resulting from an event, or of something having occurred or something having been done for the perfect, the choice of centrifugal and centripetal verbs to indicate aspect and voice-related nuances, and the choice of a verb meaning 'push' to indicate an action performed speedily and with gusto are cases in point.

Complex predicates, both verb-verb and noun-verb, behave like simple verbs in many respects. De-verbal derivations can be based on both types of compounds and both display the full range of verbal behaviour, showing their similarity to simple morphological elements. Negative and adverb scopes apply over the whole compound as over a simple verb. Two types of negative particles are used in Tamil. One is derived from the root ***al*** 'negative' which has a complete conjugation for person and number, with neutralized tense. More generally, however, the neuter form ***alla*** 'negative' common to the singular and plural is used. ***alla*** negates the whole sentence or proposition. The second negative particle is derived from the root ***il*** 'negative'. Although it is possible to conjugate this form also for number and person, in modern Tamil only the neuter form ***illai*** 'negative' is generally used. ***illai*** negates just the predicate. In some dialects and registers the second negative alone is used for both types of negation in ordinary use. Both negatives ***alla*** and ***illai***, though not always conjugated for person and number are, however, still used in high Tamil. Verb-verb complex predicates can be negated with either negative. The use of the negative is pragmatically marked. It is used to contradict an implied or asserted statement. In addition to these external negatives, the negative conjunctive participle of a given v1 can be used with three v2s: with ***iru*** 'be' in its stative and inferential uses, with ***poo*** 'go'in its use in the category of voice, and with ***cey*** as causative.

On the other hand, unlike morphologically simple verbs, complex predicates allow several elements to be introduced between them, although these are few in number, and each complex has its own coccurrence possibilities. Emphatic particles ***-taan***, ***-ee***, dubitative ***-oo***, particles of disjunction and conjunction ***-aavatu***, ***-oo***, and ***-um*** respectively, and the hesitation morphemes ***vantu*** and ***pooy*** (literally, the conjunctive participial forms of the verbs ***vaa*** 'come' and ***poo*** 'go') come under this group. In addition, echo-word formation can apply to both types of complex predicates, noun-verb and verb-verb, either the first or the second element in each minimal unit being capable of being echoed. I cite below two examples with echo words.

[25] *aTittu-k kiTittu viT- T- aan- aa?*
beat cp echo-word cp LEAVE-pa-3sm-query

'Did he beat (someone) (pfv) or any such thing?'

aTittu viTa -k kiTa-c cey- t- aan- aa?
beat cp LEAVE inf echo-word inf DO- pa-3sm-query?

'Did he do any such thing as beat (pfv) (someone)?'

Conjunction or disjunction with bound suffixes is possible. In some instances, the verb ***cey*** 'do' in the appropriate combining form, either as conjunctive participle or as infinitive has to be used as an empty v2 link between the multiple v1s and the following v2.

In sum, v2s serve as filters to block out certain areas of meaning of a given v1. The semantic fields of individual Tamil verbs are large, compared to English. v2s themselves are verbs which are broad in meaning in their avatars as independent verbs. Note that v2s which are used to denote grammatical categories like aspect, voice, and status are precisely those verbs with the broadest spectrum of meaning. Where the category "manner of action" is concerned the v2s involved are more specific and colourful. Their function is not to block out meaning but to add descriptive detail to the co-occurring v1. Complex predicates are based on the use of tropes, especially metaphors. They attest to the picture-making tendency in language and thought. Complex predicates of both types constitute a significant subsystem in Tamil. They are morphosyntactic entities, Janus-faced and versatile, vital, not moribund, an intriguing part of the grammatical anatomy and of the lexical stock of Tamil.

COMPLEX PREDICATES

Noun-Verb	**Verb-Verb**	
	serial verbs	non-serial verbs
lexical	infinitive & conjunctive participle based	infinitive based
non-predictable	lexical & grammatical	grammatical
less productive-more productive	non-productive-productive	productive
lexicalizations		modals & negatives

REFERENCES

Aronson, Howard. 1976. Interrelationships between aspect and mood in Bulgarian. Folia Slavica 1.1-39.

Comrie, Bernard. 1976. Aspect. Cambridge: Cambridge University Press.

Jakobson, Roman. 1957. Shifters, verbal categories and the Russian verb. Selected Writings II. The Hague: Mouton. [Repr. 1971.]

Jespersen, Otto. 1933. Essentials of English grammar. University of Alabama: University of Alabama Press. [Repr. 1976.]

COMPLEX VERB PHRASE:
A DIACHRONIC AND SYNCHRONIC VIEW

Vijay Gambhir
University of Pennsylvania

Abstract: In this paper, I demonstrate that the phenomenon of complex verb phrase is an indigenous Indo-Aryan phenomenon. It is found at various stages of the Indo-Aryan beginning with Vedic Sanskrit. This phenomenon was limited in early Sanskrit, but it gradually gained frequency at later stages (Hitopadesha, Ramayana, etc.) due to an ongoing simplification process within the language. Complex verbs, however, received a big impetus in modern Indo-Aryan languages when they came into contact with Persio-Arabic and English. Today, Hindi and other modern Indian languages are replete with complex verbs; many verbal concepts can be expressed through complex verbs only. I show that in Hindi even when a verb has a simple form as well as an equivalent complex form, the choice is not random. Their appropriate usage is constrained by one or more of the following factors -- form, style, semantics, and pragmatics.*

1.0 There are two main components in a verb: one that expresses meaning and the other that supplies grammatical information such as tense, aspect, mood, person, gender, and number. In simple verbs such as ARRIVE and MEET, both components -- meaning and grammar, get expressed through a single lexical item, as in examples [1] and [2] below. In complex verb phrases, however, meaning and grammatical relations are expressed by two or more words. The meaning part is generally expressed by a noun (phrase), an adjective, an adverb, or a preposition (phrase), and is commonly known as complement. The grammatical information is provided by one of the 'light verbs', such as DO or BE, which are semantically almost transparent and function more like an auxilliary or a verbalizer. Examples of complex verbs are given in sentences [3] - [6] below.

[1] ***merii gaaRii nau baje pahũcegii.***
my train nine o'clock ARRIVE-fut-3rd pers-fem-sg

'My train will arrive at nine o'clock.'

[2] ***maĩ ashok se milaa.***
I Ashok with MEET-perf-1st pers-mas-sg

'I met Ashok.'

[3] ***sab log paise se pyaar nahiĩ karte.***
all people money with LOVE(N) not DO-hab-pl-mas-3rd pers

'Every one does not love money.'

[4] *maĩ darvaazaa band karuũ?*
I door CLOSE(adj) DO-subj-1st pers-sg

'Should I close the door?'

[5] *zaraa jaldii karo.*
please HURRY(adv) DO-imp-informal-2nd pers

'Please hurry up.'

[6] *vo pahlii baar mẽ aauT huaa.*
he first time in OUT BE-perf-masc-3rd pers sg

'He was out in the first turn.'

1.1 In complex verbs, DO and BE verbalizers are almost semantically vacuous except that they express the transitivity or intransitivity of the act. In Hindi, most acts can be expressed transitively or intransitively with the help of DO and BE verbs respectively. For example, ***jaldii honaa*** 'HURRY-BE' or ***jaldii karnaa*** 'HURRY-DO', ***aauT honaa*** 'OUT-BE', or ***aauT karnaa*** 'OUT-DO', ***pyaar hona*** 'LOVE-BE' or ***pyaar karnaa*** 'LOVE-DO'.

The non-DO/BE verbalizers such as KEEP, PUT, COME are, however, not so transparent in meaning. They not only give grammatical information but also add a significant shade to the meaning of the complement. For example, the noun ***dhyaan*** by itself means 'attention', and ***dyaan karnaa*** means 'to pay attention', but when followed by the verb ***lagaanaa*** 'to attach', i.e. ***dhyaan lagaanaa,*** then it means 'to concentrate'. Similarly, when followed by ***aanaa*** 'to come' or ***rakhanaa*** 'to keep', i.e. ***dhyaan aanaa*** or ***dhyaan rakhanaa***, the meaning is 'to remember' or 'to watch', respectively. See examples **[7]** - **[9]** below.

[7] *kaam mẽ dhyaan lagaao.*
work in ATTENTION PUT-imp-informal-2nd pers

'Concentrate on your work.'

[8] *mujhe aaTh baje dhyaan aayaa ki...*
I-dat eight o'clock ATTENTION COME-perf-sg-masc that

'I remembered at 8 o'clock that...'

[9] *zaraa merii kitaabõ kaa dhyaan rakhẽge?*
please my books of ATTENTION KEEP-imp-fut-formal-2nd pers

'Would you watch my books, please?'

The above discussion on the structure of simple and complex verbs can be visually summed up as follows:

[10]

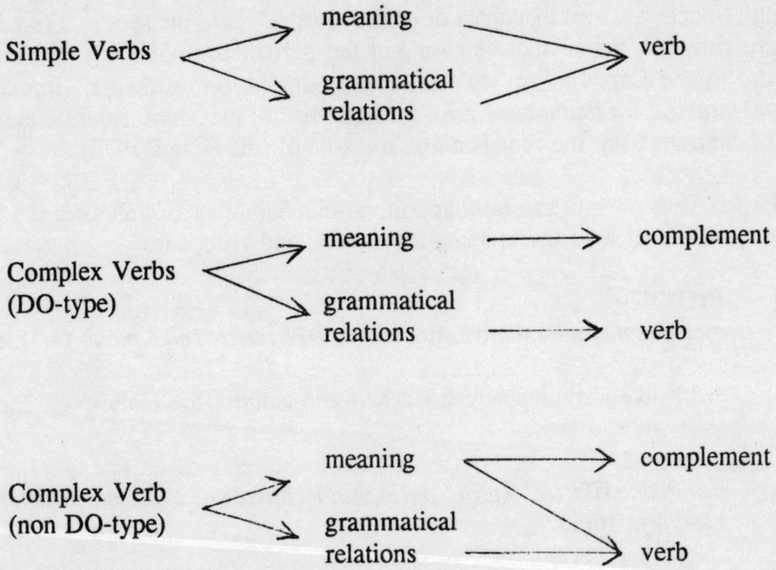

Historical Background

2.0 Examples of complex verb phrases may be found in all the natural languages of the world. In all of them, however, the periphrastic verb phenomenon is not so widespread and active as in modern Indo-Aryan languages and modern Persian. In modern Indo-Aryan languages there are many basic meanings such as LOVE, WAIT, LIKE, HATE which can be expressed only through complex verb phrases. For example in Hindi: ***prem karnaa*** 'to love', ***intazaar karnaa*** 'to wait', ***nafrat karnaa*** 'to hate'; in Bengali: ***poramorsh kor*** 'to consult', ***bhokti kor*** 'to pray'; in Nepali: ***sviikaar garnu*** 'to accept', ***nimantranaa garnu*** 'to invite'; in Sinhala: ***yojanaa karanawa*** 'to suggest', ***kataa karanawa*** 'to talk/discuss'; in Panjabi: ***marammat karnaa*** 'to repair', ***madad karnaa*** 'to help' have no corresponding simple verbs.

In modern Hindi periphrastic expressions have become so popular that they are even sometimes preferred over their simple verb counterparts, if any. For example, in Hindi the complex verbs ***sviikaar karnaa*** 'to accept', ***janm honaa*** 'to be born', and ***prakaT honaa*** 'to appear' are more frequent than their simple counterparts ***sviikaarnaa***, ***janmanaa***, and ***prakaTanaa***.

2.1 While it is true that modern Indo-aryan languages and modern Persian frequently use complex verb phrases, one should not make the mistake of saying that modern Indo-Aryan languages borrowed the phenomenon of complex verb phrases from Persian, because there are examples of periphrastic verbs even in the Rigveda. These examples are mostly of reduplicative onomatopoeic phrases where the roots ***kṛ*** 'to do' and ***bhuu*** 'to be/become' are suffixed to the preceding forms that end in ***aa*** or ***ii***; for example: ***akhkhaliikṛtyaa*** 'croaking', ***janjaNaabhavan*** 'flimmering'. There are also examples of perfect forms where the root is formed into a sort of abstract substantive in the accusative case and the perfect of an auxiliary verb such as ***bhuu*** 'to be', ***as*** 'to be' or ***kṛ*** 'to do' is added to it, for example, ***undaaM cakaara, undaaM babhuuva, undaamaasa*** are formed from the root ***und*** 'to moisten' and ***bodhayaaM cakaara*** from the root ***bodhay*** 'to explain' (cf. Beams 1970).

Complex verb phrases can be found in various Samhitas as well as in the later literature of Classical Sanskrit such as Brahmanas, Ramayana, and Hitopadesha:

[11] [a] RIGVEDA

etaa arṣantyalalaabhavantiirṛtaavariiriv sankrośamaanaaḥ (4.18.6a)

'with lively motion onward flow these waters, the Holy ones, shouting, as it were, together'

aa rikh ***kikiraa kṛNu*** *paNiinaaM hṛdyaa kave athemasmabhyaM randhaya* (6.53.7)

'Tear up and rend in pieces, sage, the hearts of avaricious churls, and make them subject to our will.'

[b] SAMAVEDA

itthaa hi som inmado ***brahma cakaar*** ... (4.7.410)

'thus being immersed in happiness, the panegyrists performed (lit., did) the praise.'

[c] SHATAPATHA BRAHMANA

... *etat* ***prajananaM kriyate*** (1.1.1.22)

'makes it creative'

[d] JAIMINIIYA UPANAISHAD BRAHMANA

tat sahaiva vaacaa manasaa praaNena ***hiMkurvanti*** (3.6.2)

'Together, they, with all their speech, mind, and the vital breath, produce the sound *hiM*.'

[e] VISHNU PURANA
evaM daitayvadhaM krisNo baladeva-sahaayavaan cakre dusTa-ksitiisaanaaM tathaiva jagatah krte (5.37.1)

'Thus, Krishana, who was helping Baladeva, killed for the sake of the world the wicked kings and the demons.'

[f] HITOPADESHA
tena tvaM yaavajjiivam ***sukhiibhavisyasi.***

'By doing that, you will be happy through your life.'

praatareva ***ksauraM kaaryitvaa*** *laguDa-hastah san svagrha-dvaari nibhrtam sthaasyasi.*

'From early in the morning, after getting shaved you will stand in front of your house quietly with a club in your hand.'

tata, kimiti tvayaasmadupeksaa ***kriyate.***

'Father, how come you are neglecting us.'
(Hitopadesha examples are from the *vigraha* section, p. 81-82)

[g] VALMIKI RAMAYAN

aaniiyataamitah senetyaajnaptah pamarsiNaa tathaa tu ***cakre*** *bharatah senaayaah* ***samupaagamam***

'Bring the army here, thus ordered by the great sage, Bharata brought (lit. did the bringing) the army accordingly.'

In general, the use of complex verbs is quite limited in the Vedic and classical Sanskrit periods. It, however, appears that there are relatively more examples of complex verbs in the genres of commentaries and story narration than in others. In commentaries, paraphrases such as ***gamanam karoti iti*** 'she does the going', ***pacati paakam kroti iti*** 'she does the cooking' are not uncommon. In stories, forms made with the Sanskrit ***cvi*** suffix, such as ***haritiikrtaa*** 'becomes green', ***jarjjariikrt*** 'wounded' are sprinkled all over.

2.2 In the Sanskrit literature there is some evidence for the gradual increased use of complex verb phrases. In the early texts, as noted by Whitney (p. 402), the use of complex verbs is mainly found in perfect and reduplicative onomotopoeic forms. Later on in Brahmanas, however, complex verbs are used in a variety of grammatical forms including optative, imperative, and indicative: ***cuulaakuryaat*** 'may roast on a spit', ***anriNaakartoḥ*** 'getting clear of debt', ***svaahaakaroti***, ***svadhaakaroti***, ***svagaakaroti*** 'makes an oblation' (frequently found in the context of ritual fire sacrifices). Still later, in Hitopadesha they are used with any noun or adjective compounded with ***kṛ, bhuu,*** or ***as***, e.g. ***stambhiibhavati*** 'becomes a post', ***ṛjuukṛtya*** 'after straightening', ***kunDaliikṛta*** 'ring-shaped', ***hetuukaraNa*** 'taking as cause'.

In modern day Sanskrit writings, the frequency of complex verb phrases is so high that it almost approximates the norms of the modern Indo-Aryan languages. This can be seen from the following examples:

[12] **[a]** *kaanicit dinaani sah itastataḥ* ***niśśankaḥ bhuutvaa*** *abhramat. ekadaa sah kancit sinhamapaśyat. sinhaat bhiitaḥ saḥ itham adhaavat yat saḥ* ***niśśvasitaḥ iva bhutvaa*** *maharṣeḥ sammukham* ***prarthanaamakarot.***

(a panchtantra story given in a school text book)

'For a few days, he roamed about without feeling concerned. One day he saw some lion, whose (sight) scared him. He ran from there, and as it were almost out of breath, he went to the sage and made a request.'

[b] *śriiraamabhadraaya namḥ. iti mantratritayen* ***aacamanaM kuryaat.*** *śriiyugala - biijamantreNa* ***praaNaayaamaM kuryaat.***

(introduction to Ramacaritamaanas, p.8)

'Salutations to Lord Rama. Thus with the three mantras sip the water from you palm. Then with the shriyugal seed - mantra do pranayam.'

2.3 The increased use of complex verb phrases from Vedic Sanskrit to modern Indo-Aryan languages can be ascribed to the simplification process in the language -- a move from the inflectional to the analytical structure. The analytical processs, according to Beams, was already prevalent in spoken vernaculars at the time of Vedic Sanskrit but occured only rarely in the actual literature because the grammarians liked to use elaborate verb forms for the sake of uniformity. Besides complex verbs, the evidence for the analytical process comes from future tense forms also, which are made from the agent-noun of the verb with the present tense form of the auxiliary ***as*** added to it. For example, the root ***budh*** 'to be aware/awake' gives the agent ***bodhitaa*** and then by adding present of ***as***, we derive the first person singular form ***bodhitaasmi***, the second person singular form ***bodhitaasi***, the first person plural form ***bodhitaasmaḥ***, and the second person dual form ***bodhitaasthaḥ***, and others.

2.4 The phenomenon of complex verb phrase was undoubtedly present in early as well as later Sanskrit; it was, however, extremely limited in its scope as compared to modern Indo-Aryan languages where it has spread all over. For instance, in modern Standard Hindi complex verb forms are found in all tenses, aspects, moods, numbers, and genders.

The widespread use of complex verb forms in Indo-Aryan languages certainly seems to have gained a big impetus when local vernaculars came into contact with Persian. At that time many new complex verbs were created with borrowings from Persian. The complex verb phenomenon, which was a common denominator in the two languages, was fully exploited by bilinguals for making their languages within easy reach by members of the other speech community. The assumption of the exploitation of this shared feature is based on the following factors:

a. Both languages had this feature present in their systems.
b. Both communities needed to develop linguistic channels to communicate with each other. This is supported by the fact that there are large numbers of borrowings in the areas of adminstration, war, and law.
c. Foreign verbal concepts are best assimilated into Hindi through the device of complex verb mechanism, as it requires no complicated phonotactic changes in the borrowed element for deriving various verb forms (as discussed in section 2.6).

Due to a long period of close language contact between Hindi and Persian, it is no wonder that many new complex verbs were created. Many existing simple verbs were either replaced by newly created periphrastic forms, or they co-existed side by side with the newly created periphrastic forms and competed with them. The competition led either to extinction of one of the two forms or to some finespun semantic distinction between them, thereby allowing the two forms to co-exist without colliding with each other. Some evidence for this comes from old Hindi verb forms, which are found mostly in verses where the frequency of simple verbs seems much higher than in the equivalent modern Hindi writings. Below are given a few examples:

[13]	**Old Hindi**	**Modern Hindi**
	andhernaa 'to darken'	*andheraa karnaa*
	iichnaa 'to desire'	*icchaa karnaa*
	adhikaanaa 'to increase'	*adhik karnaa*
	nirmaanaa 'to make'	*nirmaaN karnaa*
	cupaanaa 'to be quiet'	*cup honaa*
	agarnaa 'to move forward'	*aage honaa*
	ũũcaanaa 'to make higher'	*ũũcaa karnaa*
	prakaTnaa 'to appear'	*prakaT honaa*
	pramaananaa 'to give evidence'	*pramaaN denaa*
	adhiinanaa 'to surrender'	*adhiin honaa*

2.5 For bilinguals, the use of complex verb phrases is a very convenient and efficient way to borrow verbal concepts. In complex verbs, the complement remains invariant, i.e., it does not undergo any phonotactic changes that are required normally of a verb. It is only the verbalizer which is conjugated for various grammatical relations; for example, in ***tabaah karnaa*** 'to destroy' ***tabaah*** remains invariant, whereas ***karnaa*** is inflected for tense, mood, aspect, and gender: ***tabaah karnaa*** is the infinitive form; ***tabaah kiyaa/kiye/kii/kiĩ*** are perfective forms; ***tabaah karegaa/karegii/karẽge/karẽgii*** are future forms; ***tabaah kare/karuũ/karẽ*** are subjunctive forms, ***tabaah karo/kiijiye/kar*** are imperative forms; and ***tabaah kartaa/kartii/karte/kartiĩ*** are habitual forms.

2.6 In order to understand how easy the borrowing of verbs through complex verb phrases is, let us take a quick look at the various phonotactic changes that a simple verb in Hindi has to go through in the process of generating morphologically related simple, first causal, and second causal forms. The terms simple, first causal, and second causal are here used for forms such as ***uThnaa*** 'to wake up', ***uThaanaa*** 'to wake some one else up', and ***uthvaanaa*** 'to have some one wake up', respectively.

In Hindi, generally, the first causal form is derived by adding ***aa*** and the second causal form by suffixing ***vaa*** to the root of the simple verb, e.g. ***hilnaa***, ***hilaanaa***, ***hilvaanaa*** 'MOVE'. There are, however, exceptions to this rule depending on whether or not a root is monosyllabic or disyllabic and open or closed, etc. For instance, if the root is monosyllabic with a long vowel, then the long vowel is shortened before the first and second causal suffixes; in this case ***aa*** becomes ***a***; ***ii***, ***e***, ***ai*** and sometimes ***aa*** become ***i***; ***uu***, ***o***, and ***au***, become ***u***. For example, ***ghuumnaa***, ***ghumaanaa***, ***ghumvaanaa*** 'WALK'; ***jiitnaa***, ***jitaanaa***, ***jitvaanaa*** 'WIN'. If the root is disyllabic and has a short ***a*** in the second syllable, then the short vowel is dropped before the first causal suffix, for example, ***pakaRnaa***, ***pakRaanaa***, ***pakaRvaanaa*** 'CATCH'. Further, if the root is open, i.e., it ends in a vowel, then ***l***, is inserted before the causal suffixes, for example, ***khaanaa*** becomes ***khilaanaa*** and ***khilvaanaa***, 'EAT'.

There are still other phonotactic rules that one must know in order to generate correct forms of causal verb paradigms in Hindi. For instance, many simple verbs with monosyllabic roots enclosing a short vowel derive their first causal forms simply by lengthening that vowel; the second causal form, however, is derived in the usual way by adding ***vaa*** before the suffix. For example, ***kaTnaa*** becomes ***kaaTnaa*** and ***kaTvaanaa***, 'CUT'. Sometimes in the first causal form, instead of simply lengthening the cognate vowel, *vriddhi* takes place; for example, ***khulnaa*** becomes ***kholnaa*** 'OPEN'. There are still a few more subsets of verbs, which follow different phonotactic patterns. For instance, a few roots ending in ***T*** change ***T*** to ***R*** in their first and second causal forms, e.g., ***chuuTnaa*** becomes ***choRnaa*** and ***chuRvaanaa*** 'LEAVE'. Further, there are forms, where final guttural of the root becomes the corresponding palatal in the first causal only. For example, the first causal form of ***biknaa*** 'SELL' is ***becnaa***, but the second causal form is regular, i.e. ***bikvaanaa***.

After looking at the complex phonotactic rules involved in the Hindi verb system, it should not be hard to understand why complex verbs must have been favored over simple verbs. It is true that the phonotactic rules have patterns and they persist in modern Hindi, but the use of complex verbs which allow easy incorporation of borrowed verbal concepts without concern for their syllabic boundaries and/or phonetic characteristics has to be tempting when the focus is communication and not linguistic form.

2.7 In the more recent history of the Indian languages, the complex verb phrase phenomenon has been heavily exploited once again to accommodate English verbal concepts. Hindi has borrowed not only English verbal nouns, adjectives, and adverbs, but also prepositions and prepositional phrases such as ***on karnaa*** 'to turn on', ***off karnaa*** 'to turn off', ***look down upon karnaa*** 'to look down upon', and ***slow down karnaa*** 'to slow down'.

MODERN STANDARD HINDI

3.0 Modern standard Hindi is replete with complex verb phrases. The complement in a complex verb phrase may be a borrowing from Sanskrit, Persio-Arabic, or English. With English complements, verbalizers are almost always ***karnaa*** 'to do' or ***honaa*** 'to be'. See examples **[14]** - **[19]** below.

Sanskrit:

[14]	***is***	***baat***	***par***	***bhaartiiya***	***Tiim***	***puurii tarah***	***vibhaajit huii.***
	this	issue	on	Indian	team	complete -ly	DIVIDE BE-perf-fem-sg

'Indian team was full divided on this issue.'

[15]	***hamaare***	***ballebaazõ ne***	***cintaa***	***vyakt***	***kii***
	our	batters ag.	worry	EXPRESS	DO-perf-fem-sg

'Our batters expressed their concern.'

Persio-Arabic:

[16]	***cetan ne***	***tez gedõ kaa***	***mahatva***	***saabit kiyaa.***
	chetan ag.	fast balls of	importance	PROVE DO-perf-mas-sg

'Chetan proved the importance of fast balls.'

[17]	***sarkaar ne***	***naksalvaadii***	***guT ke 27***	***rangkarmiyõ ko***	***giraftaar***	***kiyaa.***
	government ag.	Naxalite	group of 27	artists -obj	CAPTURE	DO-perf-mas-sg

'The government captured 27 artists of the Naxalite group.'

English:

[18]	***maal***	***kab***	***saplaaii***	***hogaa***?
	goods	when	SUPPLY	BE-fut-mas-sg

'When will the goods be supplied?'

[19] *zaraa* *laaiT* *aan* *karnaa.*
please light on DO-imp-neut

'Please turn on the light.'

3.1 As pointed out earlier, the complement in a verb phrase is frequently a borrowed one; it is, however, very interesting that the verbalizer in a complex verb phrase is never a borrowed word. This fact is particularly of interest because a language like Hindi has borrowed not only substantive forms from other languages but also grammatical forms such as conjunctions ***va*** 'and', ***lekin*** 'but', and complementizer ***ki*** 'that'. The verbalizer in Hindi somehow continues to be strictly indigneous. One of the reasons, as discussed earlier, perhaps is the presence of complicated phonotactic verb derivation rules in Hindi which discourage the use of borrowed verbal concepts as verbs. The other possible reason is language typology, for the phenomenon of complex verb phrases appears to be quite active in many verb-final languages such as Indo-Aryan, Dravidian, Persian, Turkish, as well as Japanese.**

CHOICE OF COMPLEMENT

4.0 In a complex verb phrase, if there is a choice of complement among Sanskrit, Persio-Arabic, or English, it mainly depends on factors such as style, subject matter, and geographical and/or religious background of the interlocuters. Sanskrit complements are used with greater frequency in the formal speech and writing and/or in topics such as literature and philosphy; for example ***miimaãsaa karnaa*** 'to examine', ***yashogaan karnaa*** 'to praise', ***aakalan karnaa*** 'to calculate', ***vivecan karnaa*** 'to analyze', ***sanlagn honaa*** 'to be attached', ***vargiikaraN karnaa*** 'to classify', ***avagat honaa*** 'to know' (intr.), ***adhyayan karnaa*** 'to study', ***maargdarshan karnaa*** 'to guide', ***darshan karnaa*** 'to see (a deity/a holy person)', ***aaraadhanaa karnaa*** 'to pray'.

Persio-Arabic complements are frequently found in informal speech and writing and/or in topics such as history, law, and romance. For example, ***hamlaa karnaa*** 'to attack', ***caRhaaii karnaa*** 'to invade', ***ailaan karnaa*** 'to declare', ***fatah karnaa*** 'to win', ***mukadmaa karnaa*** 'to sue', ***barii honaa*** 'to be acquitted by a law-court', ***vakaalat karnaa*** 'to practise law', ***daayar karnaa*** 'to file a law-suit', ***muhabbat honaa*** 'to be in love', ***ishk honaa*** 'to fall in love', ***izhaar honaa*** 'to be manifested', ***ikraar karnaa*** 'to promise', ***bevafaaii karnaa*** 'to show unfaithfulness'.

English complements are frequently used in informal and semi-formal speech in social and professional topics. Today, periphrastic verbs with English complements abound in the speech of bilinguals and are used in almost every topic in informal and semi-formal styles. So far only a few, however, have made their way into the written language such as ***aauT honaa*** 'to be out', ***leT honaa*** 'to be late', ***bor karnaa*** 'to bore (someone)', ***sTaarT karnaa*** 'to start'. Most complex verbs with English complements are still acceptable only in the spoken style and not in the written. For example, ***pliiz karnaa*** 'to please', ***velkam karnaa*** 'to welcome',

kanfyuuz honaa 'to be confused', ***Traaii karnaa*** 'to try', ***injaay karnaa*** 'to enjoy', ***DiTekT honaa*** 'to be detected', ***smuuth karnaa*** 'to smooth' are not found in formal writing. In writing, the English complements are mostly replaced either by Persio-Arabic or Sanskrit words, depending on the topic and the level of formality in a given context.

Besides topic and style, the choice of complement also depends on the geographical and/or religious background of the interlocuters. For instance, people in Benares are likely to use more Sanskrit complements in their informal style of language than people in Delhi. People in Aligarh or Lucknow may use more Persio-Arabic complements in their formal language than people in Delhi or Agra. Further, a person may use more Persio-Arabic complements when interacting with a Muslim than with a Hindu. Hence, the choice between various complements depends on a combination of factors. In light of the knowledge on the subject, it is not possible to make any definitive statements about all the variables and the linguistic variants.

CHOICE BETWEEN A SIMPLE VERB AND A COMPLEX VERB

5.0 In a given language, there may be verbs that can be expressed either as simple verbs or complex verbs, as illustrated by Hindi examples **[20]** - **[25]**.

[20] **a.** *usne saraahnaa kii.*
he ADMIRATION DO-perf-fem-sg

'He admired (someone).'

b. *usne saraahaa.*
he admired

'He admired (someone).'

[21] **a.** *usne khaãsii kii.*
he COUGH DO-perf-mas-sg

'He coughed.'

b. *vah khaãsa.*
he coughed

'He coughed.'

[22] a. *usne khoj kii.*
he SEARCH DO-perf-mas-sg

'He searched.'

b. *usne khojaa.*
he searched

'He searched.'

[23] a. *usne snaan kiyaa.*
he BATH DO-perf-mas-sg

'He bathed.'

b. *vah nahaayaa.*
he bathed

'He took a bath.'

[24] a. *usne sĩcaaii kii.*
he IRRIGATION DO-perf-fem-sg

'He irrigated (it).'

b. *usne siĩcaa.*
he irrigated

'He irrigated (it).'

[25] a. *usne bhuul kii.*
he MISTAKE DO-perf-fem-sg

'He made a mistake.'

b. *vah bhuulaa.*
he forgot

'He forgot.'

At a first glance, the choice between simple and complex verbs in the above examples may seem arbitrary. However, if we study these examples in their broader contexts we will find that the choice between **[a.]** and **[b.]** examples in **[20]** - **[25]** is governed by one or more of the following factors: form, semantics, stylistics, and pragmatics. Let us look at each of these factors closely.

FORM

5.1 In Hindi there are verbs such as ACCEPT, PRAISE, SEARCH, TICKLE, RELINQUISH, RECOGNIZE, which, when used transitively, can be expressed as simple verbs or complex verbs. The same verbs, however, when expressed intransitively and/or causatively must be expressed as complex verbs. The reason is that the language does not have their intransitive and causative simple verb counterparts. In other words, in the verbal paradigms there are gaps in the language that are filled through periphrastic expressions of verbs. See examples given in **[26]** below.

[26]	Intransitive	Transitive	Causative
ACCEPT	****sviikarnaa*** ***sviikaar honaa***	***sviikaarnaa*** ***sviikaar karnaa***	****sviikarvaanaa*** ***sviikaar karvaanaa***
PRAISE	****sarahnaa*** ***saraahnaa honaa***	***saraahnaa*** ***saraahnaa karnaa***	****sarahvaanaa*** ***saraahnaa karvaanaa***
SEARCH	****talashnaa*** ***talaash honaa***	***talaashnaa*** ***talaash karnaa***	****talashvaanaa*** ***talaash karvaanaa***
TICKLE	****gudgudnaa*** ***gudgudii honaa***	***gudgudaanaa*** ***gudgudii karnaa***	?***gudgudvaanaa*** ***gudgudii karvaanaa***
RELINQUISH	****tyagnaa*** ***tyaag honaa***	***tyaagnaa*** ***tyaag karnaa***	****tyagvaanaa*** ***tyaag karvaanaa***
RECOGNIZE	****pahcananaa*** ***pahcaan honaa***	***pahcaananaa*** ***pahcaan karnaa***	****pahcanvaanaa*** ***pahcaan karvaanaa***

The asterisked forms in **[26]**, which are either intransitive or causative forms of the verbs ACCEPT, PRAISE, SEARCH, TICKLE, etc., do not exist in Hindi and are, therefore, unacceptable. These gaps in the language are, however, filled through the periphrastic forms, i.e. ***tyaag honaa***, ***tyag karvaanaa***, ***talaash honaa***, ***tyaag karvaanaa***, etc. Hence, if verbs like ACCEPT, PRAISE, SEARCH, TICKLE, etc. are to be used intransitively or causatively, then there is really no choice between a simple verb and its counterpart complex verb. Only if these verbs are to be used transitively, is there some choice available to the speaker or writer.

5.1. In this context, the question arises why there are no simple verb equivalents for the complex verbs such as ACCEPT or PRAISE? It seems there are different explanations for different missing forms in a given language. For instance, in Sanskrit, the usual way to form the perfect tense is by reduplication: ***tataapa*** and ***dadarśa*** are derived from the roots ***tap*** 'to be hot' and ***dṛś*** 'to see'. But if a root begins with a vowel in a heavy syllable (i.e. long by nature or by position), it cannot be reduplicated. Such forms then must make their perfect forms in a periphrastic manner -- the perfect form of the roots ***iikṣ*** 'to see', ***ujjh*** 'to forsake', ***edh*** 'to thrive' are ***iikṣaaM cakre***, ***ujjhaaM cakaar***, and ***edhaaM cakre***.

The length of a syllable is another factor that prevents a language from creating certain simple verb forms. The evidence for this comes both from Hindi and Sanskrit. In Hindi, most verb stems with two or more syllables seem to make their intransitive and causative verb forms through complex verbs only. Hence, there are no intransitive and causative simple verb forms for SEARCH, PRAISE, etc. The full causative paradigms have to be generated with complex verb forms:

[27]	***talaash honaa***	***talaash karnaa***	***talaash karvaanaa***
	gudgudii honaa	***gudgudii karnaa***	***gudgudii karvaanaa***
	saraahnaa honaa	***saraahnaa karnaa***	***saraahnaa karvaanaa***

In Sanskrit, most derived roots with more than one syllable do not have simple forms because they seem to make their perfect form as a complex verb. See some examples in **[28]** below.

[28]	***cakaas***	'to shine'	***cakaasaaM cakaara***
	bodhay	'to explain'	***bodhayaaM cakaara***
	mantray	'to counsel'	***mantrayaaM cakaara***
	bobudh	'to understand repeatedly'	***bobudhaaM cakaara***

Another possible explanation for the missing simple verb forms in a given language is that their competing complex verb forms gradually take over all the domains of simple verbs, and the use of simple verbs become unacceptable in the language. This seems to be the case for the Hindi verb RELINQUISH; the intransitive form of RELINQUISH is found in some dialects of Hindi (tajnaa) as well as in Sanskrit (tyajyate) but it is not acceptable in Modern Standard Hindi.

SEMANTICS

5.2 Sometimes the choice between a simple verb and its parallel complex verb is determined by their precise distribution of meaning. For example in Hindi, either of the simple or complex verb forms for the verb 'SEARCH', i.e. ***khojnaa*** or ***khoj karnaa***, can be used to express the meaning 'to search for something', but only the complex verb form, i.e. ***khoj karnaa***, gives the meaning 'to discover'. Similarly, the verb 'ARGUE' in its simple verb form, i.e. ***bahasnaa***, can mean only 'to argue', but in its complex verb form, i.e. ***bahas karnaa***, depending on the context, can either mean 'to argue' or 'to debate'. Hence, the simple verb and its counterpart complex verb may have some overlapping semantic area but they are not interchangeable in all their shades of meaning. See examples **[29]** and **[30]**.

[29] **a.** ***vah aajkal naukarii khoj rahaa hai.***
he nowadays job search ing is

b. ***vah aajkal naukarii kii khoj kar rahaa hai.***
he nowadays job of search do ing is

'He is looking for a job these days.'

c. ***eDiisan ne raDio kii khoj kii.***
Edison ag radio of invention did

d. ****eDiisan ne raDio khojaa.***
Edison ag radio invented

'Edison discovered radio.'

[30] **a.** ***kyõ bahas rahe ho?***
why argue ing are-second person

b. ***kyõ bahas kar rahe ho?***
why argue do ing are-second person

'Why are you arguing?'

c. ***aaj shaam kin do ummiidvaarõ mẽ bahas hogii?***
today evening who two candidates between debate be-will

d. ****aaj shaam kaun do ummiidvaar bahasẽge?***
today evening who two candidates debate-will

'Which two candidates will debate this evening?'

5.2.1 Some morphologically related pairs of simple and complex verbs have no overlap in their meaning; the forms are related but their meanings are different. For example in Hindi ***bhuulnaa*** means 'to forget' and ***bhuul karnaa*** means 'to make a mistake'; ***tarasnaa*** means 'to crave for something' and ***taras khaanaa*** means 'to have mercy on someone'. In such cases, the choice between morphologically related simple verbs and complex verbs is clearly determined by their meaning.

5.2.2 In some cases, the use of simple or its parallel complex verb form is determined by its concrete vs. abstract use.

[31] **a.** *pahle vah aadmii kaa foTograaf haasil kartii hai, phir vah us aadmii ke bhiitar chupe mard ko* ***talaashtii hai.***

'First she obtains the photograph of the person and then she searches for the man hiding inside that person.'

b. ? *pahle vah aadmii kaa foTograaf haasil kartii hai, phir vah us aadmii ke bhiitar chupe mard ko* ***talaash kartii hai.***

In example **[31a.]**, for instance, the simple form of the verb SEARCH, i.e. ***talaashnaa***, denotes search for something abstract, i.e. non-tangible (search for the manly qualities in this case). In **[31b.]** where the simple verb ***talaashnaa*** is replaced by the complex verb ***talaash karnaa***, the resulting sentence becomes connotationally inappropriate because the use of complex verb ***talaash karnaa*** denotes search for concrete or tangible objects only.

Similarly, **[32a.]**, where ***talaash karnaa*** 'to search' is used in the concrete sense, is connotationally appropriate but **[32b.]** is not, where the verb ***talaashnaa*** denotes search for some abstract qualities.

[32] **a.** *pulis ne sargarmii se apraadhii kii* ***talaash kii.***
police ag. active -ly criminal for search did

'Police actively searched for the criminal.'

b. * *pulis ne sargarmii se apraadhii ko* ***talaashaa.***

STYLE

5.3 The selection of a simple or complex verb in a given context is sometimes conditioned by stylistic factors also. For instance, in a formal register it is more apt to choose the complex verb phrases with Sanskrit complements such as ***gyaan honaa*** 'to know' (intr.), ***prasthaan karnaa*** 'to go', ***snaan karnaa*** 'to bathe', and ***darshan karnaa*** 'to see' than their simple verb counterparts ***jaananaa***, ***jaanaa***, ***nahaanaa***, and ***dekhnaa***, respectively, because the use of Sanskrit words generally indicates a higher level of formality or culturally loaded environment.

In an informal register, on the other hand, most urban educated speakers may choose complex verbs with English complements such as ***DekoreT karnaa*** 'to decorate', ***muuv karnaa*** 'to move', ***miks karnaa*** 'to mix', ***vaash karnaa*** 'to wash' over their simple verb equivalents: ***sajaanaa***, ***hilaanaa***, ***gholnaa***, ***dhonaa***, as the Hindi-English mixed code is the norm for most informal situations in urban settings.

PRAGMATICS

5.4 The use of a complex verb form over its parallel simple form may be at times geared to achieve contrastive emphasis, as in examples **[33]** and **[34]**.

[33] ***vah khaãsii kar nahiĩ rahaa use khaãsii ho rahii hai.***
he coughing do not ing to him cough happen ing is .

'He is not coughing (on purpose), he cannot help coughing.'

[34] ***seTh karoRiimal ne dhan kaa tyaag kiyaa nahiĩ, tyaag ho gayaa.***
rich krorimal ag. money of RENOUNCE DID not RENOUNCE BE-perf.

'The rich Kirorimal did not renounce his wealth himself but it got renounced.'

By using intransitive and transitive complex verbs in the same sentence, the contrastive emphasis is being placed on the volitionality and involitionality of the verbs COUGH and RENOUNCE in **[33]** and **[34]**, which cannot be expressed through the use of simple verbs because of the missing intransitive forms in the language.

5.4.1 Further, the use of complex verb phrases over simple verbs allows the speaker or writer to place a greater emphasis on the act as opposed to the action itself. See the following examples:

[35] **a.** ***usne do baar paisõ kii corii kii.***
he-ag. two times money of theft did

'He stole the money twice. (lit.: Twice he did the stealing of money.)'

b. ***usne do baar paise curaae.***
he-ag. two times money stole

'He stole the money twice.'

[36] **a.** ***bacce ne saarii raat khaãsii kii.***
child ag. all night cough did

'The child coughed all night. (lit.: The child did the coughing all night.)'

b. ***bacce ne saarii raat khaãsaa.***
child ag. all night coughed

'The child coughed all night.'

In **[35a.]** and **[36a.]** the focus is on the acts of theft and cough, and not on the actions as is the case in **[35b.]** and **[36b.]**.

SUMMARY

6.0 In this paper, I have tried to show two things: One, the phenomenon of complex verb phrase which is extremely productive and widespread in modern Standard Hindi is found at various earlier stages of Indo-Aryan languages including vedic and classical Sanskrit. In the earlier Sanskrit language, at least from the written texts, it appears that this phenomenon was restricted to those grammatical forms which could not be formulated in a regular fashion because of certain phonetic conditions. Later, in classical Sanskrit, however, the use of complex verb phrases became much more prevalent. In modern Hindi, complex verb phrases have gained a very high frequency. Language simplification and language contact seem to be two important factors that have contributed to the mushroom growth of complex verb phrases in modern Indian languages, including modern Sanskrit as spoken and written today.

Second, the choice between a complex verb and its parallel simple verb is not arbitrary. It is governed by formal, semantic, stylistic, and pragmatic factors. Further, within a complex verb phrase, when there is a choice between a Sanskrit, English, or Persio-Arabic verbal complement, the selection depends on subject matter, style, regional as well as religious background of the interlocuters.

* I am grateful to Professor George Cardona, University of Pennsylvania, for his valuable comments and suggestions. All inaccuracies, however, are my own.

** Examples of complex verb phrases:

Malayalam:	*naan*	*avanu*	*Telifon*	*ceydu*
	I	him	telephone	did
Persian:	*man*	*ura*	*telifon*	*kardam*
	I	him	telephone	did
Japanese:	*watakusi wa*	*kare ni*	*telifon*	*suru*
	I	him	telephone	did

'I telephoned him.'

REFERENCES

Acharya, Shriram Sharma (ed.) 1967. viShNu-puraaNa. Bareli, U.P.: Sanskriti Sansthan.

Bahri, Hardev. 1960. Persian influence on Hindi. Allahabad: Bharati Press Publications.

Beams, John. 1871. A comparative grammar of the modern Aryan languages of India. [2nd Indian Reprint, New Delhi: Munshiram Manoharlal, 1970.]

Grimshaw, J., and A. Mester. 1988. Light verbs and θ-Marking. Linguistic Inquiry 19:2.205-32.

Johnson, Francis (ed.) 1847. Hitopadesha. London: Wm. H. Allen and Co.

Kachru, Yamuna. 1982. Conjunct verbs in Hindi-Urdu and Persian. South Asian review: studies in South Asian languages & linguistics, ed. by P. J. Mistry. (SALA Journal, 6:3.) 117-26. Jacksonville, FL: South Asian Literary Association.

Kellogg, S. H. 1875. A grammar of the Hindi language. [Indian reprint, New Delhi: Oriental Books Reprint Corp., 1972.]

Lambton, A. K. S. 1971. Persian grammar. Cambridge: The University Press.

Tulsi Das. Raamcharitmaanas. 36th edn. Gorakhpur: Geeta Press.

Sharma, B. R. (ed.) 1967. JaiminiiyopaniShad-braahmaNam. Tirupati: Kendriya Sanskrit Vidyapeeth.

Upadhyaya, Gangaprasad (ed.) 1967. satapathabrahmana. New Delhi: Prachiin vaijnaanikaadhyayan-anusandhaan sansthaanam.

Whitney, W. D. 1879. Sanskrit grammar. [Indian reprint, Delhi: Motilal Banarsidass, 1977.]

ASPECTOGENESIS AND THE COMPOUND VERB IN INDO-ARYAN*

Peter Edwin Hook
University of Michigan

ABSTRACT. Aspectogenesis (the gradual or sudden emergence of aspectual contrast as a paradigmatic category) is a complex and largely unstudied phenomenon. In some Indo-Aryan languages (for example, Hindi-Urdu and Marwari) the compound verb has evolved into an explicit means of expressing perfective aspect. In other languages (for example, Marathi and Kashmiri) the compound verb exists but does not function as a regular exponent of aspect. This paper identifies certain features of compound verb systems as being the "signatures" of the emergence of perfective aspect as a regular grammatical category and attempts to interpret those features in a theory of aspectogenesis.

The compound verb in Indo-Aryan.

With the exceptions of the northern dialects of Shina and some languages spoken in southern Rajasthan, every form of contemporary Indo-Aryan has a set of auxiliary (or **vector**) verbs homophonous with members of its inventory of basic lexical verbs. As full lexical verbs these express a change in location or posture or actions that entail such a change: GO, GIVE, TAKE, THROW, LET GO, GET UP, STRIKE, SIT, COME, FALL, etc. A **compound verb** (CV) comprises the finite form of one of these following a non-finite or stem form of a main or primary verb. In 1h and 2h ***kar*** and ***ho*** are the non-finite forms of primary verbs, while ***liyaa hotaa*** and ***jaatii*** are the finite forms of the vectors ***le*** TAKE and ***jaa*** GO (examples marked **h** are from Hindi-Urdu):

1h agar mAI ne xaamoS rahne kaa faislaa kar liyaa hotaa[1]
if I ERG silent staying's decision do TAKEN had[2]
'If I had decided to remain silent . . .'

2h baat vahII xatam ho jaa-tii
thing there over become GO-CTF
'The matter would have ended right there.' (Vaid 1970:25)

For every CV there is almost always a corresponding non-compound or simple verb (SV) in which the auxiliary is absent and the primary verb bears the desinential affixes:

1h' agar mAI ne xaamoS rahne kaa faislaa kiyaa hotaa
if I ERG silent staying's decision done had
'If I had decided to remain silent . . .'

2h' baat vahII xatam ho-tii
thing there over become-CTF
'The matter would have ended right there.'

The compound verb is an innovation in Indo-Aryan. It is first attested in Buddhist Pali stories from Sri Lanka:

3p daruni āhari-tvā aggi-m ka-tvā da-ssa-ti
sticks bring-CPM fire-ACC make-CPM GIVE-FUT-3sg
'Bringing wood he'll make a fire.' (Trenckner 1879:77)

It is rare in Pali and non-existent in Sanskrit (aside from a few sequences that are ambiguously interpretable as compound verbs or as serial verbs):

4s tato makṣikā - uḍḍiya gatā (Tikkanen 1987:176)
then fly fly-CPM WENT
'Then the fly flew up and departed/flew away.'

The first clear instances of it known to me from texts composed on the South Asian mainland are in Svayambhu's *paumacariu*, a Ramayana composed in Apabhramsha late in the first millennium of the present era:

5a viNNi vi kumaara gaya osar-evi (*paumacariu* 65.12.1b)
two also princes WENT withdraw-CPM
'Both the princes departed.'

6a chuDu ekku gaasu mahu ho-u[3] ga-u (*paumacariu* 62.2.8)
still one bite me-DAT became WENT
'Yet (a whole elephant is (just) one bite for me.'

It appears in later Apabhramsha works such as *jasaharacariu* (2.28.8b-9a):

7a vaahI maariya mahu jaNaNi saa laiaya Nivandhivi celiyahI
hunter-INS killed my mother her TOOK tie-up-CPM cloth-INS
'The hunter killed my mother (and) tied her up in a cloth.'

Examining the text frequency of CV's at different times in the histories of modern Indo-Aryan languages, one finds some variation. For example, in Hindi-Urdu prose works of the nineteenth and twentieth centuries:

	Title	Author	Date	CVs	total	CV%
a	rānī ketkī	I.K. Insha	1818	162	1158	14.0
b	devarānī	Gauridatta	1870	193	1212	15.9
c	bhāgyavatī	Phillauri	1877	158	1193	13.2
d	parīkṣā-guru	L.S.N. Das	1884	121	1000	12.1
e	narendra-mohinī	D.N. Khattri	1910?	143	1150	12.4
f	godān	Premchand	1936	206	1271	16.2
g	śekhar	Vatsyayan	1940	149	1232	12.1
h	merā duśman	K.B. Vaid	1966	424	2363	17.9
i	ādhere band kamre	M. Rakesh	1967	208	1247	16.7
j	yārõ ke yār	K. Sobati	1968	209	1185	17.6
k	dūsre kināre se	K.B. Vaid	1970	227	1263	18.0
l	ye kahāniyā̃	M. Mohini	1985	121	812	14.9
m	śalmalī	N. Sharma	1987	150	1001	15.0

Table 1. CV percentages in Hindi-Urdu prose works since 1800.

It is possible to graph the percentage figures for compound verb occurrence versus time and extract from them a formula that describes the increase in CV text frequency over time. The formula can be used to generate a regression line. The steeper the line's slope, the more rapid the change:

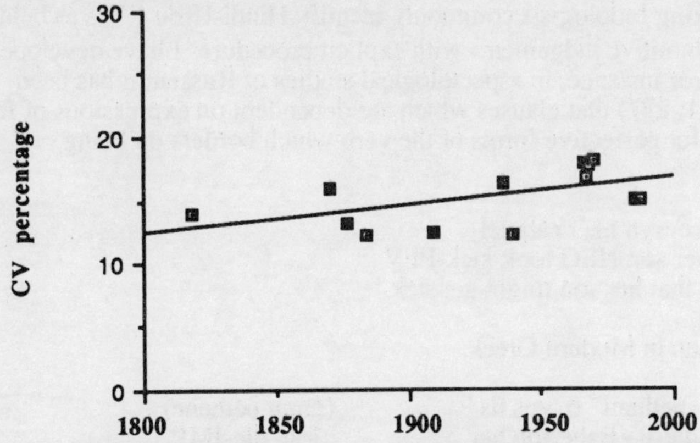

Figure 1. CV% in Hindi-Urdu prose of the nineteenth and twentieth centuries.

While change in CV frequency (and the overall direction of change) is perceptible in Fig. 1, it is not dramatic enough to exclude the possibility that what we see is nothing more than the random effect of differences in style or author.[4]

Investigation of such change in Hindi-Urdu is hampered by two factors: 1. The sequence of texts available to us is fairly short: at most two centuries separate our times from the appearance of the earliest prose works (e.g., Insha's *rānī ketkī kī kahānī* and Mir Amman's *bāgh o bahār*). 2. Urdu (and later, Hindi) was for much of this time a second language for most of its speakers, who were spread over a vast area of northern India and spoke a variety of languages as their mother tongues. Inevitably, there was wide variation in the kind of Hindi and Urdu people from different parts of northern India used. In the earliest texts the differences extend even to basic verb morphology.[5]

Thus, although we know that the compound verb is an innovation in Indo-Aryan and, in the western Gangetic area, over a period of not more than fifteen hundred years, must have undergone an increase in frequency from zero to the approximately fifteen percent that we see today, we are not able to observe the progress of that increase in an absolutely unambiguous way in the Hindi prose texts available to us. Therefore, data has to be gathered from other Indo-Aryan languages whose geographical range is smaller than Hindi-Urdu's and whose written record is longer.[6]

One such language is Marathi. From prose accounts of the lives of Mahānubhāva saints, through historical annals (known as **bakhar**'s), to modern prose (which began about a hundred and twenty years ago) we have a fairly continuous record of about seven hundred years in length. However, as fine and complete as the record of Marathi prose may be, it is not of much use in an investigation of aspectogenesis. That is because the percentage of compound verbs in contemporary Marathi is still very low. The figure for late twentieth century prose ranges between three and four percent. Furthermore, it can be shown that the Marathi compound verb (unlike the Hindi-Urdu compound verb) does not function to express perfective aspect.

Identifying perfectivity as a function of the compound verb.

In Hindi-Urdu the CV/SV opposition functions to express perfectivity in the sense which the term has in Slavistics: viewing an action or process as (summed into) a whole vis-a-vis some specific moment or interval of time. This rather cumbersome definition[7] has the merit of accommodating two divergent meanings of the perfective found in languages where it is a paradigmatic category: completeness of action and inchoation of state or activity.

Russian or Czech-speaking Indologists commonly identify Hindi-Urdu CV's as being perfectives.[8] To buttress their intuitive judgements with explicit procedures I have developed independent diagnostic texts. For instance, in aspectological studies of Russian it has been observed (Forsyth 1970: 258-61; 297) that clauses which are dependent on expressions of fear and anxiety show a preference for perfective forms of the verb which borders on being categorical:

8r mat' bojalas' kak-by eë syn ne zabolel
mother feared lest her son NEG took-sick-PFV
'The mother was afraid that her son might get sick.'

The same preference is to be seen in Modern Greek:

9mg i mitera fovotane min pethani o yos tis (*min pethene)
the mother feared lest die-PVF the son her lest die-IMP
'The mother was afraid her son might die.'

The strong preference for perfective forms in *fear*-clauses in these languages can be understood as the reflection of a language-independent fact about the semantics of perfective aspect: The very act of fearing the occurrence of an event presupposes the completeness of its conceptualization. Such an event, clearly visible to the mind's eye, seems to have a degree of mental reality that compels speakers to use a perfective form for its expression (provided their language has such forms).

There is a similar (although not quite so univocal) preference for perfective forms in clauses dependent on expressions that mean 'until' (10r from Forsyth 1970:133):

10r ona budet ubajukivat' rebënka poka on ne zasnët
she will rock child while he NEG sleeps-PFV
'She will rock the baby till it goes to sleep.'

10mg tha kunai to pedi mexri na kimithi (*...mexri na kimate)
will rock the child until that sleeps-PFV until that sleeps-IMP
'(She) will rock the child until it goes to sleep.' (Spyros Hoidas, p.c.)

There are also environments which strongly disfavor the perfective. For example, the complements of phasal verbs in Russian and Mod. Greek bar the occurrence of perfective aspect:

11r on načinaet čitat' predloženie (*načinaet pročitat')
he begin-3sg read-IMP sentence begin-3sg read-PFV
'He begins to read the sentence.'

11mg arxizi na dyavazi to vivlio (*arxizi na dyavasi)
begin-3sg that read-IMPFV the book begin-3sg that read-PFV
'He begins to read the book.'

These asymmetries[9] in the distribution of perfective forms in Russian and Modern Greek are closely paralleled by Hindi-Urdu CV's:

12h mujhe Dar thaa ki kahII tum use ciTThii na de do
to-me fear was that lest you him letter NEG give GIVE
'I was afraid that you might give him the letter.'

13h tum yahAA Thaharo jab-tak vo tumhE ciTThii na de de
you here stay until he you letter NEG give GIVE
'Wait here until he gives you the letter.'[10]

14h vo khaanaa paros-ne lagii (*paros le-ne lagii)
she food serve-INF began serve TAKE-INF began
'She began to dish out the food.'

Applying these same tests to Marathi we find that its CV/SV opposition does not regularly express perfectivity:

12m ma-laa kaaLji hoti ki tu tyaa-laa patr de-Sil (*fear*)
me-to anxiety was that you him-to letter give-FUT
'I was afraid that you might give him the letter.'[11]

13m to tu-laa patr de-i paryant itha thaamb (*until*)
he you-to letter give-INF until here wait
'Wait here until he gives you the letter.'

14m ti ann vaaDh-un ghe-u laagli (phasal verb)
she food dish-out-CPM TAKE-INF began
'She began to dish out the food.' (Chirmule 1967:60)

These data show there is a difference in the functions of the CV/SV opposition for these two Indo-Aryan languages and that the difference is statable in terms of aspect. But because Marathi's compound verb system has not yet acquired perfectivity as one of its functions and Hindi-Urdu prose texts are unavailable before the early nineteenth century we are not able to use either language for a direct look at what happens during aspectogenesis. For that we need a language which has a compound verb system as highly developed as Hindi-Urdu's and which also has a longer textual record. Such a language is Marwari, the chief regional language of Rajasthan.

The evidence from Marwari.

In Rajasthan there is a tradition dating back several centuries of maintaining historical records. Some of these are in the form of verse; some, in prose. Using the latter we can obtain a frequency measure of the compound verb from as far back as the early seventeenth century for Marwari. (The fifth and sixth sets of figures are from collections of contemporary short stories):

	Title	Author	Date	CVs	total	CV%
A	daḷpat vilā̃s	Anon.	@1600	13	1020	1.3
B	naiṇsī rī khyāt	M. Nainsi	1670	43	1292	3.3
C	ajit vilā̃s	Anon.	@1730	56	1010	5.5
D	mā̃nsingh rī khyāt	Anon.	@1870	101	1125	9.0
E	ūkaḷtā antarā	Moolchand	1973	158	1249	12.7
F	khiṛakī	Rathor	1989	198	1118	17.7

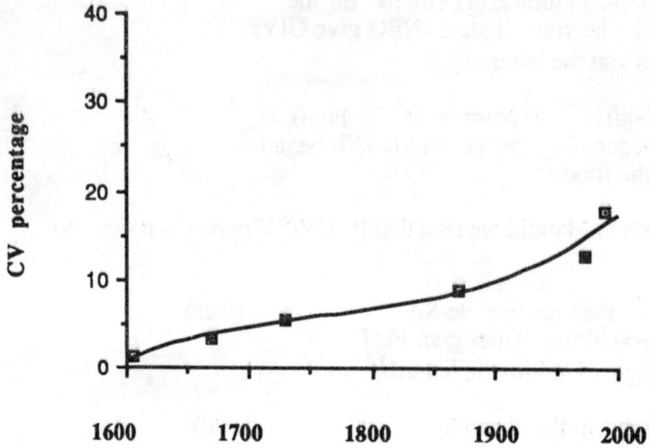

Figure 2. CV% in Marwari prose from 1600 to the present.

In Figure 2 the CV percentages are plotted in a scattergram and fitted to a line of regression describing a regular growth in compound verb frequency over time.

It can be shown that modern Marwari has the expression of perfective aspect as one of its functions [13] For example, when asked to translate a *fear*-clause from English to Marwari, native speakers invariably use a compound verb:

15M manai bhai to ki aap unhE ye kaagaj de devolaa
me-DT fear was that you him the letter give GIVE
'I was afraid that you would give him the letter.'

While we have no access to native Marwari speakers from the seventeenth century it is possible to identify *fear*-clauses in texts. One candidate occurs in Nainsi's description of Mulraj Solanki's successful plot to overthrow the Chavoras (joint rulers of Patan). Mulraj realizes that his mother has learned of the plot and fears that she may reveal it:

16M aa niice paavaRiyAA utarNa laagii tarai iN diTho,
she down steps descend began then he-ERG saw
"aaloc baarai phuuT-sii; dhartii haath nahII aavai."
plan out break-FUT realm hand not come
'As she began to go down the stairs, he thought to himself,
"My plan will get out; I won't get the kingdom"' (Nainsi 1.268.-3)

The form ***phuuTsii*** is not compound even though the event it denotes is feared by the subject of ***diTho***. In another example from Nainsi (2.28.2), a king expresses his apprehension of treachery. The verb (***dai***) is in non-compound form:

17M raajaa kahyo, "o khoTo aadmii chai. koh-ek dago dai."
king said this false man is some betrayal give
'The king said, "This man is false. He may betray (us)."'

In the one clear instance I found in *daḷpat vilās* (20.6-7), the verb expressing the feared event is not compound: (Note the code mixing in the quotation: Marwari ***ju*** 'that' and Urdu ***kii*** GEN):

18M mirjai ibraaham im kahiyo ju na karai khudaay ju ghar kii
Mirza Irbahim thus said that NEG do-SBJNC God that house-GEN
paatisaahii khovUU
empire lose-SBJNC
'Mirza Ibrahim said. "God forbid I lose my kingdom!"'

In the next example the speaker is anxious over the fate of a son who disappeared many years before (Nainsi 2.20.1):

19M na jaaNAA mUvo kinaa kaThii-hii jogii sanyaasii huy gayo
not know died or lest yogi sanyasi become WENT
'I don't know if he died or became a yogi or sanyasi.'

Here one of the verbs is compound (***hu***- 'become') while the other (***mar***- 'die') is not. Although the total of clear examples of *fear*-clauses in the older texts is not high, very few of them have compound verbs. Examples of until-clauses or of compound verbs dependent on phasals (as in (14m)) are absent altogether [14]

Other evidence can be gleaned from a closer examination of what kinds of predicates can appear in compound form in medieval as opposed to modern Marwari. In the sample from Nainsi about twenty-five different verbs are found in compound form of which twenty (80%) are predicates denoting a physical motion of subject or object: 'go', 'come', 'send', 'bring', 'run away', 'put in', 'pull out', 'disappear', 'leave behind', etc. Of the others, four are actions that either presuppose physical movement or result in it: 'kill', 'break', 'create', 'summon'. Only one is abstract in its meaning: ***log aapraa kar raakh*** 'to make people one's own; to suborn them'. In the modern sample only some 50% of verbs that show up in compound form denote physical motion. Types that make up the other 50% include abstract ('work', 'accomplish', 'arrange', 'shelter'); mental ('understand', 'forget', 'decide'); perceptual ('hear', 'catch a glimpse of'); change of state ('die', 'go to sleep'); linguistic ('say', 'refuse'); and phasal ('start/stop V-ing') verbs.

Of course, part of this difference may follow from the difference in genre: the modern sample is from a collection of short stories; the medieval one is an historical account. And part of it may reflect three hundred years of evolution in what writers consider worthy of being recorded. A rather unadorned account of historical events may contain a higher propostion of motion verbs than a modern short story which describes the thoughts, feelings and perceptions of its protagonists as well as their acts. But in both the modern and medieval texts, a lot of attention is paid to what is said. It is very interesting to see that out of seventy-five instances of the verb ***kah*** 'say' in the sample from Nainsi, not one of them is compound; while in the prose sample from the twentieth century, nearly twelve percent of the tokens of ***kah*** are compound. (See Table 3).

Even more dramatic is the change in the frequency of compounding in phasal verbs ('begin V-ing', 'stop V-ing'). In the sample from Nainsi there are fourteen tokens of the verb ***laag*** used with a dependent infinitive in the meaning 'begin to V'. None of these are compound. In the twentieth century sample ***laag*** shows up with a dependent infinitive in twenty-nine tokens of which seven (one fourth) are compound.

This stands in contrast to the frequency of compounding in verbs which express physical motion. In a count of seven of them ('go', 'come', 'send', 'take', 'leave behind', 'go out', 'take out') I found that three percent of the total tokens in *daḷpat vilās* were compound (6/186), and six percent of the total tokens in Nainsi were compound (13/219); while fifteen percent of their twentieth century counterparts show up in compound form. This change in frequencies (500%) is less than that found for verbs overall (1000%).

Ratio of CVs to total tokens of:		motion verbs	'say'	'begin'
A dalpat vilās	@1600	6/193	0/54	0/10
B nainsī rī khyāt	1670	13/219	0/75	0/14
C ajit vilās	@1730	28/237	0/31	0/02
D mansingh rī khyāt	@1870	23/157	1/18	0/00
E ukaltā antarā	1973	26/173	3/26	7/29

Table 3. Change in CV frequency for selected predicates.

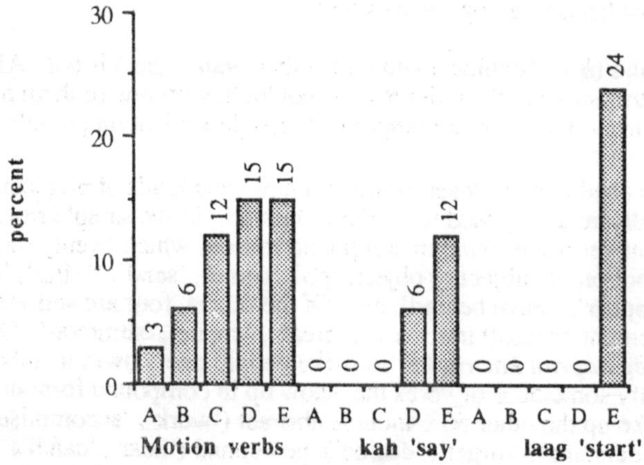

Figure 3. Change in CV frequency for selected predicates.[15]

An explanation of these asymmetries is the subject of the next section.

A theory of aspectogenesis in Indo-Aryan.

We have seen that the difference in text frequency that distinguishes the Marathi from the Hindi-Urdu CV can be correlated with a fundamental difference in function. Studying medieval and modern Marwari texts has provided us with some evidence for a parallel correlation of frequency and function in the CV systems of different periods of one and the same language. While all predicates share in the general increase in CV manifestation shown in Figure 2, certain subsets of them exhibit the even more dramatic change shown in Table 3. Does the disproportionate increase in CV manifestation for communication verbs like ***kah*** or phasal verbs like ***laag*** have any connection with the emergence of perfective aspect as one of the CV's significata?

If we assume that innovations enter linguistic systems in order to resolve communicative problems (Traugott 1988: 414), it follows that they would take root first in domains where they are maximally informative. An inspection of the verbs that appear compound in the earliest prose text that is available (*dalpat vilās*) shows that over 75% of them are verbs of general motion: 'come', 'go', 'flee', 'withdraw', 'pull out'. A common characteristic of general motions is that they admit of degrees; they are continuous. An object can come closer and closer or go further and further without its having to cross some threshold or minimum distance before the speaker may felicitously describe its motion as one of coming or going. Of course, in real life situations there are such thresholds: motion to or from some reference point is not of much interest to speakers or hearers unless it brings objects or persons into or out of range of a subsequent action. Speakers can indicate the crossing of such thresholds explicitly with a locative phrase (***here***, ***there***, ***to me***, ***to Bombay***, ***home***, etc.) or implicitly by referring to a subsequent action that presupposes crossing some relevant threshold in performing the earlier action:

20e *The guard pulled a rope and a bell began to ring.*

What the use of the compound form seems to do for verbs of general motion is to conceptually establish such a limit or term of motion, a "bound of relevance", without requiring that bound to be specifically named. In *dalpat vilas* it is possible to see this effect of CV form most clearly with the verb ***naas*** 'flee'. There is a partial alternation of the compound form ***naasi jaav*** with explicit locatives:

21M su (diikraa) naasi ar samudra rai kAAThai nUU gayaa
they (the sons) flee-CPM ocean 's edge to went
'They fled to the shore of the sea.' (*DV* 16.-1)

22M burai havaal raav candseN naasi gayo
bad condition-OBL king Chandrasena flee WENT
'King Chandrasena fled in distress.' (*DV* 31.1)

But the textual distribution of compound forms and explicit locatives is not complementary even at the incipient stage of development represented by *dalpat vilās:* Compound forms co-occur with locative phrases and simple forms occur without them, so that inferring thresholds of relevance from context remains a requirement in the interpretation of the narrative.

Since most verbs of articulate communication express activities that are either inherently bound or are clearly delimited in temporal extent we should expect a system that formally marks completeness to be extended to them rather later than it would be to classes of verbs expressing continuously divisible motions or verbs whose aspectual values are inherently less determined. The same would apply even more markedly to verbs of phase since their function is the simple demarcation of the temporal extent of other actions.

Over time, as the frequency of explicit marking of completeness grows, predicates that express actions and events which are complete by their very nature are drawn into the domain of the compound verb. We can see this in the sudden increase in CV manifestation in Marwari of inherently perfective predicates like 'say' and 'begin' and we may expect to find similar diachronic profiles for other subsets of predicates that have similar inherent aspectual values: 'arrive', 'forget', 'catch', 'find', 'realize', etc. Efficient investigation of such predicates will require researchers to enter text from different periods into electronic files and use key-word searches to find changes in the CV ratio for each of them.

Granting this staggered sweeping of predicates and predicate types into CV systems as an empirically verifiable fact, we still need to address the question of why this has taken place. Why should the use of vectors with unbounded verbs of movement (where they are maximally informative) be extended over time to verbs expressing actions and events which are inherently bounded and where use of vector verbs is minimally informative, if not altogether redundant? This question is essentially a psychological one and probably is unanswerable in any other way than by conducting controlled experiments on living speakers. But the written record does suggest at least one plausible hypothesis.

In my sample of medieval Marwari texts ***mar***, the common verb meaning 'die', is rarely compound (1/69). In contemporary Marwari, as in Hindi-Urdu, this verb is invariably in CV form unless there is some specific factor (such as negation or participial form) that favors or requires the use of a non-compound form. In its commonest uses ***mar*** describes an inherently bounded change of state. We do not usually speak of individuals as partly or completely dying (unless we are speaking figuratively). How then can we explain the replacement of ***mar*** by ***mar jaav*** as the normal expression in modern Marwari for 'die'? I think part of the answer is in the use of metaphorical equivalents for ***mar*** which are drawn from the pool of unbounded motion verbs. When a motion verb is used in the sense of 'die', it is often given a compound form:[16]

23M su vaat kartAA raaj soLanki ro hans raajaa uR gayo (Nainsi 1.265)
so thing saying king Solanki 's swan king (soul) fly WENT
'As a result King Solanki's soul flew away (as if in the midst of a sentence).'

24M DaavaDaa nUU kAAii balaai huii su jiiv niisar gayo
child DAT some disease became so soul leave WENT
'The child got sick and died.' (Nainsi 1.144.-3)

This is because, while the event expressed is an inherently bounded one, the events of flying or leaving to which it is implicitly compared are not bounded. As such metaphors lose their original force and become fixed euphemisms for 'die', users are apt to transfer their formal characteristics to all expressions meaning 'die', including ***mar***. This kind of metaphorical extension may have contributed over time to the assimilation of more and more inherently perfective predicates to the compound verb system and to the eventual emergence of the CV form as a universal (or nearly universal) morphological category of the modern Marwari and Hindi-Urdu verb.

Such a view has an interesting consequence. If we assume metaphorical extensions of meaning to be universal in human communication, it follows that, once the compound verb has established itself as an option for concrete motion predicates, it will in time invade other more abstract areas of meaning. That is, given enough time, the verb-compounding systems of languages like Marathi, Kashmiri, or Middle Marwari will inevitably come to resemble those of Hindi-Urdu and modern Marwari. Indeed, this view may provide us with a testable hypothesis (and a specific mechanism) to account for one aspect of the phenomenon known since Sapir's day as **drift**. (See Kahr 1976)

The theory of aspectogenesis that I have presented here makes the following four predictions:

(1) As a compound verb system evolves predicates expressing physical displacement will show an earlier onset of CV manifestation than will predicates expressing inherently abrupt events or sudden changes of state.

(2) At a later stage some of the latter ('begin', 'forget', 'find') will show a fairly sudden change in CV manifestation, from well below the average to well above it.

(3) An evolving CV system will satisfy the diagnostic tests for perfective aspect only when CV manifestation becomes an option for nearly every non-stative predicate.

(4) The signatures of aspectogenesis described under (2) and (3) will be associated with an overall CV frequency rate of between nine and twelve percent.

There is a fifth feature of aspectogenesis that I have set forth elsewhere (1988, In press):

(5) As SV/CV oppositions evolve into a system of aspectual contrasts, constraints on the syntactic distribution of the CV become tighter.

These predictions await confirmation and refinement from parallel studies in Dravidian and Altaic as well as other Indo-Aryan languages with long textual traditions (e.g., Braj, Awadhi, Gujarati, Sindhi, Bangla,[17] Sinhala).

NOTES

* The present study continues a line of enquiry which I have been pursuing over the past four years. Earlier stages in it have been (or are about to be) published as Hook 1988 and 1989 (and Hook, In press). In the preparation of this paper I greatly benefitted from the generous help provided by Dr. Richard Saran in suggesting (and providing me with) samples of Marwari prose from the seventeenth through the nineteenth centuries, and in making available to me citations from his extensive glossaries of the works of Nainsi. An earlier version of this paper appears under the same title in a commemorative volume for Dr. Bholanath Tiwary, edited by R.N. Srivastava and published by Sahakar in Delhi.

1. The transcription system used for Marathi, Hindi-Urdu, Marwari, and other NIA languages is the one generally found in the Indo-Aryan linguistics literature with the following exceptions: Contrastive length in vowels is indicated by doubling the symbol (not by a macron or colon); nasality in vowels, by capitalization (not by a tilda or following capital N); retroflexion of apical stops and flaps, by upper case letters (not by sublinear dots); and palatal fricatives, by capitalization of the symbol for the corresponding alveolar fricatives. However, in transcribing titles of books in Hindi, Marathi, and Marwari I have used diacritics. Data from Russian, Pali, and Sanskrit are presented in the traditional transcription.

2. Abbreviations used in this paper include:

ACC	accusative case
CPM	conjunctive particle marker
CTF	counter-factual mood
DAT	dative case or postposition
EMP	emphatic particle
ERG	ergative case or postposition
FUT	future tense
GEN	genitive case or postposition
IMPER	imperative
IMP	imperfective
INF	infinitival form
NEG	negative particle
NF	non-finite form
OBL	oblique form or case
pl	plural number
PFV	perfective form
SBJNC	subjunctive
sg	singular number

3. Note that *both* the main and vector verb are in finite form. This may be a characteristic of incipient systems: cf. the system in Brahui, (Bray, Vol 1, para 351).

4. The slope is somewhat improved by including data from *bāgh-o-bahār* written by Mir Amman of Delhi and published at Fort William in 1802. In a sample of 1333 verb tokens in *bāgh-o-bahār* 7.7% were compound. I decided to ignore this datum for the following reasons. The percentage of CV's in Insha's *rānī ketkī ki kahānī*, published only sixteen years later (1818), is double that of *bāgh-o-bahār*'s. It does not seem likely that the frequency of compound verbs in the language that I am assuming texts to represent would double in such a short time and then not change much at all over the next 150 years. Furthermore, I feel that it is not possible that literary works would, as it were, ***over***report the frequency of the compound verb. If anything, it seems to me likely that texts probably ***under***report the frequency of the compound verb that existed in speech, (especially under the literary influence of the Sanskrit, Persian, Arabic, and English models of Amman's time, all of which completely lack the compound verb). I should note here that I was not sufficiently aware of this difficulty with *bāgh-o-bahār* in an earlier study (Hook 1989). Moreover, I had only carried out half as many counts at that time. As a result the rate of change in the Hindi compound verb system which I report in that article is much too high.

5. Some examples of this kind of variation in morphology:

(a) tab madanbaan ne vo sab baatE kholiyAA
then Madanban ERG those all things opened-fpl
'Then Madanban revealed all those things.' (*ketkī*, p. 131)
(Feminine plural noun forms extended to participles.)

(b) aur jo mAI kahUU ciTThii mE likh dii-jo
and what I say letter in write GIVE-FUT-IMPER
'and be sure to write what I say in the letter.'
(Future imperative in *-jo*. (*devarānī*, p. 13)

(c) tumhaarii maa tum ko bahut yaad kar-e hai
your mother you DAT much memory do-SBJNC is
'Your mother misses you very much.' (*devarānī*, p. 17)
(Use of ***laṭ*** instead of ***śatṛ*** to form present tense.)

6. I do not exclude the possibility of carrying out such a study on a text base of Hindi narrative verse. This would allow us to reach several centuries further into the past. However, it would require the texts from later periods also to be in verse, if a valid comparison is to be made.

7. It derives from Comrie (1976:16) and Timberlake (1985).

8. Pořizka (1967) and the Barannikovs (1956) inter alia.

9. Parallels exist in secondary aspectual functions, too:
In both Russian and Hindi-Urdu, non-perfective forms in the imperative are felt to be more polite than perfectives:

A. teacher: vojdite v klass — klass mE aa jaa-iye
enter-PFV in class — class in come GO-IMPER
'Come into the classroom!' (official tone)

B. host: vxodite — andar aa-iye
enter-IMPFV — inside come-IMPER
'(Please) come in!' (hospitable tone)

Russian data from Isačenko (1954) cited in Babby (1964:10).

10. The procedure used to obtain the data in 12h-13h was to ask several dozen English-knowing speakers of Hindi-Urdu to translate from English into their native tongue. In about 95% of their translations CV's appeared as indicated.

11. Of course, a CV in 12m-13m would not be ungrammatical. Rather, when asked to translate from English into Marathi, speakers of Marathi did not use CV's any more frequently in these environments than in other environments.

12. With the exception of Nainsi, all the counts were made from the beginning of each work. For Nainsi, I counted from 1.163.1 to 1.276.-1 and from 1.53.-10 to 1.65-1. In making these counts I regarded verbs extended with ***par@*** or ***ur@*** as the functional equivalents of compound verbs as defined in the first section of the paper. Evidence for this identification is presented in Hook and Chauhan (1988) and supports Kellogg's observations (1938:303). Against our identification one could claim that ***ur@*** and ***par@*** were used in Middle Marwari in their earlier etymological senses of 'here' and 'away' and had not (yet) reached the grammaticized state we report for them in Bhitrauti (a closely related language spoken in the vicinity of Mt. Abu). For example, in (a):

(a) punpaaL nUU pUUgal de nai uThii nUU paro meliyo
Punyapal DAT Pugal give CPM there to AWAY sent
'giving Punyapal (the jagir of) Pugal, sent him there.' (Nainsi 2.42.-1)

one could argue that Jaitsi (<Jayant Singh?), the agent of ***mel*** 'send', wanting to be rid of Punyapal, sent him **away** to Pugal. However, close examination of ***ur@*** and ***par@*** in other contexts show that very often they either occur redundantly with locative phrases or are used in contradiction with or orthogonally to their etymological meanings:

(b) tarai iNAA gaRh uubho-mel nai vikUUpur uraa aayaa
then they-OBL fort abandon CPM Vikumpur HERE came
'Then they left the fort and came to Vikumpur.'
(Nainsi 2.118.1; The narrator is not in Vikumpur.)

(c) hajrat hukam karo to mhe (pokaraN) uri lyAA
majesty order make then we Pokaran HERE take-SBJNC
'If your majesty should command let us capture Pokaran.'
(Nainsi 2.105.7; Pokaran is a town, immoveable.)

(d) raavjii hukam karai to laRaaii parii thaapAA (Nainsi 3.10.-5)
majesty order make then battle AWAY fix-SBJNC
'If your majesty commands it, let us arrange (the manner of conducting the battle.'

In view of examples like these I have treated all instances of verb plus ***par@*** or ***ur@*** as CV's. In any event, even if we do exclude all such extended verbs from the set of Marwari CV's, the direction or progression of change that I show in Table 2 is not materially affected:

	Title	Author	Date	CVs	total	%
A	dalpat vilās	unknown	@1600	12	1020	1.2
B	naiṇsi ri khyat	M. Nainsi	1670	28	1292	2.2
C	ajit vilās	unknown	@1730	29	1010	2.9
D	mānsingh ri khyat	unknown	@1870	93	1125	8.3
E	ūkalta antara	Moolchand	1973	156	1249	12.5

Table 2'. CV percentages in Marwari prose works since 1600 (excluding verbs extended with ***par@*** or ***ur@***).

13. Another function which the Marwari compound verb has in common with that of Hindi-Urdu is the power to express anteriority of one action to another. (In Hook (1974) I had identified anteriority or "relative tense" with perfective aspect. Later I realized the two categories are independent and, at times, in conflict. See discussion in Hook (1978)). When English-knowing speakers of Hindi or Urdu are asked to translate the gloss of (a) into their mother tongue, they invariably use the compound verb to express the earlier action and the simple verb to express the later one:

(a) tumhaare aane se pahle hii us ne mujhe ciT de dii thii
your coming from before EMP he ERG me note give GIVEN had
'By the time you came here he had given me the note.'

That this constraint is a property of the construction and is not some irrelevant property of the lexical items or of the actions they express can be demonstrated by switching the contents of the two clauses:

(b) tumhaare ciT dene se pahle hii vo yahAA aa gayaa thaa
your note giving from before EMP he here come GONE had
'By the time you gave me the note he'd already come here.'

Modern Marwari exhibits a similar distribution of compound and simple forms in constructions contrasting anterior with subsequent action:

(c) aap aThai aayaa uN su pahlaa ve manai kaagaj de diyo tho
you here came that from before he me-DAT letter give GIVEN had
'By the time you came here he had (already) given me the letter.'

(d) aap manai jab kaagaj diyo vo aThai aa gayo tho
you me-DAT when letter gave he here come WENT was
'When you gave me the letter he had (already) come here.

It is possible that the power to indicate anteriority is a precursor of the power to express perfectivity. It should be possible to confirm or disprove this hypothesis by examining the geographical distribution of the two functions.

14. It also seems not to have been regularly used to indicate anteriority. Compare (c) with (a) and (b) in fn 10:

(c) su the mo aav-tAA pehalii gAAv choR-ijyo (Nainsi 1.63.2)
so you me com-ing before town leave-FUT-IMPER
'. . . so you be sure to leave town before I get there!'

15. In making the counts for these lexical items I took ***padhaar, sidhaar***, and ***farmaav*** to be the respective [+honorific] suppletions of ***aav*** 'come', ***jaav*** 'go' and ***kah*** 'say'. I took ***caaliy@ jaav***, ***par@ jaav*** and ***buuh@ jaav*** as the compound counterparts of ***jaav***.

16. There are also instances of motion verbs used in the sense of 'die' that are not in compound form:

(a) itrai hemai ro hii hans uRiyo (Nainsi 2.297.12)
Then Hemo 's EMP swan flew
'At that point Hemo passed away.' (cf. example 23M)

(b) jiiv niisariyo huto paN saabato huto (Nainsi 3.112.6)
soul gone-out was but complete was
'(His) soul had left but (his body) was in one piece.' (cf. example 24M)

The contrast is between ***mar***, rarely compound, and metaphors for 'die', very often compound (other exx: Nainsi 3.92.-1 & *DV* 40.8). Because these metaphors are relatively uncommon, a meaningful quantitative measure cannot be given.

17. Figures are available from Zbavitel (1970) that show the increase over time in the frequency of the compound verb in Bangla. Since Zbavitel used texts in verse as well as prose and made his counts on a different basis (and had a somewhat different definition of "compound verb" in mind when he made them), his figures are not strictly comparable with those in Table 2. Nevertheless, they reveal a 1000% increase in compound verb frequency for Bangla over the past six centuries:

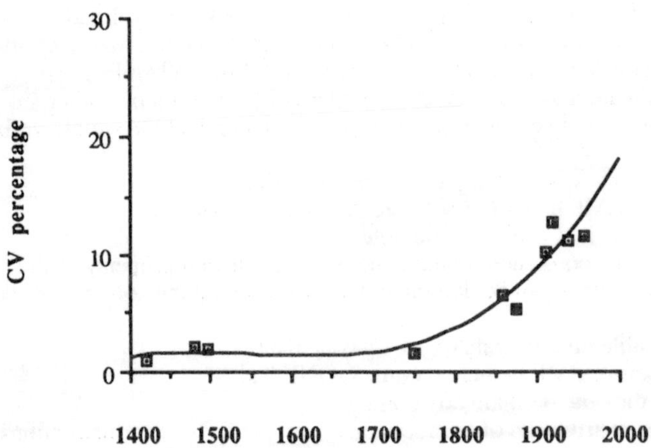

Figure 4. CV% in Bangla from the fifteenth through twentieth centuries.

	Title	Author	Date	CVs	total	%
a	rāmāyaṇ	Krittibas	@1420	51	4862	1.0
b	śrīkṛṣnakīrtan	Chandidas	@1480	99	4778	2.1
c	manasābijay	Bipradas	1495	95	5127	1.9
d	annadāmangal	Bharatchandra	@1750	77	4738	1.6
e	alaler gharer . . .	P.C. Mitra	1858	332	5113	6.5
f	biśabṛkṣa	Bankimchandra	1873	257	4927	5.2
g	gorā	R.N. Tagore	1910	523	5103	10.2
h	śrīkāntā	Sharatchandra	1917	707	5576	12.7
i	putulnācer . . .	Bandyopadhyay	1936	591	5313	11.1
j	ghanādar galpa	Premendra Mitra	1956	599	5155	11.6

Table 4. CV percentages in Bangla literary works since 1400 (based on counts in Zbavitel 1970 and dates in Zbavitel 1976)

BIBLIOGRAPHY

Primary sources:

Apabhramsha:

Svayambhu. 1958-71. *paumacariu*. H.C. Bhayani, Ed. Gloss in Hindi by D.K. Jain. Kashi: Bharatiya Jnanapitha.
Pushpadanta. 1972. *jasaharacariu*. P.L. Vaidya, Ed. Gloss in Hindi by Harilal Jain. New Delhi: Bharatiya Jnanapitha.

Hindi-Urdu:

Amman. See Mir Amman.
Das, L.S.N. 1974. *parīkṣā guru*. New Delhi: Rishabh Charan Jain evam Santati. (first published in 1884)
Gauridatta. 1966. *devarānī jeṭhānī kī kahānī*. Gopal Ray, Ed patna: Granth Niketan. (first printed in 1870)
Insha, I.Kh. 1974. *rānī ketkī kī kahānī*. A.S. Dalvi, Ed. Bombay: M. Gandhi Memorial Research Center.
Khattri, D.N. 1966. *narendra-mohinī*. Thirteenth edition. Varanasi: Lahari Book Depot. (first printed in 1910?)
Mir Amman of Delhi. 1861. *bāgh o bahār*, 6th edition. London Sampson Low, Marston & Co. (first printed in 1802)
Mohini, Manika. 1985. *ye kahāniyā̃*. Gorakhpur: Shaiwai Press.
Phullauri, S.R. 1973. *bhāgyavatī*. New Delhi: Sharda Prakashan. (first published in 1870)
Premchand. 1936. *godān*. Allahabad: Saraswati Press.
Rakesh, Mohan. 1967. *ādhere band kamre*. New Delhi: Rajkamal Prakashan.
Sharma, Nasira. 1987. *śalmalī*. Delhi: Saraswati Vihar.
Sobati, Krishna. 1968. *yārõ ke yār*. Delhi: Rajkamal.
Vaid, Krishna Baldev. 1970. *dūsre kināre se*. Delhi: Radhakrishna Prakashan.
__________. 1966. *merā duśman*. Delhi: Rajkamal.
Vatsyayan, S. 1958. *śekhar: ek jīvanī*. Varanasi: Saraswati Press. (first published in 1940)

Marathi:

Chirmule, S.V. 1967. *śrīśillak*. Bombay: Mauz Prakshan Grih.

Marwari:

ajit vilās (author unknown). Edited by N.S. Bhati. 1969. Published as vol. 27 of Parampara. Jodhpur: Rajasthani Shodh Sansthan. Describes events through v.s. 1766.
daḷpat vilās (author unknown). Edited by R. Saraswat. 1960. Bikaner: Sadul Rajasthani Research Inst. (v.s. 1657?)
mahārājā mānsingh rī khyāt (author unknown). Edited by N.S. Bhati. 1979. Jodhpur: Rajasthan Oriental Research Inst. Describes events through v.s. 1900.
Moolchand "Pranesh". 1973. *ūkaḷtā āntarā śiḷā sās*. Bikaner: Rajasthani Bhasa Prachar Prakashan.
Nainsi, M. 1960. *munhatā nainsī rī khyāt*. Edited by B.P. Sakaria. Jodhpur: Rajasthan Prachavidya Pratishthan.
Rathod, Manohar Singh. 1989. *khiṛakī*. Pilani: Ved Prakasan.

Secondary literature:

Babby, Leonard H. 1964. *Aspect Selection in the Negated Imperative Compared to the Affirmative in Modern Russian*. Unpublished MA thesis, Harvard University.

Bahl, K.C. 1972. *On the Present State of Modern Rajasthani Grammar*. Jodhpur: Rajasthani Shodh Sansthan.

Barannikov, A.P., and P.A. Barannikov. 1956. *Khindustani: Khindi i Urdu*. Moscow: Foreign Literature Publishing House.

Bray, Denys. 1977. *The Brahui Language*. In 2 vols. Quetta: Brahui Academy. Reprint of the 1907 edition.

Brinton, Laurel J. 1988. *The Development of English Aspectual Systems*. Cambridge University Press.

Brugman, Claudia, and G. Lakoff. 1988. "Cognitive Typology and Lexical Networks." In *Lexical Ambiguity Resolution*. G. Cottrell & S. Small, Eds. Palo Alto: Morgan Kaufman.

Chatterjee, Ranjit. 1988. *Aspect and Meaning in Slavic and Indic*. Amsterdam: John Benjamins.

Comrie, B. 1976. *Aspect*. Cambridge University Press.

Dowty, David. 1972.*Studies in the Logic of Verb Aspect and Time Reference in English*. Austin.

Flier, M.S. and R.D. Brecht, Eds. 1985. *Issues in Russian Morphosyntax*. Columbus, Ohio: Slavica.

Forsyth, J. 1970. *A Grammar of Aspect: Usage and Meaning in the Russian Verb*. Cambridge University Press.

Givon, T. 1975. "Serial Verbs and Syntactic Change: Niger-Congo." In C. Li, Ed., *Word Order and Word Order Change*. Austin: University of Texas Press.

Grierson, G.A. 1919. *Linguistic Survey of India*. Calcutta: Govt. of India. (1968 reprint by Motilal Banarsidass).

Hendriksen, Hans. 1944. *Syntax of the Infinite Verb Forms of Pali*. Copenhagen: Einar Munksgaard.

Hook, Peter E. To appear. "The Compound Verb in Gujarati and its Use in Connected Text". In a commemorative volume for Dr. U.P. Shah. Edited by R.T. Vyas and S.D. Sabnis. Baroda: Oriental Institute (M.S. University of Baroda).

__________ In press. "The Emergence of Perfective Aspect in Indo-Aryan." In E.C. Traugott and B. Heine, Eds., *Grammaticalization*. Amsterdam: John Benjamins. Pp. 59-89.

__________. 1989. "Determining Thresholds for the Emergence of Perfective Aspect in Indo-Aryan Languages." *Papers from the Twenty-fifth Regional Meeting*. Chicago: The Chicago Linguistics Society. 203-12.

__________. 1988. "Paradigmaticization: A Case Study from South Asia." In *Proceedings of the Fourteenth Annual Meeting of the Berkeley Linguistics Society*. 293-303.

__________1978. "The Hindi Compound Verb: What it is and What it does." In *Readings in Hindi-Urdu Linguistics*. K.S. Singh, Ed. Delhi: National Publishing House. 129-54.

__________. 1977. "The Distribution of the Compound Verb in the Languages of North India and the Question of its Origin." *International Journal of Dravidian Linguistics* 6:336-51.

__________. 1974. *The Compound Verb in Hindi*. Ann Arbor: Center for South and Southeast Asian Studies, University of Michigan.

Hook, P.E., and M.M. Chauhan. 1988. "Resultatives in Vedic and the Extended Adverb in Rajasthani." *Gaveshana* 26.

Hopper, Paul. In press. "Some Heuristic Principles of Grammaticalization." To appear in E.C. Traugott and B. Heine, Eds., *Grammaticalization*. Amsterdam: John Benjamins.

Isačenko, A.V. 1954. "O imperative v ruštine a slovenštine: využitie vidovych odtienkov v imperative." *sovetska jazykoveda* 4.

Kahr, J.C. 1976. "Drift versus Diachronic Universals." *Proceedings of the Second Annual Meeting of the Berkeley Linguistics Society*. H. Thompson et al., Eds. 220-6.

Kapp, Dieter B. 1972. *Das Verbum paraba in seiner Funktion als Simplex und Explikativum in Jayasis Padumavati*. Wiesbaden: Verlag Otto Harrassowitz.
Kaul, Vijay K. 1985. *The Compound Verb in Kashmiri*. Unpublished PhD dissertation, Kurukshetra University.
Kellogg, S.H. 1938. *Grammar of the Hindi Language*, 2nd ed. London: Routledge and Kegan Paul.
Lehmann, C. 1985. "Grammaticalization: Synchronic Variation and Diachronic Change." *Lingua e Stile* 20:303:318.
Lord, C. 1973. "Serial Verbs in Transition." In *Studies in African Linguistics* 4.3.
Magier, David. 1982. "Marwari Honorifics." In *South Asian Review* 6:160-173.
Masica, Colin P. 1976. *Defining a Linguistic Area: South Asia*. Chicago: University of Chicago Press.
Nespital, Helmut. 1981. *Das Futursystem im Hindi und Urdu*. Wiesbaden: Franz Steiner Verlag.
Pořízka, Vinčenc. 1967-69. "On the Perfective Verbal Aspect in Hindi (Some features of parallelism between New Indo Aryan and Slavonic languages)." *Archív Orientalni* 35:64-88, 208-231; 36:233-251; 37:19-47, 345-364.
Regnell, C.G. 1944. *Uber den Ursprung des slavischen Verbalaspektes*. Lund.
Seiler, Hansjakob. 1952. *L'Aspect et le Temps dans le Verbe Neo-Grec*. Paris: Les Belles Lettres.
Singh, R.A. 1980. *Syntax of Apabhramsha*. Calcutta: Simant.
Smith, J.D. 1975. "An Introduction to the Language of the Historical Documents from Rajasthan." *Modern Asian Studies* 9:433-64.
Talmy, Leonard. 1988. "Force Dynamics in Language and Cognition." *Cognitive Science* 12:1.
Tikkanen, Bertil. 1987. "The Sanskrit Gerund: a Synchronic, Diachronic and Typological Analysis". *Studia Orientalia*, Vol. 62. Helsinki: Finnish Oriental Society.
Timberlake, Alan. 1985. "The Temporal Schemata of Russian Predicates." In Flier and Brecht, Eds. Pp. 35-57.
Traugott, E.C. 1988. "Pragmatic Strengthening and Grammaticalization." *Berkeley Linguistic Society 14*. Pp. 406-416.
Trencker, V. 1879. *Pali Miscellany*. London: Williams & Norgate.
Vendler, Zeno. 1967. "Verbs and Times." In *Linguistics and Philosophy*. Ithaca. Pp. 97-121.
Zbavitel, Dušan. 1976. *Bengali Literature*. Wiesbaden: Otto Harrassowitz.
Zbavitel, Dušan. 1970. *Non-finite Verbal Forms in Bengali*. Prague: Czechoslovak Academy of Sciences.

Version of 24 April 1991.

Address all correspondence to:

Peter Edwin Hook
Program in Linguistics
1076 Frieze Building
University of Michigan
Ann Arbor, MI 48109-1285
U.S.A.

VERB SERIALIZATION IN SYNTAX, TYPOLOGY AND HISTORICAL CHANGE

Yamuna Kachru
University of Illinois at Urbana-Champaign

1.0 The serial, or compound verbal constructions in South Asian, West African, and other groups of languages have attracted the attention of linguists of several persuasions, although most attempts at describing the phenomenon still remind one of the story of several blind men groping to comprehend the form of an elephant (see, for example, the studies listed in Kachru 1978, Li and Thompson 1973, Foley and Olson 1985, among others).[1] This paper is not an exhaustive study of verb serialization in the languages of the world. I am basically concerned here with those aspects of the serial verbal constructions which are of interest to linguists both from the point of view of synchronic descriptions and that of historical syntax of the South Asian languages. For ease of discussion, I will use the terms serial verbs and verb serialization for the phenomenon regardless of the morphological shape of the first or main verb in the sequence and other such details.[2]

1.1. The present study is organized as follows. Section 2.0 discusses the existing studies of the phenomenon and reviews the findings briefly. Section 3.0 draws some conclusions from the wide range of data discussed in existing descriptions and provides more data from South Asian languages, especially Hindi-Urdu. This section also includes a brief discussion of the similarities and differences between the various groups of languages. Section 4.0 evaluates the historical syntactic claims based upon verb serialization. Section 5.0 discusses the syntax of the serial verbs. In the final Section, certain questions are raised which have serious implications for both synchronic and diachronic syntax and the lexicon of these languages.

2.0. I shall discuss first the synchronic description and subsequently, the historical account of verb serialization, mainly in South Asian and West African languages. References to other groups of languages will be made where relevant.

2.1. In the case of West African languages, generally three types of studies have discussed verb serialization in detail: one, descriptions of individual languages or groups of languages (e.g. Bamgboṣe 1966, Boadi 1968, Callow 1966, Pike 1966, Stewart 1963, Ward 1936, Williamson 1965, among others); two, limited typological studies of African language structures (e.g. Welmers 1973); and three, works that attempt to determine either a coordinate or a subordinate source for serial verbs (e.g. Hyman 1971, Stahlke 1970 and 1974, among others), or those that present a monoclausal source for the serial verbs (e.g. Lord 1975 and Schachter 1974a).[3]

In the case of the South Asian languages, the phenomenon usually forms an integral part of the traditional grammars and contemporary descriptions of individual languages (e.g. for Hindi, Guru 1922, Kellogg 1875, Bahl 1967, Kachru 1965, 1966, 1979, 1980, McGregor 1972, Shapiro 1974; for Bengali, Anderson 1920; for Gujarati, Cardona 1965; for Kannada, Spencer 1914; for Tamil, Bright and Lindenfeld 1968, Fedson 1981, Schiffman 1969, Steever 1988, among others). In the case of Hindi-Urdu, at least one detailed study attempts to determine the syntactic and semantic properties of the serial verb (Shapiro 1974) and one attempts, additionally, to isolate the syntactic environment in which the construction may or may not occur (Hook 1974). A few studies discuss the semantic and pragmatic aspects of serial verbs (e.g. Sinha 1972, Kachru 1979, for Hindi). Very little typological work involving Indian languages has been attempted so far (see, however, Kachru and Pandharipande 1980, Masica 1976 for an initial attempt).

2.2. The historical syntactic descriptions of verb serialization are of the following nature. In the case of the West African languages, a few interesting studies have discussed the relationship between serial verbal constructions and word order change via the development of prepositions from serial verbs (e.g. Lord 1973, 1977, Givón 1975, Hyman 1975, among others; see also Li and Thompson 1973 for Mandarin Chinese).

In the case of the South Asian languages, most historical studies of Indo-Aryan and Dravidian languages mention the phenomenon (e.g. Bloch 1954, Chatterji 1926, Caldwell 1913, Tiwari 1960, among others). Bloch 1954, and to a lesser extent, Subrahmanyam 1971 discuss the serial verb in Dravidian languages. Recently, a specific type of serial verbs has been discussed in some detail in Steever 1988 and Hock 1988. Both Chatterji 1926 and Tiwari 1960 mention that in the course of historical development, as a result of phonological and other changes, Old Indo-Aryan root-modifying prefixes were lost. In addition, certain verbal declensions were lost. The serial verbal constructions were developed in NIA to compensate for these losses.[4] Similar observations have been made with regard to the development of the phrasal verb in English. No detailed studies of syntactic change in either Dravidian or Indo-Aryan, however, are available.

3.0. The African and South Asian language data are available in several studies (e.g. the studies mentioned above and the additional studies listed in Kachru 1978). As such, I shall provide more data from South Asian languages only when it becomes crucial for the discussion.

3.1. The data, no doubt, show individual differences among languages. Nevertheless, there is remarkable similarity between both genetically related and unrelated groups of languages. An example of a former type of similarity is the use of the verb 'fall' for passivization, or 'obtain, require' to denote a reflexive meaning in Dravidian languages (e.g. see Pillai 1964 for Tamil and Spencer 1914 for Kannada).[5] Within the NIA, the use of 'come' and 'go' in the deictic sense, 'go' in the completive sense (with certain classes of verbs), 'take' versus 'give' in the reflexive versus benefactive sense, and 'give' in the permissive sense are widely shared. The use of serial verbs to express certain aspectual meanings (such as durative, completive, etc.), and the use of 'give' in a benefactive sense, are examples of features shared by both Dravidian and NIA languages (see, Bloch 1954, Schiffman 1969, Rajpurohit 1973, among others, for Dravidian, and Guru 1922, Kellogg 1875, Bahl 1964, Kachru 1965, 1966, 1979, 1980, Shapiro 1974, Anderson 1920, Cardona 1965, among others, for NIA).[6]

Givón 1975 presents the following table, summarizing the similarity of diachronic development of prepositions denoting specific case meanings from serial verbs for the Niger-Congo languages (Givón 1975:93):[7]

[1] CASE	VERB(S)	PREPOSITION SENSE
accusative	'take', 'get', 'do'	Acc.
locative	'go', 'come'	'to'
	'exit', 'leave'	'out', 'from'
	'enter'	'into', 'in'
	'be at', 'live', 'sit'	'in/at/on'
	'rise', 'climb'	'up'
	'fall', 'descend'	'down'
dative/benefactive	'give', 'present', 'send'	'to/for'
benefactive	'benefit', 'help'	'for'
instrumental	'take', 'hold', 'use', 'be with'	'with'
associative	'be at', 'be with', join', 'meet'	'with'
conjunction	'be at', 'be with', 'join', meet'	'with', 'and'
	'add', 'repeat'	'and'

It is clear that some similarity is observable between South Asian and West African languages in the use of explicator verbs to express certain meanings (e.g. deictic and benefactive). There is also similarity in the use of specific verbs for denoting such meanings, e.g. COME and GO for deictic and GIVE for benefactive.[8]

Compare the above with the following regularities observed in the South Asian language data:[9]

[2] EXPLICATOR VERBS	MEANING
COME vs. GO	deictic meaning (Bengali, Hindi-Urdu, Marathi); Continuation vs. completion (Bengali, Gujarati, Hindi-Urdu, Kannada, Tamil, Telugu)
GO	Passive in Indo-Aryan languages
TAKE vs. GIVE	Benefactive (Bengali, Gujarati, Hindi-Urdu, Kannada, Kui, Marathi, Punjabi)
FALL	passive in Dravidian; suddenness in Indo-Aryan
POUR, PUT, THROW PUSH	violence, 'to get it over with' (Bengali, Gujarati, Hindi-Urdu, Kannada)
KEEP, PUT, PLACE	completion, action accomplished for future use (Bengali, Hindi-Urdu, Kannada, Marathi, Tamil)

It is obvious that South Asian languages share many more meanings and explicator verbs that express them.

3.2 There are certain formal similarities, too. In works such as Lord 1973, it has been shown that not all serial verbs in West African languages are at the same stage of grammaticization. Some retain their verbal characteristics to a great extent whereas others have become more like prepositions (see also Li and Thompson 1973 for Mandarin Chinese). The same is true of South Asian languages, more so of the Dravidian group (e.g., Rajpurohit 1973, Schiffman 1969, among others, discuss the loss of independent verbal status of certain verbs in serial constructions). The defining characteristics of serial verbs are very similar in several groups of languages. These are obvious from the discussion on the syntax of serial verbs in section 5.0 of this study.

3.3. The similarities notwithstanding, there are important differences, too. The differences are observable on the semantic as well as formal level. In most South Asian languages, certain serial verbs express speaker attitudes, intentions, judgements, beliefs, etc. Consider the following examples:

[3] ***... vah aavaaz de kar ro uThii aur merii god mẽ gir aaii.***
(JK 1968:77)[10]
she noise give CP cry rose and my lap in fall came
She began crying loudly and fell into my lap.

The context is that of a father narrating the event of a sorrowing daughter falling into his lap, crying. Notice that ***gir aanaa*** is an unusual, a novel, combination. The author coins the new combination since the usual serial verb, ***gir paRnaa*** 'fall drop' meaning 'to fall down' would not convey the sympathetic attitude of the father.

[4] ***maanya mitra bole, 'anaasakti!' aur muskaraa aaye.***
(JK 1968:116)
distinguished friend said 'detachment' and smile came
My distinguished friend said 'detachment!' and smiled.

Again, given the context of the troubled character attempting to smile, the usual serial verbs ***muskaraa paRnaa*** 'smile drop' or ***muskaraa denaa*** 'smile give' would not have captured the sympathetic attitude of the narrator; these would simply suggest a ready smile.

[5] ***mãĩ ne jitne bhii phal laa rakhe the, kambaxt bandar sab khaa gaye.***
I ag. whatever fruit bring kept had darned monkeys all eat went
The darned monkeys ate up all the fruit I had brought.

[6] ***ram kuch aisii baatẽ kah gayaa jo use kahnii nahĩĩ caahiye thĩĩ.***
Ram some such things say went which he to say not ought was
Ram blurted out some things that he should not have.

Note the attitude expressed by the explicator verb *jaanaa* 'go' in contrast with the attitude expressed by the explicator *aanaa* 'come' as illustrated above. Obviously the speaker thinks of the events of the consumption of fruit in **[5]** and the revelation of certain matters in **[6]** as undesirable.

Consider the use of explicator *lenaa* in the folowing example:

[7] ***DeviD thoRii-bahut hindii bol letaa hai.***
David less more Hindi speak takes
David manages to speak a little Hindi.

The sentence in **[7]** makes it clear that the speaker thinks David manages to speak the language with some competence. Note that a first person subject with a main verb denoting a skill with the explicator *lenaa* 'take' would suggest modesty rather than a relative lack of control of the skill (see Kachru 1979 for a detailed discussion of this phenomenon).

Another such explicator verb is *dhamaknaa* as in the following example:

[8] ***subah subah amit aa dhamkaa, mãĩ ne tab tak caay bhii nahĩĩ pii thii.***
morning Amit come thumped I ag. then till tea even not drink had
Amit turned up so early in the morning, I hadn't even had tea as yet.

The explicator *dhamaknaa* 'thump' is restricted and denotes an unexpected, and generally unwelcome, occurrence.

This kind of use is not restricted to Indo-Aryan, as is clear from the following Tamil example:

[9] ***ate uTi tolecci caapiTT-iTTu poongaL-en.***
Why (don't you) pour it (out), eat it up, and get going, for the love-of-mike?
(Schiffman 1969:52-3)

According to Schiffman, the explicator verb *tole* 'to lose, get lost' is 'extremely expressive and often has more to do with the feelings and opinions the speaker has about the personality and status of his interlocutor.' In the sentence in **[8]**, *tole* is said to indicate the speaker's disgust or impatience with the addressee.[11]

In the West African language data, it is difficult to discern such meanings. More importantly, from the studies on West African languages, it appears that use of the serial verbal construction to denote certain meanings is virtually obligatory. In other words, serial verbs are grammaticized to a great extent. In case of the South Asian languages, this is rarely the case, even when the serial verbal construction involves an aspectual meaning. Compare the following from Hindi-Urdu:

[10] *baccõ ne khaanaa khaayaa*
children ag. meal ate
The children ate their meal.

[11] *baccõ ne khaanaa khaa liyaa*
children ag. meal eat took
The children ate (their) meal, i.e., The action was self-directed and completed.

[12] *bacce khaanaa khaa cuke*
children meal eat completed
The children ate (their) meal, i.e., They completed the act.

All three roughly mean the same thing, i.e., the children have eaten, they are no longer hungry, they do not have to be fed any more. It depends on the speaker intentions as to which one is used on any given occasion.[12] The same is true of the following set from Bengali:

[13] *aami kaaj-Taa kare niye-chi*
I work class. do CP taken have
I have done the work.

[14] *aami kaaj-Taa kare rekhe-chi*
I work class. do CP put have
I have done the work (it is already finished).

[15] *aami kaaj-Taa kare-phele-chi*
I work class. do abs. thrown have
I have done the work (once for all).

Also, unlike in West African languages, the serial verbs have not developed into prepositions (or postpositions) in South Asian languages. This is discussed more fully in the next section.

4.0. Givón 1975 proposes four hypotheses regarding the paths a mature SOV language may take in shifting to an SVO syntax. These are as follows:

[16] "(i) A 'mature' SOV language may first shift to SVO ... and then develop verb serialization as a means of marking case functions of nominals (most Benue-Kwa, Moree).

(ii) A 'mature' SOV language may first shift to SVO and then develop prepositions via the genitival noun-compound pattern in a N-Poss syntax (Fula, P-Bantu).

(iii) A 'mature' SOV language may re-develop a new generation of noun-derived postpositions via the genitival pattern and this will considerably retard the move toward SVO or even completely arrest it (Mande, Wara).

(iv) A 'mature' SOV language may develop serialization directly, without changing to SVO (Ijo)."

Most Niger-Congo languages considered in Givón 1975 seem to conform to pattern (i) - (iii).[13] There is only one language, Ijo, that takes path (iv).[14] According to Givón 1975, for a language to be both SOV and verb serializing is rather exceptional, as such a development leads to perceptual complexity. Note, however, that what is exceptional in Niger-Congo is normal in South Asian languages. All Dravidian and South Asian languages are both SOV and verb serializing. Also, unlike in Niger-Congo and Mandarin Chinese, there does not seem to be any move in South Asian languages toward reinterpreting serial verbs as preposition (or postpositions).[15]

In case of most South Asian languages, the predominant meaning of the serial verb has been claimed to be either aspectual (Hook 1974, Pal 1972, Schiffman 1969, etc.) or definitive (Guru 1922), or adverbial (temporal, directional, or manner; see Kachru 1977, 1979, 1980 and Shapiro 1974 for a discussion of these meanings in Hindi-Urdu). According to Hyman 1975, the types of information presented in adverbials, relative clauses, prepositional phrases, etc. are likely to be forgotten by a speaker in verb-final utterances and later tacked on as after-thought. This conflict between syntax and pragmatics gives rise to SVO features in SOV languages, and in fact, there are languages such as Kpelle (Welmers 1964) which have benefactive, dative, locative, instrumental, etc. after the verb. Afterthought, thus, is an important factor in change of word-order in West African language. Although there are some SVO features in NIA languages, there is no discernible move yet toward a change in word order as in West African languages or Mandarin Chinese. Language contact (with Dravidian) may have played a role in verb serialization in NIA languages, as may have the loss of OIA root-modifying prefixes (Chatterji 1926). More research on historical syntax of both Dravidian and IA is needed before any historical explanation of the phenomenon of serialization in South Asian languages can be proposed.

5.0. As regards the synchronic syntactic description of serial verbs, there are considerable differences of opinion between linguists working with West African languages. The basic agreement seems to be in the following areas. Most verbs in a serial verbal construction retain their transitivity characteristics and tense-aspect and agreement markings. All the verbs in a series, however, agree in respect of tense-aspect (Stahlke 1970).[16] A few verbs in serial construction have lost their verbal features and have become fully grammaticized (Lord 1973). Not all verb sequences are serial verbs, some verbal sequences arise from the deletion of linking particles such as *and*. Serial verbs are distinct from sequences of verbs in that in a serial verbal construction, the meaning conveyed is not the sum of the parts conveyed by each verb in the series (Awobuluyi 1967 and 1973, Bamgbose 1973 a and b among others).

5.1. As far as a grammatical account of the phenomenon is concerned, there are several opinions. For example, Awobuluyi 1967 and 1973 discuss serial verbs in terms of 'splitting' versus 'causative' verb construction. Bamgbose 1972, 1973a and 1973b classify serial verbs into 'linking' versus 'modifying' types. A majority of linguists have suggested both coordinate and subordinate sources of derivation for serial verbal construction, although the details have been under dispute (Awobuluyi 1973, Stahlke 1974, among other). Schachter 1974a and Lord 1975 argue against biclausal derivation of serial verbs and instead, propose a monoclausal derivation to account for the phenomenon. Stahlke 1974 gives several syntactic arguments against deriving serial verbs from concatenated verb phrases in the base, as suggested in Schachter 1974a. More recently, Foley and Olson 1985 has proposed a monoclausal structure for verb serialization of a slightly different sort. In order to account for the internal differences between different types of serial verbs, the researchers propose a layered structure according to which some serial verbs are combined at the nuclear layer, others at the core layer and still others at the peripheral layer. This accounts for the semantics of the serial verbs rather neatly in that the aspectual serial verbs are nuclear, and the adverbial ones are either core or peripheral depending upon several other considerations. A detailed description of language specific facts, of course, would have to be worked out to see how adequate this account is for a particular language.

In the case of the South Asian languages, there are very few studies that deal with the syntax of the serial verbs. Most accounts of serial verbs are contained in traditional grammars. More recent attempts at describing the verbal syntax of the NIA languages either propose concatenatation of verbs in the base (Kachru 1965) or do not explicitly discuss the biclausal derivation in detail (Bahl 1964, Hook 1974, among others). In case of the Dravidian languages, Bright and Lindenfeld 1968 as well as Rajpurohit 1973 propose concatenated verbs in the base, Murti 1973 discusses only causatives in Telegu, and Schiffman 1969 does not formulate explicit rules for the derivation of the aspectual markers in Tamil.[17]

5.2. No matter whether one prefers a monoclausal source, as suggested in Kachru 1965, Schachter 1974a, Lord 1975, and Foley and Olson 1985 or a biclausal approach, as suggested in Stahlke 1974, there are certain regularities in the South Asian data that have to be taken into account in any grammatical description of the serial verbs in these languages. The regularities I am referring to are observed in cases of the serial verbal constructions such as the following: the use of 'come' and 'go' with verbs of motion to indicate deictic meaning; the use of 'take' and 'give' with transitive verbs to indicate 'self directed' versus 'other directed' action in NIA and some Dravidian languages; the use of 'sit' to indicate 'unexpectedness, impudence'; the use of certain verbs to indicate aspectual meaning; etc. Most of these have been exemplified in works referred to above (see also the table in **[2]**). Notice, however, that deriving all serial verbs from the same source may not be justifiable in South Asian languages either. Historically speaking, it is probably accurate to say that the serial verbs developed from the conjunctive participial construction as exemplified in **[16]** - **[21]** below; synchronically, however, the sentence pairs **[16]** - **[17]**, **[18]** - **[19]**, and **[20]** - **[21]** (Hindi-Urdu) are not identical, they express distinct meanings:

17. ***vah kitaab le kar gayaa***
he book take abs. went
He took the book and left.

18. ***vah kitaab le gayaa***
he book take went
He took away the book.

19. ***vah kitaab le kar aayaa***
he book take abs. came
He took the book and came.

20. ***vah kitaab le aayaa***
he book take came
He brought the book.

21. ***vah miThaaii khaa kar gayaa***
he sweets eat abs. went
He ate the sweets and left.

22. ***vah miThaaii khaa gayaa***
he sweets eat went
He ate up the sweets.

It is conceivable that some of the serial verbs have a regular monoclausal or biclausal derivation and the specific meanings such as disgust, disapproval, etc. are to be accounted for in terms of Gricean Conversational Principles. This alternative, however, has to be explored further in detail to tease out the semantic from the pragmatic facts.

6.0. To sum up and conclude this discussion, then, the following points are obvious. In all the languages mentioned in this study, there is a need to distinguish serial verbs from other V+V sequences. The serial verbs, however, are not a closed system. Kachru 1979 cites examples from literary works in Hindi to show how verb serialization is exploited as a stylistic device in Hindi.[18] Neither in West African, nor in South Asian languages have the serial verbs become fully grammaticized. That is, the second and subsequent members of the series retain their verbal characteristics to a greater or lesser extent. In view of these facts, the controversy regarding the number of explicator verbs is rather futile.[19] Also, since in a majority of cases, the use of the serial verb as opposed to the simple verb, depends upon speaker attitudes and intentions (Kachru 1977, 1979, 1980, Kachru and Pandharipande 1980, Schiffman 1969, and others), any attempt to isolate the syntactic environments in which a serial verb may or may not occur can only be partially successful, if that.[20] The syntactic constraints on serial verbs are to be explained in terms of their semantic characterization. For instance, in South Asian as well as West African languages, it has been observed that certain serial verbs do not occur in negative sentences (Burton-Page 1957, Kachru 1965, Bendor-Samuel 1968, etc.). Negation in these works has been used as one of the criteria that separate serial verbs from other sequence involving two or more verbs. The non-occurrence of certain serial verbs in negative sentences is not surprising. It is a well-known fact that certain sentences containing affective elements either have no negative counterparts, or if they have a parallel negative, the affective elements attract negation, i.e., they invariably come under the scope of negation (see Quirk et al. 1972 for English). Since serial verbs primarily denote aspectual or adverbial meanings or indicate speaker attitude and beliefs, they are not felt to be appropriate in negative sentences. More detailed work on the semantics of the serial verbs may throw some light on their syntactic behavior.

6.1. Some relevant questions that arise out of this study are as follows. The NIA languages such as Hindi-Urdu, Gujarati, Bengali, Nepali, etc. may have developed serial verbal construction under the influence of Dravidian languages.[21] The question that now arises is how and why the Dravidian languages, which are SOV, developed the serial verbal constructions, if the combination of these two characteristics leads to 'perceptual complexity', as claimed in Givón 1975. All cases -- and prepositions parallel to them -- are probably verbal in historical origin. It is interesting to enquire how and why English developed phrasal verbs parallel to serial verbal constructions in South Asian and West African languages. Notice that the prepositions or particles in English follow the main verb, just as the vector verbs do in South Asian languages. Moreover, the phrasal verbs share a number of important semantic and syntactic properties with the serial verbs. The answer to these questions may contribute significantly to our understanding of languages universals.

It has been noted in several studies (Awobuluyi 1967, Bamgboṣe 1973a, Hook 1974, Kachru 1965 and 1977, 1979, 1980 etc.) that serial verbs range over a continuum at one end of which the two (or more) verbs have almost independent verbal status whereas at the other end, the construction is more like a frozen idiom.[22] The latter cases almost demand characterization as lexically complex items, to be listed as such in the lexicon. This raises interesting questions with regard to the nature of lexical entries, and the need for principled criteria to distinguish between syntactic constructions and lexical items.

NOTES

1. Although the term 'compound verb' has been most widely used in the context of South Asian languages and 'serial verbs' in the context of West African languages, the use of 'compound verb' to refer to sequences of verbs in West African languages is not totally unknown. Ogumbowale 1970 and Ward 1952, for instance, refer to 'compound verbs' in Yoruba.

2. This is different from how the terms are used in Steever 1988 and its review in Hock 1988.

3. This is not to imply that all the studies grouped here under one category or the other agree in all the details of the processes they discuss. For instance, the proposals in Lord 1975 and Schachter 1974a are quite distinct: the former suggests a lexicalist approach whereas the latter proposes concatenation of VPs to account for verb serialization.

4. Chatterji 1926 contains the following remarks:

> "The use of . . . 'compound verb' or 'group verb' construction amply compensates for the loss of the root-modifying prefixes which form such a characteristic feature of Sanskrit and of the Indo-European speeches outside India." (p. 1049)

5. Note, however, that according to Bh. Krishnamurti, 'fall' for pasivization is a very recent development in Dravidian under the influence of English. (personal communication)

6. See Bloch 1954, Hook 1974, Kachru 1977, 1979, 1980, Kachru and Pandharipande 1980, Kellogg 1875, Pal 1972, Rajpurohit 1973, Schiffman 1969 and others in Kachru 1978. In fact, in some of these works, the primary meaning of the serial verbal construction is claimed to be aspectual.

7. According to Givón 1975, Mandarin Chinese data show an "amazing consistency as to what verbs may give rise to what prepositions."

8. Foley and Olson 1985 mentions intransitive verbs of motion, location, and posture as being the frequent 'explicator' verbs. These classes of verbs are widely attested in South Asian as well as West African languages.

9. This is a slightly expanded version of the table that appears in Kachru and Pandharipande 1981.

10. JK refers to the novel <u>Anantar</u> by Jainendra Kumar (Purvoday Prakashan, Delhi, 1968).

11. See Fedson (in this volume) for further examples of "manner of action" complex verbs.

12. According to Hook 1974, serial verbs are more completive than simple verbs in the perfective. He gives the following examples in support of his argument (the numbering and the English translations are from Hook 1974, the English glosses are mine):

C1 ***raajaa ne tasviir banaaii magar ban nahĩĩ paaii***
king ag. picture made but make (intr.) not managed
The king tried to make a picture but couldn't.

C3 ****raajaa ne tasviir banaa lii magar ban nahĩĩ paaii***
king ag. picture make took but make (intr.) not managed.
*The king made a picture but couldn't.

The difficulty with any such proposal is that it would claim that the meaning of the perfective in Hindi is something like "TRY TO V", which is clearly false. Notice that C1 becomes contradictory if the serial verb in the second conjunct is replaced by a simple verb:

C1a. ****raajaa ne tasviir banaaii magar nahĩĩ banii***
king ag. picture made but not made (intr.)
*The king made a picture but it didn't get made.

Notice that C1 involves a non-causative verb ***ban*** in the second conjunct and its causative (transitive) counterpart in the first conjunct. In case the verbs involved are such that the transitive verb has no intransitive counterpart, such sentences are ungrammatical:

a. ****baccõ ne khaanaa khaayaa magar nahĩĩ khaa paaye***
children ag. meal ate but not eat managed
*The children ate but didn't manage to eat.

As pointed out in Kachru 1976, the causative verb in Hindi is factive. The meaning of C1 is actually as in b:

b. The king made the picture but it didn't turn out well.

Such meanings are derivable from principles other than those involved in straightforward semantic interpretation of syntactic structures. A detailed discussion of such principles (e.g. conversational implicature, etc.) is, however, beyond the scope of this paper. The serial verbs as a class denote a meaning of accomplishment of the action/process denoted by the main verb. This is what has been termed the 'perfective' meaning in several studies. For a discussion of the perfective aspectual meaning in Hindi-Urdu (i.e. the meaning of the verbal affix ***-aa*** as in ***dekh-aa*** 'saw'), see Kachru 1966, 1979, 1980, Kachru and Pandharipande 1980, Hackman 1976, and Pandharipande and Kachru 1977.

13. See, however, Hyman 1975 for a dissenting view about the relationship between verb serialization and word order change.

14. See Williamson 1965 for a description of Kolokuma, a dialect of Ijo.

15. The few verbs that in their absolutive forms come close to a prepositional sense are TAKE in Bengali, Hindi-Urdu; LEAVE (i.e. ***choR***) and INCREASE (i.e. ***baRh***) in Hindi-Urdu. Consider the following from Hindi-Urdu:

a. ***vah haath mẽ kitaab le kar khaRaa thaa.***
he hand in book take abs. standing was
He was standing with the book in his hand.

b. ***siimaa bacee ko god mẽ liye calii aaii.***
Sima child obj. lap in take abs. moved came
Sima arrived with the child in her arms.

c. ***raam ko choR kar aur sab aaye.***
Ram DO leave CP other all came
Everyone except Ram came.

d. ***paRhne mẽ raam shyaam se baRh kar hai.***
studies in Ram Shyam than increase CP is
Ram is cleverer than Shyam in studies.

Also, see Chatterji 1926:767-77 for a discussion of postpositional use of some verbal forms in IA.

16. Boadi 1968 characterizes the serial verbal constructions as follows:

"... string of two or more verb phrases which form a single internally coherent structure. The constituent verb phrases are governed by one noun phrase subject and are separated neither by pause nor coordinators. What joins them together is agreement in mood and between certain preverbal affixes (referred to as PREV's) across the sentence. Thus, all conjoined and certain types of embedded verb phrases are either affirmative or negative, interrogative or declarative. Besides, the tenses which occur in these verb phrases are identical." (p. 84)

It is difficult to characterize serial verbs in South Asian languages in such general terms. In a V+V sequence, the first V may occur in a variety of forms, although, in most languages, it is in absolutive participial form. In Hindi, it may occur in six different forms (Kellogg 1875, Kachru 1965). One of the earliest works discussing the criteria for defining serial verbal constructions in Hindi is Burton-Page 1957. There is a summary and an extended discussion of the criteria proposed so far in Hook 1974.

17. Schiffman 1969 is in the framework of generative semantics. There are detailed discussions of derivations and several diagrams illustrating the proposed derivations. It would

be interesting to see if explicit rules could be formulated on the basis of the discussion and, if so formulated, what kinds of claims would be entailed by these rules.

18. The following, too, is from JK 1968:

jaisaa	*soctaa*	*hũũ*	*vaisaa*	*mãĩ*	*likh*	*chuuTtaa*	*hũũ*
as	think impf.	am	such	I	write	go free impf.	am

I write as I please.

Notice that ***chuuTnaa*** 'go free, leave', has not been included in any list of the explicator verbs proposed so far, yet ***likh chuuTnaa*** 'write leave' here is very effective in bringing out the totally unrestrained nature of the action.

19. Hook 1974 devotes an entire chapter (section 3, 17-143) to determining a list of the explicator verbs, referred to as the 'vector verbs' in the study, in Hindi.

20. Hook 1974 attempts to define likely environments for simple versus serial verbs in Hindi.

21. Just as in Dravidian, in NIA languages also, the periphrastic passive is formally similar to the serial verbal construction. In most languages, in the passive construction, the main verb is in the past participle form, and the passive marker is the verb 'go' ('come' in Kashmiri). Chatterji (1926:923) supports the suggestion in Beams 1879 that the old ***-ijja-*** passive of Apabhramsha was reanalyzed as a serial verbal construction under the analogy of other verbs involving ***jaa*** 'go' as the vector verb. About the serial verbal constructions itself, Chatterji (1926:1050) has the following to say:

> "In this point there is a remarkable agreement with Dravidian ... In the Dravidian languages, compound verbs of exactly similar formation and functions occur ... It is very likely that here we have another contribution of Dravidian in the formation of Modern Indo-Aryan speeches."

22. I am referring to serial verbs such as ***cal basnaa*** 'move settle', meaning 'to die', in Hindi-Urdu.

REFERENCES

Anderson, J. D. 1920. A manual of the Bengali language. [Republished by arrangement with the Cambridge University Press, New York: Frederick Ungar Publishing Company, 1962.]

Awobuluyi, A. Oladele. 1967. Studies in the syntax of the standard Yoruba verb. Columbia University dissertation. [University Microfilms.]

Awobuluyi, A. Oladele. 1973. The modifying serial construciton: a critique. Studies in African Linguistics 4.87-11.

Bahl, K. C. 1964. A Study in the transformational analysis of Hindi verb. Chicago: University of Chicago, South Asia Language and Area Center.

Bahl, K. C. 1967. A reference grammar of Hindi. Chicago: University of Chicago. [mimeographed]

Bamgboṣe, Ayo. 1966. A grammar of Yoruba. (West African Language Monographs 5.) Cambridge: Cambridge University Press.

Bamgboṣe, Ayo. 1972. On the derivation of adverbs from higher sentences. Proceedings of the Eleventh International Congress of Linguists, ed. by Luigi Heilmann, 507-19. Bologna: Società editrice il Mulino Bologna.

Bamgboṣe, Ayo. 1973a. The modifying serial construction: a reply. Studies in African Linguistics 4.207-17.

Bamgboṣe, Ayo. 1973b. On serial verbs and verbal status. Journal of West African Languages 9:1.17-48.

Bendor, Samuel John T. 1968. Verb clusters in Izi. Journal of West African Languages 5.119-28.

Bloch, Jules. 1954. The grammatical structure of Dravidian languages. Tr. Ramkrishna Ganesh Harshe. Poona: Deccan College.

Boadi, Lawrence. 1968. Some aspects of Akan deep syntax. Journal of West African Languages 5.83-90.

Bright, William, and Jacqueline Lindenfeld. 1968. Complex verb forms in colloquial Tamil. Studies in Indian linguistics, ed. by Bh. Krishnamurti, 30-45. Poona and Annamalai: Deccan College and Annamalai University Centres of Advanced Study in Linguistics.

Burton-Page, J. 1957. Compound and conjunct verbs in Hindi. Bulletin of the School of Oriental and African Studies 19.469-78.

Caldwell, R. 1913. A comparative grammar of the Dravidian or South Indian family of languages. 3rd edn. [Reprinted New Delhi: Oriental Books Reprint Corporation, 1974.]

Callow, Kathleen. 1966. Preliminary notes on serial constructions in Kasem. In Pike (ed.) 1966, 182-6.

Cardona, George. 1965. A Gujarati reference grammar. Philadelphia: University of Pennsylvania Press.

Chatterji, Suniti Kumar. 1926. The origin and development of the Bengali language. Calcutta: Calcutta University. [Reprinted London: Allen and Unwin, 1970.]

Fedson, Vijayarani J. 1981. The Tamil serial or compound verb. Chicago: University of Chicago dissertation.

Foley, William A., and Mike Olson. 1985. Clausehood and verb serialization. Grammar inside and outside the clause: some approaches to theory from the field, ed. by Johanna Nichols and Anthony C. Woodbury, 17-60. Cambridge: Cambridge University Press.

Givón, Talmy. 1975. Serial verbs and syntactic change: Niger-Congo. Word order and word order change, ed. by Charles N. Li, 47-112. University of Texas Press.

Guru, Kamta Prasad. 1922. Hindi vyakaran. Banaras: Kashi Nagari Pracharini Sabha. [Seventh printing, 1962.]

Hackman, Geoffrey J. 1976. An integrated anaylysis of the Hindi tense and aspect system. Urbana: University of Illinois dissertation.

Hock, Hans. 1988. Finiteness in Dravidian: Sanford B. Steever (1988) The serial verb formation in the Dravidian languages. Review article in Studies in the Linguistic Sciences 18:2.211-33.

Hook, Peter Edwin. 1974. The compound verb in Hindi. (The Michigan Series in South and Southeast Asian Languages and Linguistics.) Ann Arbor: The University of Michigan Center for South and Southeast Asian Studies.

Hyman, Larry. 1971. Consecutivization in Fe?Fe? Journal of African Languages 10:2.29-43.

Hyman, Larry. 1975. On the change from SOV to SVO: Evidence from Niger-Congo. In Li (ed.) 1975, 113-48.

Kachru, Yamuna. 1965. A transformational treatment of Hindi verbal synatx. University of London Ph.D. thesis. [Unpublished.]

Kachru, Yamuna. 1966. An introduction to Hindi syntax. Urbana, Illinois: University of Illinois.

Kachru, Yamuna. 1976. On the semantics of the causative construction in Hindi-Urdu. The grammar of causative constructions, ed. by M. Shibatani, 353-69. Academic Press, Syntax and Semantics Series.

Kachru, Yamuna. 1978. A biblography of serial verbs in South Asian and West African languages. [Mimeographed draft.]

Kachru, Yamuna. 1979. Pragmatics and verb serialization in Hindi-Urdu. Studies in the Linguistic Sciences 9:2.157-69.

Kachru, Yamuna. 1980. Aspects of Hindi grammar. Delhi: Manohar Publications.

Kachru, Yamuna, and Rajeshwari Pandharipande. 1980. Toward a typology of compound verbs in South Asian languages. Studies in the Linguistic Sciences 10:1.113-23.

Kellogg, S. H. 1875. A grammar of the Hindi language. [Oriental Reprint, New Delhi: Oriental Books Reprint Corporation.]

Leben, William (ed.) 1974. Papers from the Fifth Annual Conference on African Linguistics. Studies in African Linguistics, Supplement 5.

Li, C. N., and S. A. Thompson. 1973. Serial verb construction in Mandarin Chinese: Subordination or coordination? You take the high node and I'll take the low node, CLS 9, 96-103. Chicago: Chicago Linguistic Society.

Lord, Carol. 1973. Serial verbs in transtition. Studies in African Linguistics 4.269-96.

Lord, Carol. 1975. Igbo verb compounds and the lexicon. Studies in African Linguistics 6:1.23-48.

Lord, Carol. 1977. How Igbo got from SOV serializing to SVO compounding. Studies in African Linguistcs, Supplement 7, 145-56.

Masica, Colin P. 1976. Defining a linguistic area: South Asia. Chicago: University of Chicago Press.

McGregor, R. S. 1972. Outline of Hindi grammar. London: Clarendon Press.

Murti, K. V. S. 1973. Causative forms in Telegu. Linguistics 107.23-37.

Ogumbowale, P. O. 1970. The essentials of the Yoruba language. London: University of London Press Ltd.

Pal, Animesh K. 1972. Aspect in Bengali verbal compounds. Journal of the Asiatic Society (Calcutta) 12, 1970 (1972), 110-14.

Pike, Kenneth Lee (ed.) 1966. Tagmemic and matrix linguistics applied to selected African languages. Ann Arbor: The University of Michigan Center for Research on Languages and Language Behavior.

Pillai, S. A. 1964. Auxiliary verbs in Tamil. Tamil Culture 11.272-9.

Quirk, Randolph, S. Greenbaum, G. Leech, and J. Svartvik. 1972. A grammar of contemporary English. London: Longman.

Rajapurohit, B. B. 1973. Compound verbal constructions in Kannada. International Journal of Dravidian Linguistics 2:2.316-20.

Schachter, Paul. 1974a. A non-transformational account of serial verbs. In Leben (ed.) 1974, 253-70.

Schachter, Paul. 1974b. Serial verbs and verbs: a reply to a reply. In Leben (ed.) 1974, 278-82.

Schiffman, Harold. 1969. A transformational grammar of the Tamil aspectual system. Chicago: University of Chicago dissertation. [University Microfilms.]

Sharma, Aryendra. 1958. A basic grammar of modern Hindi. Delhi, India: Govt. of India, Ministry of Education and Scientific Research.

Shapiro, Michael C. 1974. Aspects of Hindi abstract verbal syntax. University of Chicago dissertation. [University Microfilms.]

Sinha, Anjani K. 1972. On the deictic use of 'coming' and 'going' in Hindi. Papers from the Eighth Regional Meeting of the Chicago Linguistic Society, 351-8. Chicago: University of Chiacgo.

Spencer, Harold. 1914. A Kanarese grammar: with graduated exercises. Mysore: Wesleyan Mission Press.

Stahlke, Herbert. 1970. Serial verbs. Studies in African Linguistics 1.60-99.

Stahlke, Herbert. 1974. Serial verbs as adverbs: a reply to Paul Schachter. In Leben (ed.) 1974, 271-7.

Steever, Sanford B. 1988. The serial verb formation in the Dravidian languages. (MLBD Series in Linguistics IV.) Delhi: Motilal Banarsidass.

Stewart, J. M. 1963. Some restrictions on objects in Twi. Journal of African Languages 2:2.145-9.

Subrahmanyam, P. S. 1971. Dravidian verb morphology: A comparative study. Annamalainagar: Annamalai University.

Tiwari, Udai Narain. 1960. The origin and development of Bhojpuri. Calcutta: The Asiatic Society. (Monograph X.)

Ward, Ida C. 1936. An introduction to the Ibo language. Cambridge: W. Heffer and Sons, Ltd.

Ward, Ida C. 1952. Introduction to the Yoruba language. Cambridge: Heffer.

Welmers, W. 1964. The syntax of emphasis in Kpelle. Journal of West African Languages 1.13-26.

Welmers, W. 1973. African language structures. Berkeley: University of California Press.

Williamson, Kay. 1965. A grammar of the Kolokuma dialect of Ijo. (West African Language Monographs 2.) Cambridge: Cambridge University Press.

COMPLEX PREDICATES IN TELUGU

Bh. Krishnamurti
University of Hyderabad

In 1963 I presented a paper entitled "Compound verbs in Telugu" to the Winter Seminar in Linguistics at Deccan College, Poona. The article was published five years later in a Supplement to *Indian Linguistics* vol. 27 (Krishnamurti 1968: 7-17). In that paper I discussed the morphological structure of compound verbs and constructed a diagram reflecting the ordering of the morphemes within finite compound verbs (Diagram: Appendix 1). In this diagram, the element Nc. = Nucleus is the main meaning carrier of the verb (i.e. the main verb stem); the rest of the items are modal auxiliaries, tense-mood and person -- all grammatical elements. I will deal in this paper with the internal structure of the Verb Nucleus -- simple, complex, and compound, and the semantic and syntactic consequences that can be projected from it.

1. For Telugu and Dravidian, I propose the following phrase structure rules:

[1] S --> NP Pred.

[2] Pred. --> $\left\{ \begin{matrix} \text{VP} \\ \text{NP} \end{matrix} \right\}$

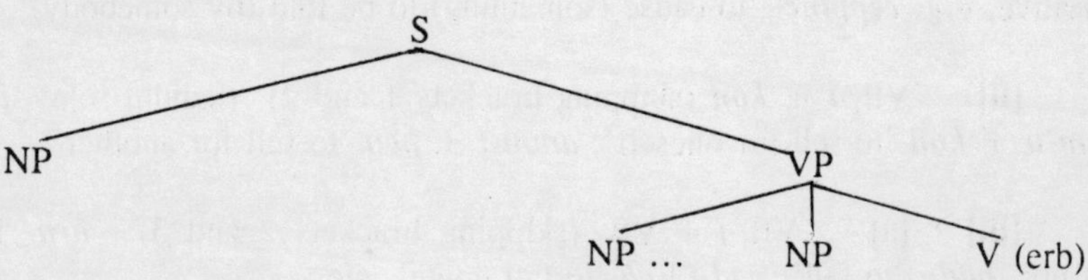

[3] V --> V Nucleus (VNc.) + (Modal (M)) + Tense-Mood (TM) + gender-number-person (g-n-p)

A finite verb consists of a Verb Nucleus followed by an optional category of Modal, followed by Tense-Mood (Past, Non-Past, Imperative, Durative) and g-n-p agreement with the subject NP. The following formula accounts for over 98% of the Telugu verb stems: simple, complex, and compound (the last two designated as complex hereafter):

[4]

$$\text{VNc} \dashrightarrow \left\{ \begin{matrix} \text{N + Enstative Aux.} \\ \text{VB}_1 \left(\left\{ \begin{matrix} \textit{-i} \\ \textit{-aN} \end{matrix} \right\} + \text{VB}_2 \right) (\textit{-inc}) \left(\textit{-i} \left\{ \begin{matrix} \textit{+kon} \\ \textit{+peṭṭ} \end{matrix} \right\} \right) \end{matrix} \right\}$$

N = a stative noun

Enstative Aux. = ***aw-*** 'to become', ***wacc-*** 'to come', etc.

VB_1 = any verb root or simple verb base, intransitive or transitive (including some morphologically derived transitives)

VB_1 + ***i*** = perfective participle of VB_1

VB_1 + ***aN*** = infinitive of VB_1

VB_2 = grammaticalized aux. verbs, e.g. ***pō*** 'to go', ***koṭṭ*** 'to beat', ***peṭṭ*** 'to put', ***wēs*** 'to throw', etc.

-inc = Causative suffix

-kon = Reflexive

-peṭṭ = Benefactive

The complex verb sequences resulting from the above formula **[4]** are:

[i] VB_1-***inc*** (skipping brackets 1 and 3): VB_1 is transitive; the resultant stem is causative, e.g. ***ceppinc-*** 'to cause (something) to be told (by somebody)'

[ii] VB_1-***i*** + ***kon*** (skipping brackets 1 and 2) (Sandhi rule: ***i*** --> ***u*** before ***kon***): ***amm-u*** + ***kon*** 'to sell for oneself'; ***amm-i*** + ***peṭṭ*** 'to sell for another'

[iii] [a] VB_1-***i*** + VB_2 (skipping brackets 2 and 3): ***āru*** 'to dry'; ***ār-i+pō*** 'to dry up', ***paḍu*** 'to fall'; ***paḍ-i+pō*** 'to fall down', etc.

[b] VB_1-***aN*** + VB_2: //ār-aN+peṭṭ// --> ***ārabeṭṭ*** 'to lay (something) to dry'; //paḍ-aN+koṭṭ// --> ***paḍ-a+goṭṭ*** 'to fell (something/someone) down'

[iv] VB_1-***inc-i*** + ***kon***, VB_1-***inc-i*** + ***peṭṭ*** (skipping the 1st bracket): ***cepp-inc-u+kon*** 'to cause (something) to be told (by somebody) for oneself'; ***amm-inc-i+peṭṭ*** 'to cause (something) to be sold (by somebody) for another's benefit'

[v] [a] VB_1-***aN*** + VB_2-***i*** + ***kon*** (skipping the 2nd bracket): //ār-aN+peṭṭ-i+kon// --> ***ār-a+beṭṭ-u+kon*** 'to dry up something (by one) for oneself (the actor)'

[b] VB_1-***aN*** + VB_2-***i*** + ***peṭṭ***: ***paḍ-a+goṭṭ-i+peṭṭ*** 'to fell something/somebody for someone (different from the actor)'

[vi] VB_1-*aN* + VB_2-*inc* (skipping the 3rd bracket): ***ār-a+beṭṭ-inc*** 'to cause (something) to be dried by somebody (two Agents)'; ***paḍ-a+goṭṭ-inc*** 'to cause (something) to be felled (by somebody)'

[vii] [a] VB_1-*aN* + VB_2-***inc-i*** + ***kon***: ***āra+beṭṭ-inc-u+kon*** '($Agent_1$) to cause something to be dried by $Agent_2$ for oneself (for the benefit of $Agent_1$)'

[b] VB_1-*aN* + VB_2-***inc-i*** + ***peṭṭ***: ***paḍ-a+goṭṭ-inc-i-peṭṭ*** '($Agent_1$) to cause something to be felled by $Agent_2$ for the sake of another (other than $Agent_1$ and $Agent_2$)'

N + aux (Stative Predicates):

2. Here N stands for a noun (or adj.) which denotes a psychosomatic or climatic state such as ***ākali*** 'hunger', ***kōpam*** 'anger' followed by an 'enstative' verb ***aw*** 'to become', ***wacc***, ***wēs*** 'to occur', etc. An enstative aux. is a grammaticalized verb which denotes an animate entity (generally human) experiencing or undergoing a state. Study the following sentences:

[5] **[a]** ***pillawāḍiki*** [1] ***ākali*** [2] ***awutunnadi /ayindi*** [3]
[The boy-to hunger become-dur-it/become-past-it]
'The boy[1] is getting/got[3] hungry[2].'

[b] ***pillawāḍu*** [1] ***ākaligā*** [2] ***unnāḍu*** [3]
'The boy[1] is/was[3] hungry[2] (hungry-like).'

The selection of the appropriate enstative is presumably determined by the semantic features of the stative noun (Krishnamurti 1970).

2.1. A large sample list of such **N + Enst. aux** is as follows:

[6] [a] ***kōpam*** 'anger', ***ēḍupu*** 'crying', ***nidra*** 'sleep', ***nawwu*** 'laughter', ***duhkham*** 'sorrow', ***dhayryam*** 'courage', ***sōṣa*** 'fainting', ***teliwi***, ***spruha*** 'consciousness', ***jwaram*** 'fever', ***kala*** 'dream', etc. take ***wacc***- 'to come'.

[b] ***ākali*** 'hunger', ***iṣṭam*** 'liking', ***santōṣam*** 'joy', ***anyāyam*** 'injustice', etc. take ***aw***- 'to become'.

[c] ***ākali*** 'hunger', ***kōpam*** 'anger', ***bhayam*** 'fear', ***duhkham*** 'sorrow', ***wisugu*** 'disgust', etc. take ***wēs*** (intr.) 'to strike', 'hit' (tr. 'to throw').

[d] ***jalubu*** 'cold', ***jabbu*** 'sickness' take ***cēs***- 'to happen' (tr. 'to do').

[e] ***jāli*** 'compassion', ***bādha*** 'distress' take ***kalugu***, ***wēs*** 'to happen'.

Notice that ***wēs*** 'to throw', ***cēs*** 'to do' are syntactically intransitives here since they do not take a direct object.

2.2. Some of the enstative auxiliaries are related as intransitive and transitive:

[7]	[a]	***-paḍu***	***-peṭṭ***
		santōṣa-paḍu	***santōṣa-peṭṭ***
		'to feel happy'	'to make (somebody) happy'
		bhaya-paḍu	***bhaya-peṭṭ***
		'to fear'	'to frighten'
	[b]	***-pō***	***-puccu***
		nidra-pō	***nidra-puccu***
		'to go to sleep'	'to put to sleep'
	[c]	***-wacc /-aw***	***-cēs***
		jnāpakam-wacc	***jnāpakam-cēs***
		'to come to memory'	'to bring to (somebody's memory)'
		pāḍ-aw	***pāḍu-cēs***
		'to get spoiled'	'to spoil'

Notice that the transitive auxiliaries here are not morphologically related to the intransitive auxiliaries thereby symbolizing the idiosyncratic lexical and semantic structure of the enstatives.

2.3. The composite stative predicates in **[6]** require a subject NP in Dative (see **[5]** above). A question arises whether the entities designated N can be treated as complement NP, since the g-n-p in the verb has agreement with a neuter subject?

Study the following contrast between NP + V sequences branching from VP as opposed to N-aux. which is a constituent of the V.

[8] [a] [S [NP ***wāḍiki***] [VP [NP ***teliwi***] [V ***undi***]]]
'He has intelligence' (lit. to him - intelligence - is)

[b] [S [NP ***wāḍiki***] [VP [V ***teliwi wacc-in-di***]]]
'He got consciousness' (lit. to him - consciousness - came)

[8] [a]

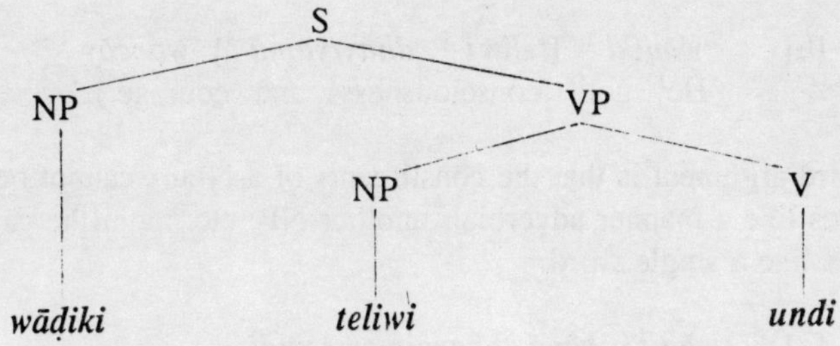

[b]

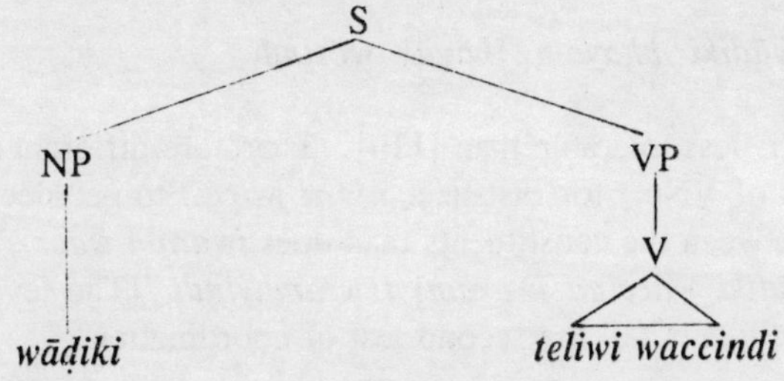

Notice that the whole clause **[8a]** can be converted into an NP as in **[9a]**:

[9] [a] [*wāḍiki unna teliwi*] *nāku lēdu*
'I do not have [the intelligence he has].'

BUT NOT **[8b]** into **[9b]**.

[9] [b] [**wāḍiki waccina teliwi*] *maḷḷī pōyindi*
'He lost [the consciousness he got].'

Here, there is a meaning difference between the two instances of ***teliwi*** in support of the syntactic difference.

The second argument is that the NP constituent of VP can be coordinated with another compatible NP but the N constituent of V cannot be coordinated with another N taking the same aux.

[10] [a] *wāḍiki* [1] *teliwī* [2] *andamū* [3] *unnāy* [4]
'He[1] has[4] [intelligence[2] (as well as) good looks[3]].'
(lit. To-him[1] intelligence[2] - (and) - beauty[3] are/were[4])

BUT NOT

[10] [b] **wāḍiki* [1] *[teliwī* [2] *dhayryamū* [3]*] waccāy* [4]
'He[1] got[4] [consciousness[2] and courage[3]].'

The third argument is that the constituents of a N-aux cannot be generally separated by other categories like a manner adverbial, another NP, etc. as in the case of NP + V; because N-aux behaves like a single word.

[11] [a] *wāḍiki bāgā bhayam wēsindi*
'He got frightened badly.'

[b] ? *wāḍiki bhayam [bāgā] wēsindi*

Sentence **[11b]** is less tolerable than **[11a]**. There are different degrees of cohesiveness among the constituents of VNc.; for instance, ***nidra wacc-*** 'to get sleep' (lit. 'sleep to-come') has greater cohesion between the constituents than does ***jwaram wacc-*** 'to get fever' (lit. 'fever to-come') because [***wāḍiki waccina jwaram***] ***tīwramayindi*** '[The fever he got] is severe' is possible. But the constituents fail the second test of coordination.

2.4. The lexical entry for such a composite predicate may be given as follows:

[12] *ākali-aw* 'be hungry'

a.	categorial features	[+V, −N]
b.	composition	[Nc: N-Enst.]
c.	Theta grid	[Experiencer + ______]
d.	case-marking	[NP Dat + ______]

The above rule **[12a]** says that *ākali aw* is a Verb Nucleus consisting of a N + aux (enstative). It belongs to the grammatical category of Verb; the V assigns a θ-role (case role) of Experiencer to the only Subject NP which must be [+animate]. There is no complement NP required by V here. The Subject NP carrying the role of 'Experiencer' takes a dative suffix when the predicate is a stative noun + enst. If the stative noun is an adverbial with *-gā*, the tensed copula ***un*** 'to be' can have neuter agreement (agreement is neutralized) with Dative subject, or normal agreement (g-n-p) with Nominative subject; e.g.

[13] [a] *wāḍiki* *kōpamgā* *undi*
him-to *ākaligā* is/was-it
bhayamgā
dhayryamgā
santōṣangā
'anger-like'
'hunger-like'
'fear-like'
'courage-like'
'happiness-like'

Each of the sentences of **[13a]** has an alternative paraphrase like

[b] *wāḍu* *kōpamgā* *unnāḍu*
he angrily is/was-he
'He is/was angry.'

[13b] represents an animate (person) being already in a state and 'not getting into a state', etc. This kind of clause alternation is not possible for all stative nouns; a large number can occur in the clause type **[13a]** and not **[13b]**.

[14] [a] *wāḍiki* *jāligā* *undi*
him-to *jalubugā* is/was-it
jwaramgā
noppigā
caligā
'compassion'
'cold (sickness)'
'fever'
'pain'
'cold (weather)'

BUT NOT

[b] *wāḍu* **jāligā* *unnāḍu*
**jalubugā*
**jwaramgā*
**noppigā*
**caligā*

Alternatively it is possible to say some of these with a 'with phrase'

[c] *wāḍu* *jālitō* *unnāḍu*
jalubutō
jwaramtō
noppitō

BUT NOT **calitō* 'with chill'.

The above differences give a sub-classification of stative nouns. It may be that the different degrees of 'compositeness' or 'cohesiveness' of stative noun + enst. aux. is related to this phenomenon; this in turn is possibly related to the semantic structure of the stative nouns. Notice that the states predicated in **[13]** are more 'internal' and psychological; those of **[14]** are more 'external' and somatic. Also note that there are no plurals to many of these nouns, e.g. **ākaḷḷu* 'hungers', **iṣṭālu* 'likes', **santōṣālu* 'joys', etc. when an enstative follows. However, it is possible to have plurals like *jwarālu* 'fevers', *bāḍhalu* 'difficulties', *jalubulu* 'colds', *kalalu* 'dreams':

[15] [a] *inṭlō* [1] *andarikī* [2] *jwarālu* [3] *waccǣy* [4]
'Everybody[2] in the house[1] got[4] fevers[3].'

[b] *inṭlō* [1] *andarikī* [2] *jalubulu* [3] *cēsǣy* [4]
'Everybody[2] in the house[1] got[4] colds[3].'

3. $\mathbf{VB_1} \left\{ \begin{matrix} -i \\ -aN \end{matrix} \right\} + \mathbf{VB_2}$. The stems which take Reflexive *-kon* and Benefactive *peṭṭ* are all transitive but not all transitives take *-kon* and *-peṭṭ*. The addition of VB_2 (a specific auxiliary) to VB_1 (basic verb) may introduce changes in the assignment of case roles to different arguments (Subject and Complement NPs) of a proposition. Reflexive *-kon* and Benefactive *-peṭṭ* are mutually exclusive, i.e., they do not co-occur as modifier auxiliaries. The auxiliaries *-kon* and *-peṭṭ* are the final constituents of a maximally extended verb stem (VNc.) which can then optionally take a Modal followed by T-M and g-n-p to make it a finite verb. Intransitive verbs cannot take the reflexive *-kon*; e.g. *weḷḷ* 'to go', *lēc* 'to get up', *āru* 'to get dried' have no **weḷḷ-u kon*, **lēc-u kon*, **ār-u kon*, etc. Perhaps reflexivity within the semantic structure precludes co-occurrence with *-kon* in the case of some transitive stems also like *win* 'to hear', 'listen to' (**win-u kon*), *namulu* 'to chew' (**namul-u kon*). This restriction could be language-specific; cf. Hindi *sun le* 'to hear for oneself', *dekh le* 'to see for oneself'.

There are compound stems with *-paḍu* 'to fall' as VB_2 which cannot take *-kon*:

[16] VB_1 + *aN* + *paḍu*

[a] *win* 'to hear' : //win-aN+paḍu// --> *winabaḍu* 'to be heard'

[b] *kan* 'to see' : //kan-aN+paḍu// --> *kanabaḍu* 'to appear'

[c] *kūl* 'to fall' : //kūl-aN+paḍu// --> *kūlabaḍu* 'to squat'

[d] *tagul* 'to catch' : //tagul-aN+paḍu// --> *tagalabaḍu* 'to catch fire, to burn'

The above and their like are one- or two-place predicates; **[a]** and **[b]** have Experiencer (Dat.) and Theme (Obj.); **[c]** has Actor (Nom.) and Location (Loc.); **[d]** has Theme (Obj.). This last has a transitive counterpart //tagul-aN+peṭṭ// --> *tagalabeṭṭ-* 'to set fire to' which has two arguments: Actor (Agent) and Patient (Object).

3.1. VB_1 + *i* + VB_2: A very large class of intransitive stems are 'change-of-state' and 'change-of-position' verbs (incl. motion verbs). All these, inflected with the perfective participial *-i*, take the auxiliary *-pō* 'to go', grammaticalized as an 'intensifier' (for listing see Appendix 2).

[17] [a] *guḍḍalu* [1] *annī* [2] *ārāy /āri pōyāy* [3]
'All[2] the clothes[1] got dried (completely)[3].'

[b] *aḍawi* [1] *kālipōyindi* [2]
'The forest[1] got burnt[2].'

[c] *wāḍiki* [1] *juṭṭu* [2] *nerisindi* [3]*/nerisi pōyindi* [3a]
[him-to hair greyed/having greyed-went]
'To him[1] hair[2] (has) greyed[3] a lot[3a].'

OR

[c̀] *wāḍi* [1] *juṭṭu* [2] *nerisindi* [3]*/nerisi pōyindi* [3a]
[his hair greyed/having greyed (went)]
'His[1] hair[2] (has) greyed[3] (very much[3a]).'

[d] *wāḷḷa* [1] *illu* [2] *kūlindi /kūli pōyindi* [3]
[their house having fallen (went)]
'Their[1] house[2] fell down (completely)[3].'

With animate subjects:

[e] *wāḍu* [1] *caccæḍu* [2]*/cacci pōyæḍu* [2]
[he having died-went]
'He died (suddenly).'

[f] *pakṣulu* [1] *egiri pōyæy* [2]
[birds having flown (went)]
'The birds[1] flew off [2].'

There are nearly 100 change-of-state and change-of-position verbs which take *-pō* as VB_2. These are mostly one- or two-argument predicates: Experiencer or Theme or sometimes both as in **[17c]** and **[17c̀]**. Some VB_1 stems have corresponding morphological transitives, e.g.:

[18] [a] *wāḍiki* [1] *kālu* [2] *wirigindi* [3]*/wirig-i pōyindi* [3a]
[him-to leg broke (off)]
'His leg broke off.'

[b] *wāḍu* [1] *kālu* [2] *wirucu konnāḍu* [3]
[he leg broke (tr.)-refl. past]
'He broke his leg.'

Notice in **[18a]** the Theta roles are Experiencer (Dat. subj.) and Theme (Obj.); in **[18b]** the Theta roles assigned by the transitive verb are Agent (*wāḍu* NP nom) and Theme (*kālu* NP acc.). Although in **[18a]** *kālu* appears to be the surface subject, it is not the grammatical subject by the following test:

[c] *wāḍiki kālu wirigi (pōyi), (wāḍu) mancamlō unnāḍu*
[him-to leg having-broken off he bed-in is/was he]
'His leg broke and he is in bed.'

In **[18c]**, the subjects of the subordinate clause and the main clause should be coreferential and identical. Both *wāḍiki* of the subordinate clause and *wāḍu* of the main clause are identical referring to the same person.

3.2. VB_1 *-i* + *wēs*. Where VB_1 is a transitive (inherently or through morphological derivation, e.g. *tiṭṭ* 'to scold', *wiruc* 'to break (tr.): *wirugu* (intr.)), its inflected perfective participle can take *wēs* as an 'intensifier' corresponding to *pō* with intransitives: ***cepp***- 'to tell': //cepp-i-wēs// --> //cepp-i-ēs// --> *ceppēs*- 'to tell fully, to reveal', so also ***koṭṭ*** 'to beat': *koṭṭēs* 'to beat thoroughly', ***tin***- 'to eat', ***tinēs*** 'to eat away'.

[19] [a] *wāḍu* ^{1} *annam* ^{2} *tinnāḍu* ^{3}
'He^1 ate^3 food^2.'

[b] *wāḍu* ^{1} *annam* ^{2} *antā* ^{3} *tinēsǣḍu* ^{4}
'He^1 ate away^4 all^3 the food^2.'

3.3. VB$_1$ + *aN* + VB$_2$. A large number of change-of-state and change-of-position verbs (VB$_1$), inflected with the infinitive *-aN*, take *-koṭṭ* 'to beat' and *-peṭṭ* 'to put' as VB$_2$. Here VB$_2$ converts VB$_1$ into a transitive and adds other semantic nuances (see Appendix 2 for listing):

[20] [a] *Rāmu* ^{1} *nā bomma* ^{2} *wiragagoṭṭǣḍu* ^{3}
'Ramu^1 broke (into pieces)^3 my doll^2.'

[b] *Rāmu* ^{1} *nī paḷḷu* ^{2} *rālagoḍatānu* ^{3} *annāḍu* ^{4}
'Ramu^1 said^4, "I will knock off^3 your teeth^2."'

[c] *Kamala* ^{1} *nīḷḷu* ^{2} *kāgabeṭṭindi* ^{3}
'Kamala^1 boiled^3 the water^2.'

[d] *Kamala* ^{1} *biyyam* ^{2} *nānabeṭṭindi* ^{3}
'Kamala^1 soaked^3 the rice^2.'

There are fine distinctions between morphologically derived transitives and those derived by the addition of *-koṭṭ* and *-peṭṭ* as VB$_2$, e.g. *kālu* 'to burn (intr.)', *kāl-uc* 'to light-up (as a cigarette)', 'to set fire to', *kāla beṭṭ* 'to burn down'.

The items which include *-koṭṭ* as VB$_2$ specify a sudden change-of-state, whereas those which include *-peṭṭ*, a gradual change-of-state. The lexical entries can be marked for the feature complex ‹+state, +change, −gradual› for VB$_1$ taking *-koṭṭ* as VB$_2$, and ‹+state, +change, +gradual› for VB$_1$ taking *-peṭṭ* as VB$_2$. The *koṭṭ* forms imply that the action of the Agent brings about the change-of-state in the object suddenly; in *peṭṭ* forms the Agent acts on the object (putting on fire, putting in sun) and something happens gradually to the object to bring about the desired state as in boiling, soaking, drying, etc. There is a strong involvement of the Agent in *koṭṭ* forms implying his/her intent, volition, deliberate action, etc.

Another transitivizer is *wēs* 'to throw' which can replace both *koṭṭ* and *peṭṭ* as VB$_2$ in some cases on VB$_1$ + *aN*; *paḍagoṭṭ*, *naḍēs* 'to fell', *nānabeṭṭ*, *nānēs* 'to soak in liquid (tr.)', but not **ceḍēs*, beside *ceḍagoṭṭ* 'to spoil'. Actually *-wēs* seems to imply that the actor 'throws away', 'puts out', 'pours in' some concrete object to bring about the change-of-state. One uses *ārēs* 'to dry' (clothes, etc.); but *ārabeṭṭ* 'to let something dry which got wet'.

3.4. Transitive stems with *-koṭṭ*, *-peṭṭ*, and *-wēs*, like transitives, minimally require a combination of two arguments whose case roles are [+Agent +Object]: *wiruc*, *wiragagoṭṭ-* 'to break' [+Ag. +Obj.] with case marking as NP nom. and NP acc., respectively. The intransitive complex stems with *-pō* as VB_2 require one or two case roles, as the case may be, excluding the above combination, e.g.:

[21] [a] [Agent]: *Rāmu* [1] *weḷḷipōyǣḍu* [2]
'Ramu[1] went away[2].'

[b] [Object, Cause]: *ceṭṭu* [1] *gāliki* [2] *paḍipōyindi* [3]
'The tree[1] fell down[3] because of wind[2].'

[c] [Experiencer]: *wāḍiki* [1] *juṭṭu* [2] *nerisi pōyindi* [3]
'His[1] hair[2] greyed (completely)[3].'

[d] [Location]: *ceruwu* [1] *enḍipōyindi* [2]
'The tank[1] dried up[2].'

[e] [Agent, Goal]: *piṭṭalu* [1] *gūḷḷaku* [2] *egiripōyǣyi* [3]
'Birds[1] flew off [3] to (their) nests[2].'

[f] [Agent, Source]: *Rāmu* [1] *ūrininci* [2] *wastāḍu* [3]
'Ramu[1] will come[3] from the village[2].'

There are some $VB_1 \left\{ \begin{matrix} -i \\ -aN \end{matrix} \right\} + VB_2$ sequences which have become idioms, e.g. ***can-i pō*** 'to die', **can-* 'to go' (archaic); ***kan-i peṭṭ-*** 'to invent' (**kan-* 'to see'), ***eg-a goṭṭ-, ega wēs-*** 'to skip payment of dues', ***pō goṭṭ*** 'to lose' (lit. to make go), ***nil-a beṭṭ*** 'to set up' (**nil-* 'to stand'), etc. The other items under VB_2 are ***taluc*** 'to intend', ***cepp-a daluc*** 'to intend to speak', ***ettu*** 'to raise', ***lēw-an ettu*** 'to lift up', ***tīs-*** 'to remove', ***wiḍ-a dīs*** 'to separate' (**wiḍ-* 'to leave'), ***lēw-a dīs-*** 'to lift up', ***cēr-a dīs*** 'to bring close, to endear', ***cepp-*** 'to tell': ***teliy-a jepp*** 'to convince', to tell to make know', ***-puccu*** 'to send', ***weḷḷ-a buccu*** 'to spend time, to let go'. Most of these are not productive. Syntactically they follow the same pattern of argument structure as those discussed earlier. Several of them retain their lexical meaning in complex stems.

3.5. V Stem *-inc*, Causative. Causative stems in *-inc* require minimally three arguments: A_1 = Causer (Instigator), A_2 = Causee (Actor), O = Patient or Theme; A_1 = NP nom., A_2 = NP instr. (*cēta*), O = NP acc.

[22] [a] *Rāmu* [1] (A_1) *kūliwaḷḷacēta* [2] (A_2) *ceṭlu* [3] (O) *paḍa goṭṭ-inc-ǣḍu* [4]
'Ramu[1] got[4] the trees[3] felled down[4] by labourers[2].'

[b] *nēnu* [1] *Rāmucēta* [2] *uttaram* [3] *rāyincǣnu* [4]
'I[1] got[4] a letter[3] written[4] by Ramu[2].'

I discussed the semantic and syntactic analysis of causative constructions in Telugu elsewhere (Krishnamurti 1971).

3.6. $VB_1 \left(\left\{ \begin{array}{l} \textit{-i} \\ \textit{-aN} \end{array} \right\} + VB_2 \right) \textit{(-inc)} \left(\left\{ \begin{array}{l} \textit{+kon} \\ \textit{+peṯṯ} \end{array} \right\} \right).$

The reflexive ***-kon*** is generally added to transitive and causative verb stems. There are, however, other idiomatic and grammatical uses of ***-kon*** which are semantically different from the transitive-based reflexive ***-kon***.

(i) **Idiomatic *-kon***: ***an-*** 'to say': ***anu-kon*** 'to think, feel, intend'; ***paḍu*** 'to fall': ***paḍukon*** 'to lie down, to sleep', ***niluc-*** 'to rise' //niluc-i+kon// --> ***nilcon /nilcun*** 'to stand'; //kūruc-i+kon// --> ***kūrcon /kūrcun*** 'to sit'.

(ii) **Medio-passive or Middle voice *-kon***: A very small set of VB_1 type (both transitive and intransitive) take ***-kon*** to form Middle voice stems; e.g. ***paṯṯ*** 'to hold': ***paṯṯ-u-kon*** 'to stick', ***mūs*** 'to close': ***mūs-u+kon*** 'something to close itself, (one) to shut (one's mouth)'; ***teruc*** 'to open': ***teruc-u+kon*** 'door, etc. to open itself'; ***cuṯṯ*** 'to roll': ***cuṯṯ-u+kon*** 'mat, etc. to roll itself'; ***pūḍ-*** 'to be buried': ***pūḍ-u+kon*** 'something to get buried'; ***pēr-*** 'to curdle': ***pēr-u+kon*** 'something to curdle itself'. These are used intransitively without either specifying or implying the participation of an Agent.

[23] [a] ***nāku*** [1] ***bhayam*** [2] ***paṯṯ-u konnadi*** [3]
'(Some) fear[2] has gripped[3] me[1].'

[b] ***āmeki*** [1] ***gontu*** [2] ***mūs-u + ku pōyindi*** [3]
'Her[1] throat[2] got blocked[3] (so she cannot speak).'

[c] ***neyyi*** [1] ***pēr-u + ku pōyindi*** [2]
'The ghee[1] thickened[2].'

[d] ***goyyi*** [1] ***pūḍ-u + ku pōyindi*** [2]
'The pit[1] got filled up[2].'

The above sentences are all [−Agentive]. The subject NP is marked for the thematic roles of [+Experiencer] or [+Theme]. Notice also that this small class is the only complex set of verbs which can occur in the position of VB_1, because they take ***-pō***, a member of VB_2, i.e. //mūs-i+kon-i+pō// --> ***mūs-u + ku pō*** (Sandhi rule: ***kon-i --> ku***) (see **[23b, c, & d]**). The resultant forms are intransitives, some of which are also stative predicates (see **[23a]**). These have to be accommodated in the formula **[4]** which can be partly revised as **[24]** incorporating also **[16]**:

[24]

$$\left\{\begin{array}{l} \text{(1) VB}_1 \left\{\begin{array}{l} \textit{-i} \\ \textit{-aN} \end{array}\right\} + \text{VB}_2 \\ \left\{\begin{array}{l} \text{(2) VB}_{1a}\ (+\ \textit{kon})\ \textit{-i} \\ \text{(3) VB}_{1b}\ \textit{-aN} + \textit{paḍu -i} \end{array}\right\} \textit{pō} \end{array}\right\}$$

(VB_2 = ***koṭṭ***, ***peṭṭ***, ***wēs***, etc.
only transitivizers)

Item **[24]** **(1)** generates only transitive stems which can then take Causatives ***-inc***, Reflexive ***-kon***, and Benefactive ***-peṭṭ***. **[24]** **(2)** and **(3)** generate terminal stems which cannot be lexically extended further. Reflexive ***-kon*** and ***-peṭṭ*** change the argument structure of clauses:

[25] **[a]** ***Rāmu*** [1] ***kaḷḷaddālu*** [2] ***pagal-a goṭṭu konnāḍu*** [3]
'Ramu[1] broke[3] (his) glasses[2].'

[b] ***wāḷḷu*** [1] ***okaritala*** [2] ***okaru*** [3] ***pagal-a goṭṭu konnāru*** [4]
'They[1] broke[4] each other's head[2,3].'

[c] ***nēnu*** [1] ***kāḷḷu*** [2] ***kaḍug-u-konnānu*** [3]
'I[1] washed[3] (my) legs[2].'

The use of ***-kon*** obviates the use of a reflexive pronoun or a determiner like 'my, his, her', etc. as in English. In **[25b]** the reciprocal use of ***-kon*** assigns Agent roles to more than one Subject NP or requires a plural subject.

[26] **[a]** ***Rāmu*** [1] ***Śankarcēta*** [2] ***Kamalaku*** [3] ***uttaram*** [4] ***rāy-inc-i peṭṭǣḍu*** [5]
'Ramu[1] got[5] a letter[4] written[5] for Kamala[3] by Shankar[2].'

[b] ***nāku*** [1] ***bajārununci*** [2] ***panḍlu*** [3] ***teppinci peṭṭanḍi*** [4]
'(Please) get[4] (some) fruit[3] brought[4] for me[1] from the market[2].'

The verb in **[26a]** minimally requires four arguments: $Agent_1$ (NP nom.), $Agent_2$ (NP instr.), Theme (NP acc.), and Beneficiary/Receiver (NP dat.). Therefore a ***peṭṭ*** construction adds one more argument with the role of Beneficiary carrying dative case.

3.7 Modal Auxiliaries: There are several modal auxiliaries which a VNc simple or complex can take (see Appendix 1 at the end). These denote capacity/incapacity (***kala /lē-***), permission/prohibition (*icc-/kūḍ-*), probability (***wacc-***), obligation (***wāls-***), etc. besides some aspectual auxiliaries. I cannot go into these in this paper. Most of these will not change the valency of complex predicates, since they are grammatical and not lexical. The only problem is with permissive ***-icc*** 'to give', which sometimes can occur as part of a complex stem according it a semi-lexical status; it also introduces changes in the argument structure of a proposition, e.g.

[27] [a] ***nēnu*** [1] ***wāṇṇi*** [2] ***ceṭlu*** [3] ***paḍ-a goṭṭ-inc-u-kō-n iccǣnu*** [4]
(I him trees fall-inf. tr.-caus.-ppl.-ref.-Perm. Past I)
'I[1] allowed[4] him[2] to cause[4] the trees[3] to be felled[4] for himself[4].'
(Sandhi rule: ***kon + aN --> kōn / __Vowel***)

Here Permissive *icc*- requires an Object argument (*wāṇṇi*: NP acc.) which is Deep Structure Causer Agent (A_1) as in

[b] ***wāḍu*** [1] ***kūlīlacēta*** [2] ***ceṭlu*** [3] ***paḍagoṭṭincukonnāḍu*** [4]
'He[1] got[4] the trees[3] felled[4] by coolies[2].'

4. The auxiliaries added to VB_1 which make up the VNc. (main verb) are called by different terms in literature, viz. 'explicator', 'operator', 'intensive auxiliary', 'vector', etc. (Hook:17). Masica (1971:141) says, 'The critical difference between V_1V_2 (=Conjunctive Participle ... V) and V_1V_2 (=Vv) is rather the aforementioned shift in the semantic centre of gravity from V_2 to V_1 with concomitant lexical emptying or grammaticalization of V_2.' He compares the presence or absence of the use of ELEVEN explicators across Indo-Aryan and Dravidian languages, with lexical meanings ‹go, come, rise, fall, sit, move, give, take, put (keep), throw, leave (release), see› along with their modified meanings as Vv (i.e. VB_2). Some of these do not suit Dravidian, e.g., ‹give› in his Table is 'Benefactive' but in Telugu 'Permissive', but ***peṭṭ*** is Benefactive. ‹Sit› does not occur in any of the South Dravidian languages. It does occur in Koṇḍa (***bas***- 'to sit') under the Indo-Aryan influence. The Telugu explicators occurring within VNc. may broadly be characterized as follows:

1.	***paḍu***	'fall'	'fall within the experience of animate entity'
2.	***pō***	'go'	'completion'
3.	***koṭṭ*** (transitivizer)	'beat, hit, strike'	'use of force, sudden completion'
4.	***peṭṭ*** (transitivizer)	'put, lay'	(a) 'gradual completion' (b) 'to act to help another person'
5.	***wēs*** (transitivizer)	'throw'	'speed, completion'
6.	***kon*** (reflexive)	'buy, take'	'result of action goes to Actor/Theme/Experiencer'
7.	***tīs*** (transitivizer)	'remove'	'take away from a position'

The above are the most productive explicators. ***Icc-*** 'to give' is not a VB_2 but occurs as a Modal aux. with occasional lexicalization; ***wacc-*** 'to come' and ***aw*** 'to become' are not found as VB_2 but they are enstatives occurring with stative nouns. Even ***wēs*** 'to throw', ***cēs*** 'to do' are intransitives when used enstatively. Hook lists 63 vector verbs (explicators) and says that there are only eight which most of his respondents and different authors agree upon, viz. ***ā***, ***uth***, ***jā***, ***ḍāl***, ***de***, ***paḍ***, ***baiṭh***, and ***le*** (Hook 1974:42-3).

In Konḍa, a South-Central Dravidian language, the following explicators are used: ***ṛis-*** 'to leave', ***sī-*** 'to give', ***pok-*** 'to throw', ***ta-*** 'to bring', ***o-*** 'to carry', ***bas-*** 'to sit' (Krishnamurti 1969:307). The other types of complex verbs in Konḍa are coordinated finite verbs, e.g., ***losnap*** + ***uṇap*** --> ***losna uṇap*** 'We will beg and eat.' Here both VB_1 and VB_2 are main verbs. There are also aspectual compounds where VB_2 is a Modal auxiliary ***man-*** 'to be', e.g., ***veyu*** [1] ***kākta*** [2] ***maRar*** [3] 'They[1] were[3] with opened mouths[2].' (Ibid. 304-11.) Such verbs, including the ones with explicators, are designated serial verbs by Steever (1988) in his thorough treatment of these in all Dravidian languages. The coordinated serial verbs, however, do not have counterparts in Telugu as part of the expansion of VNc. It is to be noted that Konḍa lacks the derivative of Proto-Dravidian ****koṇ*** /****koḷ*** being used as Reflexive.

5. One unresolved problem is with VB_2 ***wēs-*** 'to throw'. It has been shown as a transitivizer as well as an intensifier, e.g. //paḍ-a wēs// --> ***paḍēs-*** 'to knock down', //tin-i-wēs// --> ***tinēs-*** 'to eat away (completely)'; ***wēs*** following ppl-***i*** has greater mobility of position unlike the other members of VB_2; for instance, it can occur as VB_3 or VB_4 before and after (***-inc***) as intensifier, e.g., //pagal-aN-koṭṭ-i wēs// --> ***pagal-a goṭṭes-*** 'one broke (something) off completely.' This requires VB_3 position to be given to ***wēs*** between VB_2 and ***-inc***, since such stems can carry Causative, Reflexive, and Benefactive morphemes, e.g., ***pagala*** + ***goṭṭ- (i) ēy-inc-u*** + ***kon*** is possible. Also one can say //pagal-a koṭṭ-inc-i wēs// --> ***pagal-a goṭṭ-inc-ēs*** with intensity attaching to causation rather than to action. Then **[4]** can be revised as **[28]:**

[28]

$$VNc \longrightarrow \left\{ \begin{array}{l} \left\{ \begin{array}{l} (1)\ N + \text{Enstative Aux.} \\ (2)\ VB_1 \left(\left\{ \begin{array}{l} \textit{-i} \\ \textit{-aN} \end{array} \right\} + VB_2 \right) (\textit{-i+wēs})\ (\textit{-inc})\ (\textit{-i+wēs})\ \left(\textit{-i} \left\{ \begin{array}{l} (\textit{+kon}) \\ (\textit{+peṭṭ}) \end{array} \right\} \right) \end{array} \right. \\ \\ \left\{ \begin{array}{l} (3)\ VB_{1a}\ (+\textit{kon})\ \textit{-i} + \textit{pō} \\ \\ (4)\ VB_{1b}\ \textit{-aN} + \textit{paḍu} \end{array} \right\} \end{array} \right\}$$

Set **(2)** in **[28]** generates only transitive stems and sets **(3)** and **(4)** generate only intransitive stems, which can then be inflected with the optional Modals followed by T-M and g-n-p. VB_{1a} and VB_{1b} are restricted subsets of VB_1 which is a simple verb root in Telugu. The other problem relates to the relative freedom of Permissive ***icc-*** and Obligative ***wāls-*** which can move to the left of some other Modals. This has been dealt with earlier. It is to be noted that there is in Telugu, as in other Dravidian languages, demarcation (which may be fuzzy marginally) between the lexical and modal constituents of complex verbal predicates.

I have not gone into the historical aspects of explicator verbs since this topic needs a full-fledged treatment.

ACKNOWLEDGMENT

I have benefited from my discussion of several aspects of this paper with G. Umamaheswhara Rao and Nozomi Kodama of the Centre for Applied Linguistics and Translation Studies of the University of Hyderabad.

APPENDIX 1

[Diagram: The Combination of a Verb Nucleus (VNc.) with Modal auxiliaries, Tense-Mood (TM), and gender-number-person (g-n-p) in Telugu (Revised from Krishnamurti 1968:13)]

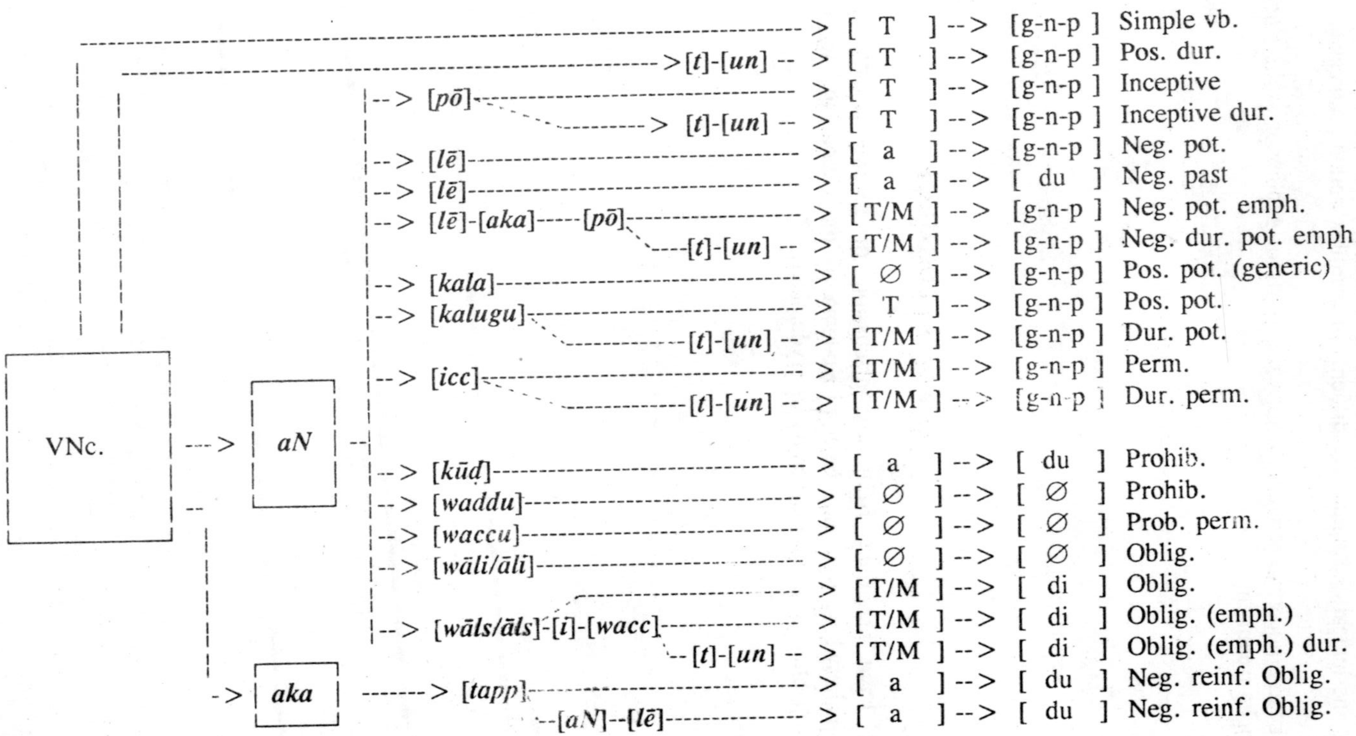

APPENDIX 2

VB_1 = Change-of-state and Change-of-position verbs and VB_2 = ***pō***- 'to go', ***koṭṭ***- 'to hit', ***peṭṭ***- 'to put', and *wēs*- 'to throw' (± = VB_2 co-occurs/does not co-occur).

VB_1	gloss	*(-i)+pō*	*(-aN)+koṭṭ*	*(-aN)+peṭṭ*	*(-aN)+wēs*
aṇugu	'to be flattened'	+	+	–	–
arugu	'to wear out'	+	+	–	–
alus	'to be tired'	+	–	–	–
āgu	'to stop, cease'	+	–	–	–
āru	'to dry'	+	–	+	+
uḍuku	'to get cooked'	+	–	+	–
ūdu	'to get loose'	+	+	–	–
ūdu	'to bloat'	+	–	–	–
**egu*	'to rise'	–	+	–	–
eguru	'to fly'	+	+	–	–
eṇḍu	'to dry up'	+	–	+	–
odugu	'to be contained'	+	–	–	–
orugu	'to slant'	+	–	? +	–
ōḍu	'to be defeated'	+	+	–	–
kadulu	'to move, shake' (intr.)	+	–	–	–
kandu	'to be scorched'	+	–	–	–
karugu	'to melt' (intr.)	+	–	+	+
kalus	'to meet, join' (intr.)	+	–	–	–
kāgu	'to boil' (intr.)	+	–	+	–
kāru	'to leak' (intr.)	+	–	+	–
kālu	'to burn' (intr.)	+	–	+	+
kuduru	'to be arranged, settled'	+	–	–	–
kuḷḷu	'to rot'	+	–	+	–
gaḍuc	'to pass (time)'	+	–	–	–
cacc	'to die'	+	? +	–	–
**can*	'to go, die'	+	–	–	–
cikku	'to become lean'	+	–	–	–
cituku	'to be crushed'	+	+	–	–
cinugu	'to tear' (intr.)	+	+	–	–
cindu	'to spill' (intr.)	+	+	–	–
ciwuku	'to rot'	+	–	+	–
ceḍu	'to go bad'	+	+	–	–
ceduru	'to be scattered'	+	+	–	–
cellu	'to pass off'	+	–	–	–
jaḍus	'to fear'	+	–	–	–

janku	'to hesitate'	+	–	–	–
jarugu	'to move, crawl'	+	–	–	–
taggu	'to abate, reduce'	+	–	–	–
tarugu	'to diminish'	+	–	+	–
tīru	'to be finished'	+	–	–	–
tunugu	'to break'	+	+	–	–
tuḷḷu	'to frisk'	+	–	–	–
tūlu	'to swing'	+	+	–	–
tegu	'to snap'	+	+	–	+
digu	'to descend, go down'	+	+	+	+
doruku	'to be found'	+	–	–	–
dorlu	'to roll'	+	–	–	–
nalugu	'to wear out, crumple'	+	+	–	–
nānu	'to soak'	+	–	+	+
niluc	'to stand, cease'	+	–	+	–
**nil*	'to stand'	–	–	+	+
nerus	'to grey'	+	–	–	–
pagulu	'to break'	+	+	–	+
paḍu	'to drop'	+	+	–	+
paṇḍu	'to ripen'	+	–	+	–
pās	'to rot (food)'	+	–	+	–
pāru	'to flee'	+	–	+	–
**pālu*	'to become pale'	+	–	–	–
pūḍu	'to get filled up'	+	–	–	–
pulus	'to ferment'	+	–	+	–
perugu	'to grow'	+	–	–	–
pēlu	'to explode'	+	+	–	–
pokku	'to blister'	+	–	–	–
pongu	'to boil, bubble up'	+	–	–	–
porlu	'to roll over'	+	–	–	–
pāku	'to crawl'	+	–	–	–
batuku	'to live'	+	–	–	–
balus	'to become fat'	+	–	–	–
bigus	'to be tight'	+	+	–	–
maggu	'to mature'	+	–	+	+
maṇḍu	'to burn'	+	–	+	–
maruc	'to forget'	+	–	–	–
māḍu	'to burn'	+	–	+	–
māru	'to change'	+	–	–	–
mās	'to get soiled'	+	–	+	–
migulu	'to be behind, remain'	+	–	+	–
mincu	'to exceed'	+	–	–	–
mīru	'to go beyond, excel'	+	–	–	–

mukku	'to rot'	+	−	+	−
mugus	'to come to end'	+	−	−	−
munugu	'to drown'	+	−	−	+
murugu	'to smell rotten'	+	−	+	−
murus	'to be joyful'	+	−	−	−
lēc	'to get up'	+	+	−	−
longu	'to surrender'	+	+	−	−
wangu	'to bend'	+	−	+	−
waṇuku	'to shiver'	+	−	−	−
wāc	'to be swollen'	+	+	−	−
wāḍu	'to wither'	+	−	+	−
wālu	'to stoop, perch'	+	−	−	−
****wiḍu***	'to separate'	+	+	−	−
wiccu	'to bloom'	+	−	−	−
weḷḷ	'to go, be out'	+	+	+	−
sāgu	'to move on, extend'	+	+	−	−

REFERENCES

Hook, Peter Edwin. 1974. The compound verb in Hindi. Center for South and Southeast Asian Studies. Ann Arbor: The University of Michigan.

Krishnamurti, Bh. 1961. Telugu verbal bases: A comparative and descriptive study (UCPL 24). Berkeley and Los Angeles: University of California Press.

Krishnamurti, Bh. 1968. Compound verbs in Telugu. Indian Linguistics (Supplement) 27.7-17.

Krishnamurti, Bh. 1969. Konda or Kūbi: A Dravidian language. Hyderabad: Tribal Cultural Research Institute, Government of Andhra Pradesh.

Krishnamurti, Bh. 1970. Stative expressions in Indian languages: Some semantic and syntactic aspects. Paper presented to a Seminar on Regional Universals in Indian Grammar, held at the University of California, Berkeley, 15-23 August 1970, MS., p. 34.

Krishnamurti, Bh. 1971. Causative constructions in Indian languages. Indian Linguistics 32.18-35.

Krishnamurti, Bh. 1975. Verbs of cognition in Telugu. Osmania Papers in Linguistics 1.1-15.

Krishnamurti, Bh., and J. P. L. Gwynn. 1985. A grammar of modern Telugu. Delhi: Oxford University Press.

Masica, Colin P. 1976. Defining a linguistic area: South Asia. Chicago and London: The University of Chicago Press.

Radford, Andrew. 1988. Transformational grammar: A first course. Cambridge: Cambridge University Press.

Steever, Sanford B. 1988. The serial verb formation in the Dravidian languages. Delhi: Motilal Banarsi Dass.

SUBAREAL VARIATION IN CONJUNCT VERBS

Colin P. Masica
University of Chicago

The phenomena now commonly called "Conjunct Verbs" (apparently beginning with Bailey 1950) have attracted the attention of students of Hindi-Urdu since the 19th century (Kellogg's *Grammar*, 1875). In the widest sense, the term refers to combinations of noun or adjective with more or less "empty" verbs such as DO and BECOME which function as lexical equivalents of single verbs in, for example, English: ***shuruu karnaa/shuruu honaa*** = 'begin (tr/intr)'.

There are a number of problems connected with them. For one thing, not all the verbs involved are quite as empty as DO and BECOME: they shade off through GIVE (***dhokaa denaa*** 'deceive') and TAKE (***mol lenaa*** 'purchase') to a few rather highly colored verbs such as BEAT (***laat maarnaa*** 'kick') and EAT (***Thokar khaanaa*** 'stumble'), thereby encroaching, as Kachru 1982 has pointed out, on the area of idioms. For another, as most studies in this century have noted (Platts 1921, Burton-Page 1957, Kachru 1982 -- further investigation must address issues raised by the latter two in particular), such combinations do not behave grammatically all in the same way.

In certain combinations, the noun involved has no grammatical relation to other parts of the sentence -- i.e., does not function as direct object of the verb, and in particular, does not control agreement in the Perfective (e.g., in **[1]** ***usne aaj kaa paaTh yaad kiyaa*** 'He/she learned [memorized] today's lesson', ***kiyaa*** [m.] is not governed by ***yaad*** 'memory' [f.] but rather by ***paaTh*** 'lesson' [m.] which seems to function as the direct object of the whole expression ***yaad kar-*** -- which corresponds to its role in the English equivalent).

In other such combinations, the noun does function as the grammatical object of the verb in the sense that it controls agreement in the Perfective (e.g., in **[2]** ***usne merii paaThyapustak kaa prayog kiyaa*** 'He/she used my textbook', the verb ***kiyaa*** lit. 'did' is governed by ***prayog*** 'use' [m.] and not by the word that corresponds to the English direct object '*textbook*', that is, ***paaThyapustak*** [f.], which is subordinated to ***prayog*** by the genitive particle ***kaa***. [All this may seem to belabor the obvious, but since non-speakers of Hindi at previous meetings of this kind have objected to the assumption that everyone knows Hindi, it may be worth spelling out by way of preliminaries.]

Some combinations are functionally intransitive (in the perhaps trivial sense of translation equivalence) but grammatically transitive (in that they demand the Agentive particle ***-ne*** in the Perfective): **[3]** ***usne [ilaahaabad vishvavidyaalay mẽ] paRhaaii kii*** 'He/she studied [at Allahabad University]' (***kii*** [f.] 'did' agreeing with ***paRhaaii*** [f.] 'study'. Others are both functionally and grammatically intransitive, even while containing (normally) transitive verbs: **[4]** ***vo*** [not ***usne***] ***[hamaare saamne] dikhaaii diyaa*** 'He/it appeared [in front of us]' (***diyaa*** [m.] lit. 'gave' agreeing with ***vo*** 'he/it' and not with ***dikhaaii*** [f.] 'showing'.

Depending on which criteria are taken as crucial, investigators have been led to conclude that some combinations (typically those where the noun-element does not function as the grammatical object) are "true" Conjunct Verbs while others are normal syntactic combinations which merely happen to coincide with single verbs in other languages.

Unfortunately such criteria are not always clear-cut: when the combination involves a masculine noun and takes a personal "object" -- or "indirect object"? -- it is not clear where the agreement lies and therefore which noun is functioning as grammatical object (N-*ko* + N + V-Pfv-masc.sg.: **[5]** ***unhõne aap KO dhokhaa diyaa*** 'They deceived you'). Such structures may also be structurally homonymous on the surface with object + complement constructions (N-*ko* + N + V-Pfv-masc.sg.: **[6]** ***unhõne aap KO mitr banaayaa*** 'They made you a friend = made friends with you'). Perhaps the passivizations and participializations beloved by modern linguists could clarify such cases, but not necessarily [see below].

At the same time it is generally admitted that on a SCALE OF DEFINITENESS the nouns in ALL these Noun-Verb combinations are MAXIMALLY INDEFINITE (see Masica 1986): they cannot, for example, themselves take the definite object marker ***-KO***. Burton-Page 1957, however, tried to explain this as a property of the class of abstract nouns typically involved in these constructions rather than of the construction itself (although not all such nouns are so abstract as to never take ***-KO*** under any circumstances -- e.g. ***kaam*** 'work, task'). Kachru 1982, on the other hand, points out that such nouns can be relativized, which is a kind of definitization: e.g., **[7]** ***aapne raaj kii JO prashansaa kii usse uskaa dimaag caRh gayaa hai***, which she translates as 'Raj has got a swollen head as a result of your praising him'. I would argue that this merely involves exploitation of structural homonymy, much as we can say in English, **[8]** *They praised him, but their praise was insincere.*

Then there are the cases involving combinations of <u>adjective</u> + DO/BECOME: ***band karnaa*** 'close', ***saaf karnaa*** 'clean', ***praapt karnaa*** 'get', ***puraa karnaa*** 'fulfill', ***pasand karnaa*** 'like', etc. A test for identifying "true" Conjunct Verbs invoked by Kachru 1982, what she calls the "past participle modifier rule", turns out to work for all such combinations: i.e. not only **[9]** ***usne gaane pasand kiye*** 'He/she liked the songs' > ***uske pasand kiye hue gaane*** 'the songs liked by him/her' (Kachru 1982:120), but **[10]** ***usne darvaazaa band kiyaa*** 'He/she closed the door' > ***uskaa band kiyaa huaa darvaazaa*** 'the door closed by him', **[11]** ***usne paanii garam kiyaa*** 'He/she heated the water' > ***uskaa garam kiyaa huaa paanii*** 'the water heated by him/her', and **[12]** ***usne mariiz KO acchaa kiyaa*** 'He/she cured the patient' > ***uskaa acchaa kiyaa huaa mariiz*** 'the patient cured by him/her'. The test excludes most Noun + Verb combinations **[13]** ***usne kitaab kii saraahnaa kii*** 'He/she praised the book' > ****uskii saraahnaa kii huii kitaab*** *'the book praised by him/her' (Kachru 1982:120), **[14]** ***usne safar kaa bakhaan kiyaa*** 'He/she described the journey' > ****uskaa bakhaan kiyaa huaa safar*** *'the journey described by him/her' (also apparently ***pyaar karnaa***, listed as a "true" Conjunct Verb by Kachru on unspecified grounds: ****uskii pyaar kii huii baccii*** *'the child loved by him'), while admitting a few: **[15]** ***usne saabun (kaa) istemaal kiyaa*** 'He/she used the soap' > ***uskaa istemaal kiyaa huaa saabun*** 'the soap used by him/her'; **[16]** ***usne sujhaav sviikaar kiyaa*** 'He/she accepted the suggestion' > ***uskaa sviikaar kiyaa huaa sujhaav*** 'the suggestion accepted by him/her'; **[17]** ***usne kitaab mol lii*** 'He/she purchased the book' > ***uskii mol lii huii kitaab*** 'the book purchased by him/her'; **[18]** ***usne zamiin daan dii*** 'He/she made a contribution of land' > ***uskii daan dii huii zamiin*** 'the land contributed by him/her'. (**[19]** ***us aadmii ne dhokhaa khaayaa*** 'That man was deceived' > ***dhokhaa khaayaa huaa aadmii*** 'the man who was deceived' is not quite the same, and raises other questions.)

This is perhaps useful, but do we really want to call e.g. ***acchaa karnaa*** -- and in fact all adjectives capable of causativization or inchoativization (i.e. ***acchaa honaa*** (which may indeed not include ALL adjectives, but is a very large and open class) -- VERBS, and list them in the dictionary? Perhaps the two questions are not the same, as we shall see.

In any case, such matters seem to have attracted the attention of students of other South Asian languages less -- unless hidden behind the opaque titles of subsequent papers in this symposium there lies a new expression of such interest. Indeed it often seems to have been possible to write grammars without discussing Conjunct Verbs at all. (Or barely mentioning them, for example in Newton's *Panjabi Grammar*, 1896, partly modelled on Kellogg.)

Does this mean they do not exist, or are unimportant? Certainly not, at least in the languages I have looked at. Some of the tests that have been proposed for true conjunctivity in the context of Hindi-Urdu, such as the participial modifier test, may have to be modified in view of the fact that in some languages (Dravidian languages, apparently in certain contexts also in Marathi -- perhaps Rajeshwariji will have something to say about this later -- one should look also at Oriya and Sinhala) such participial modifiers can be either active or passive in sense.

What I could not help noticing is also -- and this was going to be the focus of my paper -- was that the distribution of constructional types is different: e.g., the same "transitive" combination that in Hindi-Urdu takes its Patient argument as a Genitive dependent on its incorporated noun, in another language may take it as a straightforward (Dative)-Accusative:

[20] (H.) ***merii sahaaytaa karo*** 'Help me'
[21] (U.) ***merii madad karo*** 'Help me'
[22] (G.) ***ma<u>ne</u> sahaay karo*** 'Help me'
[23] (M.) ***mal<u>aa</u> saahaayya karaa*** 'Help me'
[24] (B.) ***ama<u>ke</u> shahajjo kOro*** 'Help me'
[25] (Tel.) ***naa<u>ku</u> saayam ceeyaNDI*** 'Help me'

This isn't always the pattern: sometimes OTHER languages have a Genitive argument while Hindi-Urdu takes it in some other case (such as "Instrumental" ***-SE***), or some languages (e.g. Gujarati, or Gujarati-Marathi, or Bengali) will agree with Hindi-Urdu in having a Genitive opposed to Accusative or other marking in other languages.

What the actual areal pattern is, if any, cannot be determined without extensive statistical work, which I have been unable to pull off in the time available to me, but what preliminary indications led me to suspect was that the Genitive construction is more predominant in

Hindi-Urdu, probably on the model of Persian, which may be the source of this pattern according to Bahri 1960 (see also Kachru 1982). This, however, would raise another question. If "true" Conjuncts are those that do not use this construction, and these are more common in the languages at a distance from Hindi-Urdu, we have an anomaly, in that Conjunct Verbs as such ("true" or "false") do seem to be more numerous in Hindi-Urdu -- just as, according to Kachru, they are still more numerous in Persian.[1] (I suspect also that they may be more frequent in Urdu than in Hindi.) We would have to declare that the language(s) which in fact has the most Conjunct Verbs has the least, which however acceptable and true in one purely formal sense, may well fly in the face of history.

There is also the matter of direct morphological derivation of verbs from nouns, often parallel to the "Conjunct" forms. Thus we have in Hindi ***sviikaarnaa*** 'accept' alongside ***sviikaar karnaa***, and ***saraahnaa*** 'praise' alongside ***saraahnaa karnaa***. The former method -- which I suspect is earlier -- appears to increase as we move southward, and in fact predominates in Telugu and probably in Marathi (in the former using the "causative" suffix ***-inću***), although these languages do have so-called compounds with DO also:

[26]

Hindi	Gujarati	Marathi	Telugu	
inkaar kar-	***nakaar kar-***	***naakaari-***	--	'deny'
prem kar-	***prem raakh-***	***priiti kar-***	***preeminć-***	'love'
bair kar-	***dveS kar-***	***dveS kar-***	***dveeSinć-***	'hate'
prayatn kar-	***prayatn kar-***	***prayatn kar-***	***prayatninć-***	'try'
aarambh kar-	***aarambh-***	***aarambh-***	***aarambhinć-***	'begin'

My point is not call forms like ***naakaarine*** or ***prayatninćaDam*** "Conjunct Verbs" but to suggest that both types are obviously means of deriving verbs from nouns -- the same nouns -- one perhaps more "analytic" in keeping with the analytic tendency of Hindi-Urdu especially, and need to be noted as such in the lexicon despite this difference and any differences in the grammatical construction of their arguments, which is a matter of secondary detail. The transition to the analytic formation in Hindi-Urdu may have been aided not only by the Persian model but by contamination with the conjunctive participle in ***-kar*** (e.g. ***sviikaarnaa*** 'to praise' > ***sviikaar kar-*** 'having praised' > ***sviikaar karnaa***!).

NOTES

[1]They are the normal way of verbalizing the numerous Arabic loans (nouns, and especially participial adjectives) in that language. "Compounds" (or lexicalized combinations) consisting of borrowed Chinese nouns and the verb DO (Jap. ***suru***, Kor. ***hada***) are also very numerous in and characteristic of Japanese and Korean: 'to study' = Jap. ***benkyoo suru***, Kor. ***kongbu hada***. On the basis of this inadequate sample of languages (i.e. Hindi-Urdu, Bengali, Persian, Japanese, Korean) one might be tempted to leap to the conclusion that this device is normative for languages with a heavy admixture of borrowed vocabulary. That, however, is belied by other South Asian languages such as Marathi and Telugu (and Dravidian languages generally), which rely more heavily on other devices (suffixation, etc.) -- as does that other well-known mixed language, English. Borrowed vocabulary, we might then say, seems to be a necessary but insufficient cause of conjunct verb formation. Something else is required also -- or perhaps the absence of something else, such as a ready capacity for suffixation. On the other hand, it is also very characteristic of Turkish [Lewis 1967:154], which does have such a capacity. (Turk. ***kabul etmek*** 'to accept' = Urdu ***qabuul karnaa***, Turk. ***organize etmek*** = Urdu ***"organize" karnaa***, etc.) The mystery deepens!

REFERENCES

Bahri, Hardev. 1960. Persian influence on Hindi. Allahabad: Bharati Press Publications.

Bailey, T. Grahame. 1950. Teach yourself Hindustani. London: English Universities Press.

Burton-Page, J. 1957. Compound and conjunct verbs in Hindi. Bulletin of the School of Oriental and African Studies 19.469-78.

Kachru, Yamuna. 1982. Conjunct verbs in Hindi-Urdu and Persian. South Asian review: studies in South Asian languages & linguistics, ed. by P. J. Mistry. (SALA Journal, 6:3.) 117-26. Jacksonville, FL: South Asian Literary Association.

Kellogg, Rev. S. H. 1938 (1875, 1892). A grammar of the Hindi language. 3rd edn. London: Kegan Paul, Trench, Trubner and Co., Ltd.

Lewis, G. L. 1967. Turkish grammar. Oxford University Press.

Masica, Colin P. 1986. Definiteness-marking in South Asian languages. South Asian languages: structure, convergence and diglossia, ed. by Bh. Krishnamurti, 123-46. Delhi: Motilal Banarsidass.

Newton, E. P. 1896. Panjabi grammar. Sialkot: Mission press. [Repr. as first part of Panjabi manual and grammars, Patiala: Languages Department, Punjab, 1961.]

Platts, J. T. 1921. A grammar of the Hindustani or Urdu language. London.

VERB AGREEMENT IN COMPLEX PREDICATES IN HINDI*

Tara Mohanan
Stanford University

Verb agreement in complex predicate constructions in Hindi is both descriptively and theoretically extremely puzzling. The sentences in **[1]** illustrate the well-known facts:[1]

[1] **a.** ***ilaa-ne mohan-par b^harosaa kiyaa.***
Ila-E Mohan-L trust-N (M) do-PA-M
Ila depended on Mohan.

b. ***ilaa-ne mohan-par kṛpaa kii.***
Ila-E Mohan-L favour-N (F) do-PA-F
Ila showed favour to Mohan.

With respect to a number of syntactic phenomena, the noun + verb (henceforth N+V) sequences in **[1]**, ***b^harosaa kar*** 'to trust', and ***kṛpaa kar*** 'to show favour / kindness', function as single predicates (hence COMPLEX PREDICATES (henceforth CP'S)). Furthermore, the noun in a CP, as we will see shortly, is a predicate in its own right. Nevertheless, the verb ***kar*** 'do' in **[1]** agrees with the nouns ***b^harosaa*** 'trust' and ***kṛpaa*** 'kindness'; these nouns must therefore be arguments of the verb.[2] We thus find a baffling situation: A PREDICATE AGREES WITH ONE OF ITS PARTS. The N in a CP, therefore, is simultaneously a PREDICATE as well as an ARGUMENT.[3]

The primary aim of this paper is to provide a way of representing the structure of CP'S that leads to an account of this puzzle. **§1** briefly sketches some of the factors relevant for establishing that (i) a CP functions as a single predicate, and (ii) the N in a CP is a predicate. **§2** is devoted to an analysis of the facts of verb agreement in CP'S, and to establishing the argumenthood of the N.

Because a substantial portion of the semantic burden in an N+V CP is borne by the N, the V in a CP has been referred to as a LIGHT VERB (Jespersen 1954, Cattell 1984, Grimshaw & Mester 1988, and others).[4] And the element that the light verb combines with to form a CP has been called the HOST. This is the terminology I adopt to refer to the parts that compose a CP.[5]

1. Predicatehood

1.1. The Structure of Complex Predicates[6]

A light verb and its host together exhibit a certain integrity that cannot be violated: they act like a single predicate. Thus, in coordination, although a noun and a verb can each be gapped alone, if the conjuncts are CP constructions, neither the N alone nor the V alone can be gapped. Further, a null pronominal, which is allowed in Hindi in all argument positions, cannot occur in the position of the nominal host in a CP. In other words, if part of a CP is overtly expressed, the entire CP must be expressed.

Although a CP is a single predicate, we find that it could not be a single lexical unit. The independent word ***nahīĩ*** 'no / not' can intervene between the N and the V. Also, the V may occur in clause initial position, separated from the N by the subject and other phrases, for special discourse effects. Therefore, the parts of a CP must be phrasally concatenated.

Unlike the other arguments of a verb, the N in a CP is not free to "scramble". If we assume that Hindi has a phrase structure representation such that the subject, object, and verb are direct sisters, it can be independently shown that all and only the daughters of S can scramble. Word order then tells us that the N in a CP is not a direct daughter of S, but forms a phrasal constituent with the V.

Finally, the nominal host in a CP does not yield *wh*-questions, allows no modification, adjectival or otherwise, does not participate in relativization, and cannot be conjoined. These facts follow naturally if we assume that the nominal host of a light verb is a lexical category.

In short, then, complex predicates act as single predicates, they must be phrasally concatenated, and must be single phrase structure constituents. The nominal in a complex predicate, moreover, must be a lexical category. In the light of these generalizations, a tentative skeletal structure of the N+V CP in **[1a]** may be given as in **[2]**:

[2]

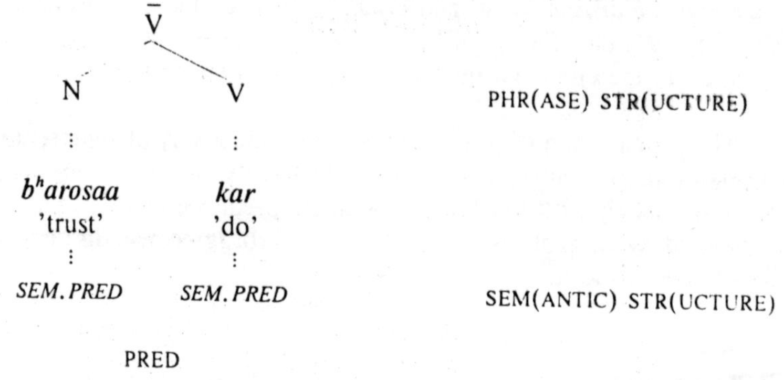

The dotted lines indicate the linking of, or association between, different dimensions of structure, as opposed to the solid lines that indicate constituency. The structure will become clearer as we proceed.

1.2. The Nominal Host as a Predicate: its Linking Properties

Let us now examine in greater detail the LINKING in complex predicates. Linking here implies roughly the matching up of different types of information about the arguments of these predicates, namely, their semantics, their grammatical functions such as subject and object, and their overt expression in terms of case marking, word order, and the like.[7]

Consider **[3]** and **[4]** below:

[3] a. *raam-ne apnaa homwark kiyaa.*
Ram-E self's homework-N do-PA
Ram did his homework.

b. *niinaa-ne raam-ko kitaab dii.*
Nina-E Ram-D book-N give-PA
Nina gave Ram a book.

[4] a. *raam-ne kahaanii yaad kii.*
Ram-E story-N remembrance-N do-PA
Ram recalled / memorized the story.

b. *niinaa-ne raam-kii kahaanii-par d^hyaan diyaa.*
Nina-E Ram-G story-L attention-N give-PA
Nina paid attention to Ram's story.

In **[3a]**, we have a doer, Ram, and the done thing, the homework. Likewise in **[4a]**, where the done thing is the act of recalling / memorizing. But in **[4a]** there is a third argument, ***kahaanii*** 'story', which could not have been sanctioned by the verb ***kar*** 'do', because it is diadic. The only plausible account for this argument, then, is that it is sanctioned by the noun ***yaad*** 'remembrance'. In that event, ***yaad kar*** 'recall' must be a complex predicate, taking ***raam*** and ***kahaanii*** as its arguments.

Similarly, **[4b]** has a giver, Nina, a givee, Ram's story, and a given thing, attention, exactly as in **[3b]**. Now, goals in Hindi are normally encoded with the dative ***-ko***, as in **[3b]**. The givee in **[4b]**, however, is marked with the locative ***-par*** 'on'. The verb ***de*** 'give' does not sanction this case. We must assume, therefore, that it is sanctioned by the noun ***d^hyaan*** 'attention'. Under the assumption that the case marking of an argument systematically correlates with its meaning, the argument meaning must also be contributed by the noun ***d^hyaan***.

Thus, the differences between **[3]** and **[4]** in valency, meaning, and case marking can be accounted for if we assume that the sentences in **[4]** are CP constructions. In short, the nominal host of a light verb has the capacity to be an active part of a predicate. It contributes to (a) the number of arguments (valency), (b) the argument meanings (roughly, THETA ROLES), and (c) the overt expression (case marking) of the arguments within the clause. These, which we call the linking properties of complex predicatehood, may be viewed as the uncontroversial overt symptoms of complex predicatehood.[8]

Now, although the semantic and syntactic properties of the light verb in a CP are not identical to those of its full counterpart, it is clear that there is a systematic synchronic relation between the two, which needs to studied and precisely characterized. One way of formally expressing this relation is on the basis of the assumption that THE STRUCTURE OF THE LIGHT VERB IS A PROPER SUBSTRUCTURE OF THE STRUCTURE OF THE FULL VERB. I will adopt this assumption here without trying to defend it.[9]

In order to understand how a nominal host contributes to the valency and argument meanings of a CP, it is useful to separate these two aspects of structure. The former can be represented as ARG(UMENT) STR(UCTURE), and the latter as being part of the SEM(ANTIC) STR(UCTURE). These two types of information carried by the FULL verb ***kar*** 'do' and by the predicative nominal ***yaad*** 'remembrance' in **[4a]** can be tentatively schematized as in **[5]** and **[6]** respectively:[10]

[5] ['doer' 'done thing'] *DO* SEM STR
⋮ ⋮ ⋮
⟨ ARG$_1$ ARG$_2$ ⟩ PRED ARG STR

[6] ['cognizer' 'cognized'] *REMEMBRANCE* SEM STR
⋮ ⋮ ⋮
⟨ ARG$_1$ ARG$_2$ ⟩ PRED ARG STR

In **[7]**, we put together the information in **[5]** and **[6]** to derive the representation of the complex predicate ***yaad kar*** 'recall':

[7] ['doer' 'done thing'] *DO*
| |
['cognizer' 'cognized'] *REMEMBRANCE* SEM STR
⋮ ⋮ ⋮
⋮ ⋮ ⋮
⟨ ARG$_1$ ARG$_3$ ARG$_2$ ⟩ PRED ARG STR

In short, the syntactic predicate at the level of argument structure has three arguments. Corresponding to it are two semantic predicates, *DO* and *REMEMBRANCE*, each of which has two semantic participants. Let us now put together, in **[8]**, the information in **[7]** and in **[2]**, replacing the nominal ***bʰarosaa*** 'trust' in **[2]** with the nominal ***yaad*** 'remembrance':

[8]

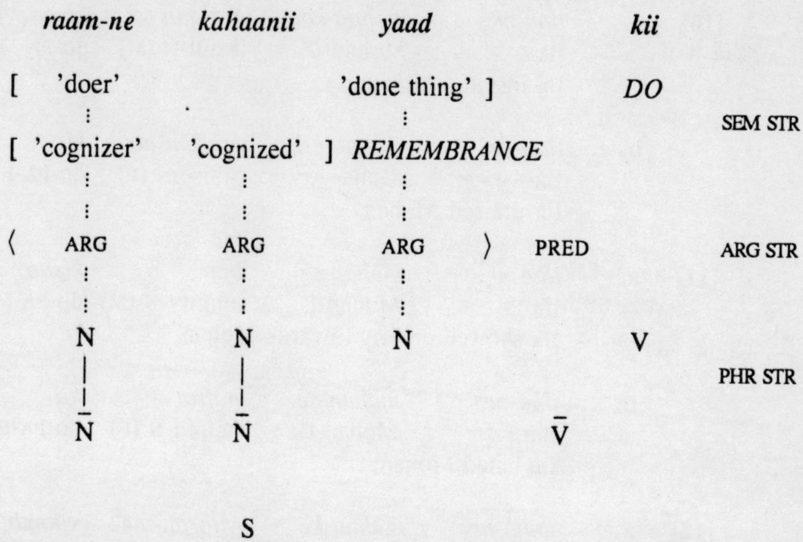

In the representation in **[8]**, the nominal host *yaad* is a lexical category, an independent semantic predicate contributing to the predicate argument structure, as well as part of the complex syntactic predicate in ARG STR. It forms a constituent with the light verb in PHR STR. However, this nominal host (as also in **[6]** and **[7]**) is also an ARG in ARG STR. We have seen that it is a predicate. In the following section, we provide evidence for its argumenthood.

2. Agreement and Argumenthood

2.1. Agreement

We now return to our original puzzle, that of agreement in CP'S. In a CP construction, if the subject is not nominative, and there is no other nominative argument in the clause, the light verb may agree with its nominal host, as in **[1a,b]**. Consider the examples in **[9]** - **[12]**, all with the same verb ***kar*** 'do'. The verb in **[9a,b]** agrees with the nominative subject. When the subject is not nominative, agreement shifts to the nominal in the CP in **[10]** - **[12]**. The difference between **[a]** and **[b]** in each of these pairs is in the gender of the host nominal, and consequently, in the verb agreement:

[9]	**a.**	*raam*	*mohan-kaa*	*apmaan*	***karegaa.***
		Ram-N (M)	Mohan-G	insult-N (M)	do-FU-M
		Ram will insult Mohan.			
	b.	*ilaa*	*mohan-kaa*	*apmaan*	***karegii.***
		Ila-N (F)	Mohan-G	insult-N (M)	do-FU-F
		Ila will insult Mohan.			

[10]	a.	*ilaa-ne*	*mohan-kaa*	*apmaan*	***kiyaa.***
		Ila-E	Mohan-G	insult-N (M)	do-PA-M
		Ila insulted Mohan.			
	b.	*ilaa-ne*	*mohan-kii*	***prašamsaa***	***kii.***
		Ila-E	Mohan-G	praise-N (F)	do-PA-F
		Ila praised Mohan.			
[11]	a.	*ilaa-ne*	*mohan-se*	*bair*	***kiyaa.***
		Ila-E	Mohan-I	enmity-N (M)	do-PA-M
		Ila showed enmity towards Mohan.			
	b.	*ilaa-ne*	*mohan-se*	*nafrat*	***kii.***
		Ila-E	Mohan-I	hatred-N (F)	do-PA-F
		Ila hated Mohan.			

[12]	a.	*unhõ-ne*	*gẽhuu-ke*	*vitaraṇ-mẽ*	*vilamb*	***kiyaa.***
		they-E	wheat-G	distribution-L	delay-N (M)	do-PA-M
		They delayed (too much) the distribution of wheat.				
	b.	*unhõ-ne*	*gẽhuu-ke*	*utpaadan-mẽ*	*pragati*	***kii.***
		they-E	wheat-G	production-L	progress-N (F)	do-PA-F
		They showed progress in the production of wheat.				

In all of the pairs in **[10]** - **[12]**, the verb agrees with its nominal host. Now we said in §**1** that the syntactic predicate of the clauses in **[9]** - **[12]** is the complex predicate, that is, ***apmaan kar***, ***prašamsaa kar***, etc. The facts of agreement, then, must be interpreted to mean that A SYNTACTIC PREDICATE MAY AGREE WITH AN ELEMENT INTERNAL TO ITSELF. This may appear to be a somewhat unusual conclusion. However, it is perfectly natural given the type of representation in **[8]**.

To repeat the facts of agreement in Hindi: a verb in Hindi agrees with a nominative subject, in the absence of which it agrees with a nominative object, and if it has neither a nominative subject nor a nominative object, it registers default agreement, which is masculine singular. Under the assumption implicit in this statement that what a verb agrees with is one of its arguments, the nominal host must also be an argument. Further, it must be either the grammatical subject or the primary object of the clause. Given that it is not the subject, it must be the primary object.

Thus, the sentence in **[1a]** must have two different structures:

[13] a. [*ilaa-ne*] [*mohan-par*] [*b*^{h}*arosaa* *kiyaa*]

b. [*ilaa-ne*] [*mohan-par*] [*b*^{h}*arosaa*] [*kiyaa*]

[13a] is the structure required by the phenomena discussed in §1, and **[14b]** the one needed for agreement. In fact, this duality is already expressed in the type of representation illustrated earlier in **[7]** - **[8]**. The structure of **[1a]** along the lines built up in **[7]** and **[8]** is given in **[14]**, with the additional information that the nominal host bears the argument function OBJ(ECT), represented in G(RAMMATICAL) **F**(UNCTION) **STR**(UCTURE):

[14]

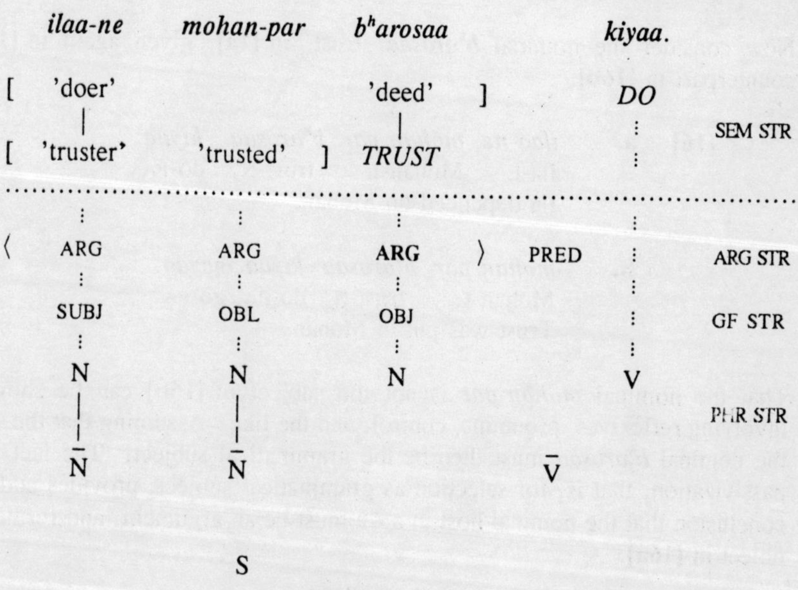

In **[14]** again, there are two semantic predicates at the level of SEM STR, each with two participants. There is a single syntactic predicate at the level of ARG STR, with three arguments, corresponding to **[13b]**. The nominal semantic predicate, which is both an ARG and part of the PRED in ARG STR is the OBJ in GF STR, with which the light verb agrees. In PHR STR, the nominal host which is an N is dominated by a V̄, and forms a phrasal constituent with the light verb, as in **[13a]**. In this representation, thus, the nominal host of a light verb is transparently thus a semantic predicate, part of the syntactic predicate and of verbal element in phrase structure, as well as an argument of a predicate.

2.2. Passivization

The agreement facts motivated the status of the nominal host in a CP as an argument and an object. Their argumenthood and objecthood is further endorsed by the facts of passivization. The primary object of the active sentence in **[15a]** alternates with the subject of the passive in **[15b]**:

[15] **a.** ***niinaa-ne raam-ko kitaab dii.***
Nina-E Ram-D book-N give-PA
Nina gave the book to Ram.

b. ***kitaab raam-ko dii gayii.***
book-N Ram-D give-PA go-PA
The book was given to Ram.

Now consider the nominal ***bʰarosaa*** 'trust' in **[1a]**, given again in **[16a]**, and its passive counterpart in **[16b]**:

[16] **a.** ***ilaa-ne mohan-par bʰarosaa kiyaa.***
Ila-E Mohan-L trust-N do-PA
Ila depended on Mohan.

b. ***mohan-par bʰarosaa kiyaa gayaa.***
Mohan-L trust-N do-PA go-PA
Trust was put in Mohan.

That the nominal ***mohan-par*** is not the subject of **[16b]** can be shown with various tests involving reflexives, pronouns, control, and the like. Assuming that the sentence has a subject, the nominal ***bʰarosaa*** must then be the grammatical subject. The fact that it is available for passivization, that is, for selection as grammatical subject, provides additional support for the conclusion that the nominal host in a CP must be an argument, and furthermore, a grammatical object in **[16a]**.

2.3. Absence of Agreement: an apparent anomaly

We have assumed in our discussion that a light verb can agree with its nominal hosts. There are, however, a few exceptions, often considered idiosyncratic, or even a separate class of complex predicates (Bailey 1956). Instances of the failure of agreement are given in **[17]**:

[17] a. *ilaa-ne* *mohan-ko* ***pasand*** *kiyaa.*
Ila-E Mohan-A approval-N (M) do-PA-M
Ila approved of Mohan.

b. *ilaa-ne* *mohan-ko* ***yaad*** *kiyaa.*
Ila-E Mohan-A remembrance-N (F) do-PA-M
Ila remembered Mohan.

c. *ilaa-ne* *mohan-ko* ***kṣamaa*** *kiyaa.*
Ila-E Mohan-I forgiveness-N (F) do-PA-M
Ila pardoned Mohan.

In the sentences in **[17]**, the only nominative elements are the CP internal nominals. Each of them is feminine, and yet, the light verb bears masculine marking. That the nominal hosts are indeed feminine is established by the genitive agreement in **[18]**:

[18] a. ***bacce-kii*** ***yaad*** ***mãã-ko*** ***sataatii*** ***tʰii.***
child-G-F remembrance-N mother-D torment-HAB be-PA
The remembrance of the child used to torment the mother.

b. ***mãĩ*** ***aapkii*** ***kṣamaa*** ***caahtaa*** ***hũũ.***
I-N you-G-F forgiveness-N desire-HAB be-PR
I wish for your forgiveness.

The question is, why does the light verb not agree with the nominal hosts in **[18]**. The answer, I suggest, lies in the argument functions of the other nominals in the sentences. Notice that failure of agreement systematically correlates with the case marking on the second participant of the nominal predicate, which is either accusative, as in **[17]** (***mohan-ko***), or nominative as in **[19]** below. It is worth noting that primary objects in Hindi are always either accusative or nominative, and only primary objects exhibit an accusative ~ nominative case alternation.

[19] a. ***ilaa-ne*** ***kissaa*** ***yaad*** ***kiyaa.***
Ila-E incident-N (M) remembrance-N (F) do-PA-M
Ila remembered the incident.

b. ***ilaa-ne*** ***kahaanii*** ***yaad*** ***kii.*** (=[4a])
Ila-E story-N (F) remembrance-N (F) do-PA-F
Ila remembered the story.

When it is nominative, as in **[19]**, the light verb agrees with it, showing that it is either the subject or the object. Given that *Ila* in **[19]** is the subject, ***kissaa*** and ***kahaanii*** must be the objects. And if they are the objects, then ***yaad*** cannot also be the object. Assuming that agreement in Hindi is restricted to subjects and primary objects, it follows that the light verb in **[19]** cannot agree with ***yaad***. Thus, if the second participant of the nominal predicate is accusative / nominative (**[17]**, **[19]**), the light verb agrees with that argument and cannot agree with its host. In all other instances (**[1]**, **[10]** - **[12]**), the light verb agrees with its host as long as the subject is not nominative.

The question remains why the second participant of some nominal predicates is the grammatical object, and not of others. This, I suggest, must derive from the semantic relation between the nominal predicate and its participants. In order to characterize this relation, let me appeal to the intuitive notion of LOGICAL TRANSITIVITY.[11] In order to understand this notion, consider the sentence *John received a book*, which is ambiguous between John's being the agent of receiving, and John's being merely a goal. Although the sentence is grammatically transitive, only with the former reading is it logically transitive. Now, just as grammatical transitivity requires the presence of a grammatical object, logical transitivity requires the presence of a LOGICAL OBJECT. Only in the former reading of the above sentence is the book a logical object.

In complex predicates, if the nominal predicate is logically transitive, and its second participant is a logical object, this object is selected as the grammatical object of the complex predicate. The nominal hosts ***yaad*** 'remembrance', ***pasand*** 'approval', and ***kṣamaa*** 'forgiveness' all involve logical objects, which are realized as grammatical objects. These hosts themselves are thus precluded from being realized as grammatical objects, and hence from inducing verb agreement. In contrast, nominal hosts like ***b^{h}arosaa*** 'trust', ***bair*** 'enmity', and ***vilamb*** 'delay' are not logically transitive; nothing prevents these nominals from being realized as grammatical objects, and inducing verb agreement.

To conclude, a light verb and its nominal host exhibit a certain duality of behavior in that, while they behave like a single predicative "word" for some purposes, they behave like independent words for other purposes. Another duality of complex predicates is that the nominal host is simultaneously a predicate that contributes to the valency and argument meanings of the clause, as well as an argument that the light verb may agree with. Both these dualities are captured in the representations we have tried to develop.

Not all nominal hosts in a complex predicate can induce verb agreement. We explained the presence or absence of agreement in terms of its systematic correlation with the logical transitivity of the nominal host. If the host is logically transitive, its logical object is the grammatical object, and the verb cannot agree with the host. If, on the other hand, it is not logically transitive, the host itself is the grammatical object, and the light verb agrees with it.

NOTES

* I am indebted to Joan Bresnan, Paul Kiparsky, K. P. Mohanan, and Peter Sells, for their invaluable advice and comments on earlier versions of this work. I have benefited a great deal from presenting more detailed versions of this paper in the Indian Linguistics class at Stanford in spring 1989, and in the Department of Linguistics at the State University of New York at Stonybrook.

1. For a detailed review of previous work on complex predicates, see Bahl 1974.

2. This agreement is clearly agreement between a verb and one of its arguments (not between parts of a predicate) because, if the subject is nominative, the verb agrees with the subject, not with the N in the CP.

3. Since the puzzle is naturally restricted to complex predicates containing nominals, we are concerned exclusively with N+V CP'S. Some of the generalizations about CP'S discussed here, however, are perhaps true of other types of CP'S as well.

4. Gilchrist (1796) called them "subservient" verbs.

5. In a sense, the relation between ***bʰarosaa*** 'trust' and ***bʰarosaa kar*** 'to trust' is analogous to the relation between ***glory*** and ***glorify*** in English. This is the analogy reflected in the use of the term HOST (in the structure stem+affix, the stem is the host).

6. Given that the focus of this paper is verb agreement in CP'S, this section is necessarily brief. For detailed arguments for the generalizations summarized in this section, see T. Mohanan 1989, and the references therein.

7. In Levin 1987, Bresnan and Kanerva 1989, and related works, the focus of LINKING is the association between thematic roles and grammatical functions. LINKING in Hale 1983 also refers to the relation between LEXICAL STRUCTURE (i.e. the structure that expresses grammatical functions) and PHRASE STRUCTURE. In Kiparsky 1987, it is claimed to be the association between thematic roles and their MORPHOSYNTACTIC REALIZATION.

8. The generalizations stated in **§1.1.** may be used as diagnostics, in unclear instances, to distinguish N+V sequences that are CP'S from those that are not.

9. Also see K. P. Mohanan, The compositionality of complex predicates in Malayalam. [See References.]

10. The labels used in the SEM STR are crude mnemonic devices, resorted to for lack of more abstract structures, and also because they are convenient, and not opaque. The subscripts on the two ARG'S in ARG(UMENT) STR indicate their relative prominence on the "thematic hierarchy".

11. I am grateful to Joan Bresnan for suggesting this notion for explaining the concept of logical objecthood.

REFERENCES

Bahl, K. C. 1974. Studies in the semantic structure of Hindi. India: Motilal Banarsidass.

Bailey, T. G. 1956. Teach yourself Urdu. J. R. Firth & A. H. Harley, eds. London.

Bresnan, J., and J. Kanerva. 1989. Locative inversion in Chichewa: A case study of factorization in grammar. Linguistic Inquiry 20:1.1-50.

Cattell, R. 1984. Composite predicates in English. North Ryde, New South Wales: Academic Press Australia.

Gilchrist, J. B. 1796. A grammar of the Hindustani language. Calcutta. [Repr. Menston: The Solar Press Limited, 1970.]

Grimshaw, J., and A. Mester. 1988. Light verbs and θ-marking. Linguistic Inquiry 19:2.205-32.

Hale, K. 1983. Walpiri and the grammar of non-configurational languages. Natural Language and Linguistic Theory 1:1.5-47.

Jespersen, O. 1954. A modern English grammar on historic principles. London and Copenhagen: George Allen and Unwin, and Ejnar Munksgaard.

Kiparsky, P. 1987. Morphology and grammatical relations. Stanford, California: Stanford University, MS.

Levin, L. 1987. Toward a linking theory of relation changing rule in LFG. (CSLI Report No. CSLI-87-115, November 1987.) Stanford, California: Center for the Study of Language and Information.

Mohanan, K. P. 1989. The compositionality of complex predicates in Malayalam. Paper read at the South Asian Languages Roundtable - XI, University of Wisconsin-Madison, 2-4 June 1989.

Mohanan, T. To Appear. Grammatical subjecthood in Hindi. Papers on argument structure, ed. by A. Zaenen. Stanford, California: Stanford University CSLI Publications.

SERIAL VERB CONSTRUCTION IN MARATHI

Rajeshwari Pandharipande
University of Illinois at Urbana-Champaign

1. Introduction

Serial verb construction (SVC hereafter) in Marathi has been discussed in traditional grammars (e.g. Damle 1911, etc.), typological studies (Kachru and Pandharipande 1980, and Masica 1976), and in Pandharipande 1989. However, a number of basic and important issues remain unresolved till today: [a] does Marathi have a SVC? (the issue of defining the status of SVC in Marathi), [b] why does SVC in Marathi have split properties, i.e., why does it share morphological, syntactic, and semantic properties with other (non-SVC) constructions in the language?, and [c] what are the constraints on the compatibility (pairing) of the verbs in SVC.

This paper attempts to resolve the above issues. The major claim of the paper is that in order to resolve the above issues it is necessary to take into account first the mechanism of the derivation of SVC and secondly to examine the morphological, syntactic, semantic, and pragmatic properties of SVC in Marathi.

2. SVC in Marathi

First, I will illustrate the SVC construction in Marathi and then argue that it has to be treated as a SVC as opposed to either a compound verb construction (CVC hereafter) or a verb + auxiliary construction.

A SVC in Marathi, similar to SVC verbs in other Indian and African languages, typically involves a sequence of a verb (V_1) + verb (V_2), in which V_1 has generally been called the main verb, while the V_2 has been called an explicator (since it explicates/extends the meaning of the V_1). The most frequently used explicators in Marathi (see Damle 1911) are listed in **[1]**. The explicator verbs include both transitive and intransitive verbs and can follow both transitive and intransitive main verbs (see **[1]** below).

[1] Serial verb = main verb (V_1) + explicator (V_2)
stem + ***ūn***

Explicator Verbs:	General meaning:
[a] ***de*** 'give' (tr.)	[action performed for someone other than the agent]
[b] ***ghe*** 'take' (tr.)	[for agent]
[c] ***ṭāk*** 'deep' (tr.)	[to get rid of]
[d] ***bas*** 'sit' (intr.)	[inadvertently]
[e] ***dzā*** 'go' (intr.)	[by mistake, action away from the agent/speaker]
[f] ***ye*** 'come' (intr.)	[action toward agent]

[g] ***kāḍh*** 'draw' (tr.) ['draw' to the last point]
[h] ***soḍ*** 'leave' (tr.) ['leave' at the point, of completion]
[i] ***bagh*** 'see' (tr.) [try]
[j] ***ṭhev*** 'keep' (tr.) [completion of an action]

[2] Examples:

[i] ***karūn de*** 'to {do / work} for someone other than the agent of the action'
do give

[ii] ***karūn ghe*** 'to {do / work} for the agent of the action'
do take

[iii] ***bolūn bas*** 'to say inadvertently'

[iv] ***raḍūn ghe*** 'to cry for oneself'

2.1 Morphology of SVC

In a SVC, V_1 consists of a stem + the suffix ***-ūn*** which it commonly shares with the V_1 in the conjunctive participle construction (see examples **[3]**, **[4]**, and **[5]**). V_1 has the invariant stem form. V_2 takes all markers of tense, aspect, and agreement. Consider examples **[3]** and **[4]** where the form of V_1 ***karūn*** **[3]** and ***bolūn*** **[4]** remains unchanged, while the explicator verbs ***ṭāk*** **[3]** and ***gelā*** **[4]** respectively, take the markers of agreement, tense, and aspect. The question is whether it is merely by accident that the suffix ***ūn*** on V_1 is homophonous with the suffix on V_1 in the conjunctive participle construction, or whether the SVC shares some other features with the conjunctive participle construction.

Examples:

[3] ***tū he kām karūn ṭāk***
you this work do drop
2p.sg.Imp.
Get this work done.

[4] ***Madhū he bolūn gelā***
Madhū this say went
3p.sg.mas.
Madhū said this (inadvertently).

[5] ***Madhū he bolūn gharī gelā***
Madhū this having said home went
3p.sg.mas.
Having said this, Madhū went home.

Note the suffix *-ūn* on V_1, and the tense and agreement markers on V_2.

In Marathi there are V + V sequences other than the type discussed above. The question is whether all of them qualify as SVC, and more importantly, what the criterion is for determining a V + V sequence to be a SVC.

Let us consider the following V + V sequences:

[6] V + ***śak -ṇe*** 'to be able to'
(can)

[7] V (imperf.) + ***as -ṇe*** 'habitual action (i.e. to habitually perform an action)'
(to be)

[8] V (imperf.) + ***rāh -ṇe*** 'continuous action' (i.e. to keep doing an action)'
(remain)

[9] V (imperf.) + ***dzā -ṇe*** 'habitual/repeated/regular action (i.e. to perform an action habitually/repeatedly/regularly)'
(go)

The following examples **[6a]** - **[9a]** illustrate the use of V + sequences in **[6]** - **[9]**.

[6a] ***to he kām karū śakto***
he this work do can
He can do this work.

[7a] ***mī he gāṇa mhaṇat ase***
I this song sing used to
I used to sing this song.

[8a] ***to te gāṇa mhaṇat rāhilā-tyātsā artha na samadztā***
he that song sing kept on - its meaning not understanding
He kept on singing that song without understanding its meaning.

[9a] ***tū hirvyā bhādʒyā khāt dzā mhanḍʒe tuḍʒʰī tabyet tsānglī hoīl***
you green vegetable eat regularly then your health good will be
Eat green vegetables regularly, then your health will improve (literally, will be good).

Note that morphologically, the verbs in **[6a]** - **[9a]** can be labelled as SVs. However, they are different from the SVs in **[1]**. Śakṇe 'can' **[6a]** is an auxiliary and is never used as an independent verb. In this sense, it is similar to the verb 'can' in English. In contrast to this the explicator verbs in **[1]** are used as single verbs independently of SVC. Verbs (V_2s) in **[7a]** - **[9a]** can be used as independent, single verbs elsewhere. However, the meaning of these V_2 is completely grammaticalized, i.e., the V_2s are completely 'bleached' of their meaning and function as aspectual markers. Therefore, $V_1 + V_2$ of the type in **[6a]** - **[9a]** is an open set. Practically, any V_1 can be paired with V_2 to convey the meanings (mostly aspectual) mentioned above. The pairing of V_1 and V_2 is restricted, not on the basis of the compatibility of the lexical meaning of V_2 with V_1, but rather, on the basis of the compatibility of V_1 with the grammaticalized/aspectual meaning of V_2. For example, a verb such as ***mar -ṇe*** 'to die' can not be combined with ***as -ṇe*** **[7]**, ***rāh -ṇe*** **[8]**, or ***dzā -ṇe*** **[9]** because of the ontological incompatibility of V_1 to take the aspectual meanings conveyed by the above.

The V_2s in this class of verbs are totally affixal in their function. They do not have a syntactic or semantic status of a verb, i.e., they do not have any arguments, or meaning (independently of V_1). They do not convey the meanings independently of V_1. Marathi does not have other affixes (besides those auxiliary verbs) to carry out their grammatical function. Also, similar to V + affix combinations, the SV in this class do not allow any intervention of any morpheme between V_1 and V_2. Moreover, similar to affixes or auxiliary verbs, the sequential order of V_1 and V_2 is irreversible. V_2 may take inflections of tense, gender, and number agreement (if it is the last element in the sentence).

The set of SV described in **[1]** is different from this class (as will be demonstrated in detail in section (3). In the SV in **[1]**, the V_2s are not as grammaticalized as the V_2 in **[6]** - **[9]**, in the sense that they are not completely 'bleached' of their lexical meaning. For example, unlike those in **[6]** - **[9]**, all V_2s (which are used also as independent single verbs) retain their features of a $\pm$volitionality, and argument structure in the SVC. Moreover, the SV in **[1]** allow an emphatic particle to intervene between V_1 and V_2 and optionally, the order of V_1 and V_2 can be reversed. One of the major differences between the two sets is that in the SV in **[1]**, V_1 is not an open set. Unlike V_2 in **[6]** - **[9]**, V_2 is not freely attachable to any V_1 in SV in **[1]**. There are syntactic/semantic constraints (see section 8) which determine the compatibility of V_1 and V_2.

The above discussion shows that the two sets of SVs need to be treated differently. In the set in **[1]**, the V_2 retains more verbal properties than the V_2 in **[6]** - **[9]**. In the former, we are dealing with SV with a pair of (structurally and functionally) two verbs while in latter, we are dealing with a $V_1 + V_2$ (which is syntactically, semantically, and functionally a grammatical inflection). In the following discussion, I will discuss the set of verbs in **[1]** as SVs.

3. Split properties of SVC: Morphology

In my earlier paper (Pandharipande 1989) it is pointed out that SVC shares morphological, syntactic, and semantic properties with other constructions in the language. In order to facilitate the discussion, I will present the relevant data to substantiate this claim. In section (1) it is already pointed out that V_1 in SV obligatorily takes the suffix ***ūn*** which it shares with the conjunctive participle (CP hereafter) construction in Marathi.

Another morphological property of a SVC is that it does not readily allow intervention of any element between V_1 and V_2. This property is commonly shared by a compound. Consider the following examples:

[10] * ***to he bolūn kāl gelā***
he this say yesterday went
He said this (inadvertently) yesterday.

Note that when an adverbial element ***kāl*** 'yesterday' intervenes between V_1 - ***bolūn*** 'say' (literally 'having said') and V_2 - ***gelā*** (inadvertently, literally 'went'), the resulting sentence is ungrammatical.[1] This property of SVC points out an intimate combination of verbs in a SVC (Foley and Van Valin 1984). However, the following example **[11]** shows that an emphatic particle can intervene between V_1 and V_2.

[11] ***to he bolūn tar gelā***
he this say (emph.) went
indeed
Indeed, he said this inadvertently.

Moreover, the order of V_1 and V_2 may be optionally switched as in **[12]**.

[12] ***tyāne kām ṭakla karūn***
he-ag. work threw do
V_2 V_1
He did the work (and got rid of it).

The above discussion points out that SVs are not as intimately combined as compounds nor are they as loosely combined as the pairs of verbs in **[6]** - **[9]**.

4. Split properties of SVs: Syntax

A close examination of the syntactic properties of SVs in the following discussion shows that some syntactic phenomena (such as passivization, participialization, and verb-agreement) refer to/operate only on V_2. Causativization refers to both V_1 and V_2.

4.1 Passivization

Consider the following example **[13]** where the SV is in the passive form. Note that while V_1 (***toḍūn*** 'cut') remains unchanged, all the markers of passive, i.e. perfective form of the V_1 ***ṭāklī*** 'dropped' and the agreement markers (3 person, neuter, plural), are on V_2.

[13] ***sarkārī*** ***hukumānusār*** ***sagḷī*** ***dzʰāḍa***
government's order-according to all trees
3p.plu.neut.

toḍūn ***ṭāklī*** ***gelī***
cut drop went
3p.neut.plu.perfect 3p.neut.plu.perfect
According to the government's orders, all the trees were cut down.

4.2 Past Participles

Except for one type of sequence of V_1 + V_2 (i.e. V_1 (intransitive) + V_2 (transitive)), all other sequences of V_1 + V_2 (in a SV) may undergo (past) participialization. Consider examples **[14]** - **[17]**. Notice that the SV with the V_1 (trans.) + V_2 (trans.) undergoes the process of (past) participialization yielding the participle (***toḍūn ṭākleli*** 'cut off') in **[14]**. Similarly **[15]** and **[16]** show that the SV with the V_1 (trans.) + V_2 (intrans.) in **[15]** and V_1 (intrans.) + V_2 (intrans.) in **[16]** undergo (past) participialization deriving the participles, i.e. ***cūk karūn baslelā*** 'the boy who made a mistake inadvertently' **[15]**, and ***tuṭūn gelelī*** 'being cut off' **[16]**, respectively. However, when the SV with V_1 (intrans.) + V_2 (trans.) sequence is (past) participialized, the resulting sentence **[17]** is ungrammatical.

Past Participles: V_1 (tr.) + V_2 (tr.)

toḍ + ***ṭāk*** = ***toḍūn ṭākṇe*** 'to cut off'
cut/break drop

[14] ***tyāne*** ***toḍūn*** ***ṭāklelī*** ***dzʰāḍa*** ***titha*** ***paḍlī*** ***hotī***
he-ag. cut drop trees there lay aux.
The trees cut down by him lay there.

[15] V_1 + V_2
tr. + Intr.

cūk ***karūn*** ***basle lā*** ***mulgā***
mistake do sit boy
3p.sg.mas.
The boy who made a mistake (inadvertently).

[16] V_1 + V_2
Intr. + Intr.

tuṭūn gelelī phāndī
break go branch
(Intr.) 3p.sg.fem. 3p.sg.fem.
The branch (which was) broken off.

[17] When V_1 is intransitive and V_2 is transitive, the formation of past participle is blocked.

* ***dzʰopūn ghetle lā mulgā***
sleep take boy
The boy who slept (for himself).

4.3 Present Participles

The process of (present) participialization is blocked for the SVs. Consider example **[18]** where the SV ***lihūn/ṭākṇe*** 'to write (to finish off the job of writing)' has undergone the process of (present) participialization. The resulting sentence is ungrammatical.

[18] * ***patra lihūn ṭākat aslelī mulgī***
letter write drop aux. girl
The girl who is writing a letter (in order to finish off the job of writing).

4.4 Causativization

Notice that when the SV **[19]**, ***karūn gheṇe*** 'to work for oneself' is causativized in **[19a]**, V_1 changes from ***karūn*** 'to work' to ***karvūn*** 'to make/do work'. No change (other than the tense aspect and the agreement marker) takes place in V_2. (Compare **[19]** and **[19a]**.)

[19] ***mī kām karūn ghetla***
I work do took
I did the work (for myself).

[19a] *mī kām sudhā kaḍūn* ***karvūn*** *ghetla*
I work Sudhā by do-caus. took
I got the work done (for myself) by Sudhā.

Note that the causative marker can also be placed on V_2 as shown in sentence **[20]**.

[20] ***mū sudhālā kām karāylā lāvle***
I Sudha-acc. work do-caus. attach + past
I made Sudha do the work.

5. Verb Agreement

The verb-agreement in Marathi is sensitive to the argument structure of the verb (for further discussion see Pandharipande 1981a): (a) a verb agrees in number, (gender), and person with the agent or patient (subject), if it is not followed by a postposition (PP hereafter), (b) if the agent/patient is followed by a PP, it agrees with the theme or object (if it is not followed by a PP), (c) if both (i.e. subject and object) are followed by PPs, the verb remains in its unmarked (3 person, sg. neut.) form. In SVC the verb agreement is sensitive to the arguments of V_2. Consider the following examples:

V_1 (tr.) + V_2 (tr.)
[21] ***sudhā patra lihūn ṭākte***
Sudhā letter write drops
Sudhā writes a letter (to get rid of the responsibility of writing it).

V_1 (intr.) + V_2 (intr.)
[22] ***Sudhā nighūn gelī***
Sudhā leave went
Sudhā went away.

V_1 (tr.) + V_2 (intr.) Note the absence of ***-ne***.
[23] ***sudhā kām karūn baslī***
Sudhā work do sat
Sudhā did the work (inadvertently).

V_1 (intr.) + V_2 (tr.) Note the ergative marking on the agent.
[24] ***tyāne dz^h^opūn ghetle***
he-erg. sleep took
(intr.) (tr.)
He slept.

In **[21]** and **[22]**, it is not clear whether it is the argument of V_1 or V_2 which controls agreement, since V_1 and V_2 in **[21]** and **[22]** have an identical argument structure (they are both transitive in **[21]** and intransitive in **[22]**). However, **[23]** and **[24]** clearly show that it is the argument of V_2 which controls agreement. In **[23]** the agent ***Sudhā*** does not take the regular marker of the agent of the transitive verb ***karṇe*** 'to do'. ***Sudhā*** (which controls the agreement), should have taken the agent-marking ***-ne*** and the verb should have agreed with the theme ***kām***. Instead, ***Sudhā*** fails to take the marking ***-ne*** and the SV agrees with ***Sudhā***. If ***Sudhā*** is taken to be the THEME (subject) of ***basṇe*** (V_2) 'to sit', then it is clear that ***Sudhā*** being the theme (subject) of an intransitive verb does not take ***-ne*** and consequently the SV agrees with ***Sudhā***. In **[24]** ***to*** 'he' is the agent of V_2 ***gheṇe*** 'to take'. Therefore ***to*** 'he' takes the agentive marker ***-ne*** (and as a result the SV fails to agree with it). Had it been the theme (subject) of V_1 -- ***dz^h^op-ṇe*** 'to sleep', it should not have taken the marker ***-ne*** and the verb would have agreed with it.

6. Split properties of SVC: Semantics

If we look at the semantic structures of SVC in Marathi, the following two points are immediately clear: (a) the semantic structure of both V_1 and V_2 is relevant for the semantic representation of a SV in which V_1 conveys the primary meaning of the SV and V_2 conveys the adverbial meaning (see discussion in section 1). For example in a SV ***karūn gheṇe*** 'to do for oneself', ***karūn*** 'do' (literally 'having done') conveys the primary meaning, while ***gheṇe*** 'take' conveys the adverbial meaning. The meaning of a SV is further split up between V_1 and V_2 in that it is V_2 which determines the transitivity/intransitivity of the SV (recall **[23]** and **[24]**) and thereby, the agreement pattern is also determined by V_2. However, the lexical meaning of V_1 is retained while that of V_2 is not.

7. Derivation and function of SVC

In order to explain the split nature of the SVC, it is crucial to discuss the derivation and function of the SVC. It is important to remember that two verbs (i.e. V_1 and V_2) will have to be compatible in order for the combination of primary meaning of V_1 and adverbial meaning of V_2 to get properly orchestrated.

A close examination of the semantic representation of V_1 and V_2 shows that (a) in order for the lexical meaning of V_1 to take on the additional adverbial meaning (conveyed by V_2), it is crucial for V_1 to match the semantic features of V_2. (b) In the above process the semantics of V_1 is modified; (c) this change in semantics of V_1 changes the nature of the argument of V_1, and (d) this change is reflected in the syntactic properties of the arguments of V_1.

The supporting evidence for this analysis comes from behavior of the arguments with reference to certain syntactic processes which apply to V_1 when it is used as a single verb but fail to apply to it when it is as a V_1 in a SVC.

7.1 Semantic properties of V_1 and V_2: the question of compatibility

Compatibility of V_1 and V_2 can be determined on the basis of the pairability of their semantic features (which as will be seen, affect their compatibility at the syntactic level as well). A further breakdown of the semantic features of V_1 and V_2 is necessary to investigate their compatibility. Note that the V_2, in addition to conveying the adverbial meaning, also determines the overall $\pm$volitionality of a SV (and thereby the $\pm$control of the agent/subject over the action expressed by V_1. It is to be further noted that the transitive V_2 conveys +volitional action and +control of the agent; while an intransitive V_2 conveys −volitional action and −control of the agent. Thus the V_2s (see the list of V_2 in section 1) such as ***de*** 'to give', ***ghe*** 'to take', ***kāḍh*** 'to draw', ***soḍ*** 'to leave', ***bagh*** 'to see', and ***ṭhev*** 'to keep' share two features: (a) +volitionality and (b) +control of their agents.

In Pandharipande 1982, the tests for determining $\pm$volitionality and $\pm$control have been discussed. It is pointed out that the verbs which express +volitional act and +control of their agent, invariably participate in the causative, passive, and imperative constructions and readily take the adverbials such as 'try to' or 'intentionally', etc. It was further demonstrated that most generally, transitive verbs express +volitional acts and +control of their subjects/agents while intransitive verbs are lower on the scale of volitionality as well as of the control of their subjects over the actions expressed by them.

The SVs with the intransitive V_2s (see the list in section 1) such as ***bas*** 'to sit', ***ye*** 'to come', and ***dzā*** 'to go', have a theme rather than an agent, and therefore they are less volitional and convey some control of the subject only if it is +human. The following two examples show that if V_2 is transitive (and therefore +volitional +control of the agent), the SV participates in the imperative construction; while with the intransitive V_2, a SV fails to participate in it.

[25] *tū thoḍa raḍūn ghe*
you a little cry take
Cry a little (for yourself).

[26] * *tū te kām karūn bas*
you that work do sit
Do the work inadvertently.

Note that it is the V_2 which determines the overall volitionality of a SV. For example, in **[26]** V_1 ***kar*** 'to do' is a transitive verb and thereby it is +volitional and +control (of the agent). However, since the V_2 ***bas*** 'sit' is intransitive (and is -volitional here), the SV ***karūn basṇe*** 'to do inadvertently' is viewed as −volitional −control (of the agent). Similarly V_1 in **[25]** ***raḍṇe*** 'to cry' is lower on the scale of volitionality and control (since it is generally accepted that one does not have an intention to cry and control over the action of crying). However, the V_2 (in **[25]**) is a transitive verb -- ***gheṇe*** 'to take' which is higher on the scale of volitionality and control. As a result, the SV is treated a +volitional and +control (of the agent) verb, which explains why it participates in the imperative construction. Examples **[24]** and **[25]** point out that it is the features of volitionality and control of V_2 which determine the overall features of volitionality and control of the SV. Thus it is only expected that the V_1 is selected on the basis of the compatibility of its features with those of the V_2, or its modifiability of its features to match those of V_2. If the features of V_1 and V_2 match then V_1 does not need to be modified. In contrast to this, if they do not match, the semantic representation of V_1 has to be modified. This is exemplified in the following:

[27]

[a] V_1 (transitive) + V_2 (transitive)
‹agent› [+volitional +control] ‹agent› [+volitional +control]
‹theme› ‹theme›

Resulting SV: ***karṇe*** 'to do' + ***gheṇe*** = ***karūn gheṇe*** 'to do for oneself'

[b] V_1 is intransitive + V_2 (transitive)
‹theme› [−volitional −control] ‹agent› [+volitional +control]

Change = V_1 +volitional +adverbial meaning of V_2
Resulting SV:
= ***dzʰopṇe*** 'to sleep' + ***gheṇe*** 'to take' = ***dzʰopūn gheṇe*** 'to sleep for oneself' (volitional)

[28] If V_2 is intransitive (i.e. ***basṇe*** 'to sit', ***dzāṇe*** 'to go', etc.) it adds the feature of −volitionality to V_1.

[a] V_1 (transitive) + V_2 (intransitive)
‹agent› [+volitional +control] ‹theme› [+volitional +control]
‹theme›

Change = V_1 −volitional +adverbial meaning of V_2
Resulting SV: ***karṇe*** 'to do' + ***basṇe*** 'to sit' = ***karūn basṇe*** 'to do inadvertently'

[b] V_1 (intransitive) + V_2 (intransitive) =
‹theme› [+volition +control] ‹theme› [+volition +control]

V_1 +volition +adverbial meaning
Resulting SV: ***basṇe*** 'to sit' + ***dzāṇe*** 'to go' = ***basūn zāṇe*** 'to sit down inadvertently'

[c] V_1 (intransitive) + V_2 (intransitive)
‹theme› [−volition −control] ‹theme› [+volition +control]

= V_1 +adverbial meaning
sukṇe 'to wither' + ***dzāṇe*** 'to go' = ***sūkūn dzāṇe*** 'to wither away'
Resulting SV: = ***sukūn dzāṇe*** 'to wither completely'

Note that when the features of volitionality and control match (between V_1 and V_2) no modification in V_1 takes place (see examples **[27a]** and **[28b]**). When the features of V_1 and V_2 do not match, V_1 undergoes change. For example, in **[27b]**, V_1 is lower on the overall volitionality scale than V_2. In this case, V_1 becomes +volitional +control (although it is still lower than V_2 on the scale since its subject argument is a theme (as opposed to an agent)). Similarly, in **[28a]** the mismatch between V_1 and V_2 is due to the fact that unlike V_1 which has an agent argument, V_2 has a theme argument. In order to be compatible with V_2, volitionality of V_1 is lowered. In **[28c]** the V_2 ***dzāṇe*** 'to go' is lower on the scale of volitionality and control since it has a theme argument. V_1 matches the volitionality feature of V_2 and since the argument of V_1 is human, the adverbial meaning 'inadvertently' is redundant. In this case, the V_2 only adds the adverbial meaning 'completely' to V_1.

8. Constraints

In the following discussion, I will discuss some of the constraints on pairing of V_1 and V_2. Let us consider the following combinations of V_1 and V_2 which are not possible in Marathi.

[29] If V_1 cannot have a volitional agent, V_2 (transitive) cannot be paired with V_1, i.e.:

[a] *V_1 (−volitional + V_2 (transitive)
+agent)

****śinkūn gheṇe** = 'to sneeze intentionally for oneself'
sneeze take

[b] Experiencer (dative-subject) verbs

*V_1 (−volitional + V_2 (transitive)
−agent
+patient)

rāg yeūn ṭākṇe
anger come drop
'(For X) to get angry to get rid of it'

[c] If V_1 cannot have a −volitional agent V_2 (intransitive) cannot be paired with it.

V_1 (+volitional + V_2 (intransitive)
+agent)

****prayatna karūn dzāṇe***
effort do
'To try inadvertently'

Examples **[29a]** - **[29c]** point out that if the semantic features of V_1 do not match with those of V_2 and the modification in the features of V_1 is not possible due to the ontological nature of the action expressed by V_1, then, V_1 cannot be paired with that V_2.

In order to match V_2 in **[29a]**, which is +volitional and +control (of the agent) verb, it is necessary to modify V_1 (which is −volitional and −control). However, ontologically, the action of sneezing is −volitional and −control (of the agent) in its nature. Therefore, V_1 cannot be paired with V_2. Similarly, in **[29c]**, V_1 expresses action (***prayatna karṇe*** 'to try') which is ontologically impossible to perform without volition and control (of the agent). Therefore, it cannot be paired with an intransitive V_2. The constraint on pairing of V_1 and V_2 also explains why the dative-subject-verbs (i.e. the verbs which have experiencer subjects) cannot take transitive V_2 (see example **[29b]**). Experiencer/dative subject-verbs typically express a −volitional action over which the subject does not have any control (for further discussion on experiencer subjects in Marathi see Masica 1976, and Pandharipande 1989). Therefore, their incompatibility with transitive (+volitional +control) verbs is only expected.

8.1 Interaction of syntax and semantics

The assumptions in (7) also explain the split syntax of SVC. For example, recall **[23]** and **[24]**. ***Sudhā*** (agent) in **[23]** fails to take the expected agentive -***ne*** marking while ***to*** in **[24]** which should not take -***ne*** obviously takes it. According to our hypothesis, in **[23]**, the semantic features of V_1 (+volition, +control (of the agent)) are modified to become compatible with V_2 (intransitive) which has a theme subject. As a result, volitionality as well as control of the agent ***Sudhā*** is lowered. Consequently, ***Sudhā*** no more claims to be the volitional agent of the action (of doing the work) expressed by V_1. Since the -***ne*** marking typically marks an agent (see Damle 1911, Pandharipande 1981), it is only expected that ***Sudhā*** (in **[23]**) is not marked with it. Therefore the SV agrees with it. In contrast to this, in **[24]**, V_1 has a theme subject and V_1 ***dzʰopṇe*** 'to sleep' is low on the scale of volitionality and control. However, as a result of its pairing with V_2, ***gheṇe*** 'to take', which is transitive, and has the features +volitional, and +control (of the agent), the volitionality and the control of the agent is raised. Therefore, the subject of V_1 is the SV ***dzʰopūn gheṇe*** 'to sleep for oneself' is more agent-like than the subject of single verb ***dzʰopṇe*** 'to sleep'. Thus it is not a surprise that it takes the agentive marker -***ne*** and the SV fails to agree with it.

The hypothesis about the modification of the semantic features of V_1 further explains why the syntactic processes of passivization, and (perfective) participialization fail to apply to **[13a]** (see **[13b]**) even though the theme argument (i.e. ***cūk*** 'mistake') is present in the sentence. Since (as discussed above) the agent is downgraded (due to the influence of V_2), the theme (***cūk*** 'mistake') is further downgraded and does not have the status of the theme argument. Therefore, the syntactic constructions of passivization and (perfective) participialization do not treat it as a 'real' theme of a transitive verb and thereby fail to operate on it (see **[15a]**). In contrast to this, the SV in **[17]** treats the subject as agent and therefore, following the ergative pattern, the (perfective) participialization fails to operate on it (see **[17]**). This operation can be summarized as follows: if semantic structure of V_1 is modified, then the nature of its arguments change and this change is reflected in the syntax of V_1.

More evidence for the hypothesis comes from the process of causativization. (Recall examples **[19]** - **[26]**.) Note that the V_1 and V_2 in the SVC in **[19]** have identical semantic features. Therefore, it is only as expected that the causative marking may be placed either on V_1 **[19a]** or V_2 **[19b]**. Ungrammaticality of **[20]** is justifiable on the basis of ontological incompatibility of the adverbial meaning 'inadvertently' with the causative meaning 'to make causee do x (action)', i.e., a causee cannot be caused to perform an action inadvertently. Therefore **[20]** is ungrammatical.

9. Conjunctive participial suffix *-un* and SVC: more evidence for compatibility of V_1 and V_2

In section (1.0) (examples **[1]** and **[2]**) it is noted that in SV, V_1 shares the suffix ***ūn*** with the conjunctive participial construction in Marathi. The use of ***ūn*** in SVC is convincingly justified within our hypothesis as follows: the suffix ***ūn*** in SVC, similar to the conjunctive participial construction, signals (a) identity or compatibility of the arguments of V_1 and V_2 and (b) completion of the action in V_1 as exemplified in **[30]**.

Conjunctive participle:
[30] *to dzʰaḍ toḍūn gharī gelā*
he tree having cut home went
Having cut the tree, he went home.

Note that the agent of V_1 and V_2 is identical[2] in **[30]** and the action in V_1 is complete. Our earlier discussion shows that the arguments of V_1 and V_2 have to be compatible. The claim that in SVC action expressed by V_1 is interpreted to be completed or realized, is supported by the fact that a progressive participle cannot be derived from a SVC (as noted in **[18]**). This interpretation of the realization/completion of the action expressed by V_1 overrides the tense/aspect of overall SVC (indicated by the marking on V_2), as in **[31]** where the SV clearly denotes the non-perfective aspect.

[31] *to patra phekūn deto*
he letter throw give
He throws away the letter.

Thus it is not implausible to assume that the completion of the action in V_1 is signaled by the suffix ***ūn*** and that this interpretation is valid at the discoursal level. More evidence to support the hypothesis regarding the completion of the action comes from the fact that a SV can not be readily negated, as illustrated in **[32]**. Our hypothesis nicely predicts and accounts for the ungrammaticality of **[32]** since the interpretation of the completion of the action is incompatible with its negation.

[32] * *to he bolūn baslā nāhī*
he this say sat not
He did not say this inadvertently.

10. The affixal nature of V_2 in SVC

The analysis of the syntactic as well as semantic behavior of SVC is further supported by the fact that the V_2 in SVC is affixal in nature. The following evidence supports this hypothesis: (a) they, similar to other verbal/nominal affixes and postpositions, are dependent on the V_1 for the realization of the adverbial meaning. (b) V_2 occurs in the position of tense, aspect, and agreement markers which categorically follow and not precede the main verb,

(c) similar to postpositions, V_2 influences the meaning of V_1 and more importantly, changes its thematic role. Consider the following examples **[33]** and **[33a]**. When the postposition ***kaḍūn*** is added on to the agent of the verb, the thematic role of the agent is changed to that of an instrument and the action of doing is treated as non-volitional.

[33] *rām ne kām kele*
Rām ag. work did
Rām did the work.

[33a] *rām* ***kaḍūn*** *kām dzʰāle*
Rām by work happened
Rām did the work (literally, Rām was instrumental in getting the work done.)

Similarly, when intransitive V_2 follows a V_1, the action expressed by V_1 is treated as −volitional and, as discussed in section (8), the nature of the arguments of V_1 is changed. (c) Another piece of evidence to support the hypothesis comes from that Marathi, similar to many other (e.g. Hindi, Gujarati, Punjabi) Indian languages uses lexical verbs as suffixes (recall discussion section (1), therefore, affixal function of verbs is independently motivated in Marathi. (d) There are no other adverbial suffixes or adverbials which carry out the function of V_2s in the language. (e) The hypothesis about the affixal function of V_2s is further supported by diachronic evidence. Beams (1872) attributes the emergence of SVs in Indo Āryan languages to the loss of Sanskrit ***upasargas*** (suffixes) during the period between Sanskrit and New Indo Āryan. Directional and aspectual Sanskrit affixes (e.g. ***ut*** 'up', ***apa*** 'away', ***pati*** 'toward', ***upa*** 'close to', etc.) were gradually lost. The distinction between verbal suffixes of ***ātmanepada*** (indicating that the action is performed for oneself) and of ***parasmaipada*** (indicating that action is performed for someone else) was neutralized. This change was gradual through Pāli and Prākṛt (the phases of Middle-Indo-Āryan following Sanskrit) but became more dominant in Apabhraṃśa (the phase following Prākṛt) where a predominantly analystical system of grammar emerged. Case suffixes of Sanskrit and Prākṛt were replaced by postpositions. The use of a verb to replace an aspectual inflection had already with Pāli. However, in Old Marathi (11-13th century A.D.) the use of inflectional affixes is still predominant while the use of a verb to convey aspectual meaning is rare. In Modern Marathi however, a majority of the derivational suffixes of Sanskrit and Prākṛt indicating the direction or beneficiary of the action are completely lost. Thus there seems to be a correlation between the loss of affixes and the emergence of SVs in Marathi. Therefore, it is not surprising that the V_2s in SVC, similar to the affixes, express the conditions under which the action expressed by the V_1 took place.

It is important to note here that not all verbs used as V_2 are fully grammaticalized as affixes. There seems to be a hierarchy of grammaticalization of verbs. For example, the verbs used as aspectual markers (e.g. ***as -ṇe*** 'to be' (habitual)), passive-marker (***dzā -ṇe*** 'to go'), and the marker of a regularly performed action (***dzā -ṇe*** 'to go') are fully grammaticalized. In contrast to this, V_2s in SVC are not fully grammaticalized. The evidence for this is discussed in section (1). Additional evidence to support this claim comes from the fact that the fully grammaticalized verbal affixes can be added on to any verb (including to the same lexical verb) while the V_2s categorically fail to be V_2s if V_1 is the same lexical verb. Consider the following:

[34] *tū śāḷet dzāt dzā*
you school-in go go
(You) go to school regularly.

The following combinations of V_1 and V_2 are unacceptable:

[35] [a] *basūn bas -ṇe* 'to sit inadvertently'
[b] *deūn de -ṇe* 'to give for someone else'
[c] *gheūn gheṇe* 'to take for oneself'

Note that in **[34]** (which does not involve a SVC construction) the verb *dzā* 'go' is used twice, first as the main verb and secondly, as the aspectual affix. Note that the resulting sentence is fine. On the other hand, in a SVC the same verb can not be used both as V_1 and V_2 since it presents semantic redundancy **[35a]** - **[35c]**. This indicates that the V_2 is as "bleached out" of its lexical meaning as the V_2 *dzā* 'to go' in **[34]**.[3]

Even within the group of V_2 some are more grammaticalized than others, i.e., *de -ṇe* 'to give', and *gheṇe* 'to take' are more grammaticalized as opposed to *pāh -ṇe* 'to see'. (In some varieties of Marathi *deūn de -ṇe* 'to give for someone else' is to a large extent, acceptable.)

The following additional evidence shows that the V_2s are not fully grammaticalized, i.e., their adverbial meaning emerges not only from its form but also from the attitudes of the speaker. For example, let us compare the adverbial meaning of the V_2 *gheṇe* 'for oneself' with the similar meaning of the reflexive particle *svataḥ sāṭhī* 'for oneself'. In **[36]**, where SV *karūn gheṇe* 'to do for oneself' is used, the use of the word indicating beneficiary other than the subject, i.e., *āīsāṭhī* 'for mother' should create discrepancy. However **[36]** does not present any discrepancy. In contrast to this, **[37]** where the reflexive particle *svataḥ* 'self' is used, the insertion of the word *āīsāṭhī* 'for mother' creates discrepancy and the sentence is not acceptable.

[36] *tyāne āīsāṭhī te kām karūn ghetle*
he-ag. mother-for that work do took
He did the work for (his) mother. (He felt that he was doing it for himself.)

[37] * *tyāne āīsāṭhī svataḥsāthī te kām karūn ghetle*
he-ag. mother-for self-for that work do took
He did the work for himself for his mother.

The difference between **[36]** and **[37]** can be explained if we assume that the reflexive meaning of *svataḥ* 'self' is fully grammaticalized, i.e., it can only refer to the subject of the sentence irrespective of the attitude of the subject or speaker. Therefore, the beneficiary of the action can not be anyone other than the subject. Thus, it is not surprising that the insertion of the word ***āīsāṭhī*** 'for mother' creates discrepancy in **[37]**. In contrast to this, if we assume that the reflexive meaning of ***gheṇe*** 'for oneself' in **[36]** is not fully grammaticalized, but rather, it depends on the attitude of the speaker, then it is expected that if according to the speaker, agent's doing the work for mother is comparable to doing it for himself, then the use of ***gheṇe*** 'for oneself' in **[36]** should not create any discrepancy.

11. **Conclusion**

The major points in the preceding discussion can be summarized as follows: (a) The SVC is different from other serial verb constructions in Marathi, since the combination of V_1 and V_2 in SVC is neither fully fixed like compounds, nor is it totally free as other serial verbs in Marathi, (b) V_1 and V_2 are paired on the basis of their semantic (and thereby syntactic) compatibility, which is subject to semantic constraints. This hypothesis is in consonance with Mishra's (1990) hypothesis of 'multiple linking' of V_1 and V_2 in Hindi SVC, (c) change in the semantic features of V_1 influence the syntactic features of its arguments, (d) V_2s are affix-like in their function. However, they are not fully grammaticalized and there is a hierarchy of grammaticalization of verbal affixes in Marathi. There is diachronic evidence for assuming that historically, SVC emerged as a result of the loss of some affixes.

The discussion in this paper points out that the split properties of SVC, the constraints the compatibility of V_1 and V_2 can be fully explained only if the morphology, syntax, semantics, and pragmatics of SVC is taken into account. Since interlinking of the levels of grammar (see sections (3) and (10)) is evident, one may ask whether it is useful or even possible to determine constraints on and properties of SVC exclusively in syntactic terms.

The paper also points out that the semantic representation of a verb not only includes its argument-structure but also other properties such as volitionality and control of the agent of the action expressed by the verb.

The discussion in this paper is also relevant for developing a typology of SVC in Indian languages in particular and SVC across different language-families in general. If the emergence of SVC in Marathi and other Indo Āryan languages is due to the loss of affixes, then it is expected that (a) the languages which have preserved a relatively more synthetic/affixal structure should have relatively fewer SVs. In fact, this seems to be true in the case of Marathi vis-a-vis Hindi. Marathi, which has retained a larger number of affixes (case-marker) than Hindi, has fewer SVs than Hindi. However, a cross-linguistic study is needed to provide a conclusive statement about the status of SVs in Indo-Āryan languages, and (b) the paper points out that the SVC in Marathi stands between compounds (which are fully fixed) and V + affix constructions (which are totally free). Perhaps, there is a scale of 'intimacy' between V_1 and V_2 in SVC across languages, on which each language occupies a particular position.

NOTES

1. The sentence in **[10]** is grammatical if it is interpreted as a Conjunctive Participle Construction. In this case the sentence will translate as 'Having said this, he went home yesterday.'

2. It is to be noted here that V_1 and V_2 may have different subjects if there is a causal connection between the actions expressed by V_1 and V_2 respectively, i.e.:

pāūs	*paḍūn*	*dhānya*	*pikla*
rain	having fallen	paddy	grew

The paddy grew due to the rainfall. (Literally, the rain having fallen the paddy grew.)

For further discussion see Pandharipande 1989.

3. It may be argued here that the same verb can not be used as both V_1 and V_2 because V_1 has all properties of V_2 (including the adverbial meaning). Therefore, repetition of the same verb causes redundancy. However, this argument fails since V_1s in **[35a]** - **[35c]** when used as single verbs do not inhere the adverbial meaning which they express when used as V_2s in SVC constructions.

REFERENCES

Beams, John. 1872. A comparative grammar of the modern Aryan languages of India. [Repr. New Delhi: Munshi Ram Manohar Lal, 1970.]

Damle, Damodar Keshav. 1911. Shastriya Marathi Vyakarana. [Repr. Pune: Damodar Sawlaram ani Mandali, 1965.]

Foley, William, and Robert D. Van Valin. 1984. Functional syntax and universal grammar. Cambridge: Cambridge University Press.

Kachru, Yamuna, and Rajeshwari Pandharipande. 1980. Toward a typology of compound verbs in South Asian languages. Studies in the Linguistic Sciences 10:1.113-14.

Mishra, Mithilesh K. 1990. Against 'object sharing' in serial verb constructions. Paper presented at Mini-Conference on Serial Verbs, Ohio State University, Columbus.

Pandharipande, Rajeshwari. 1981. Transitivity in Hindi. Studies in Linguistic Sciences 11:2.161-79.

Pandharipande, Rajeshwari. 1981a. Syntax and semantics of the passive construction in selected South Asian languages. Urbana-Champaign: University of Illinois dissertation.

Pandharipande, Rajeshwari. 1982. Volitionality: more evidence for a constraint on passive in Hindi. South Asian Review VI:3.89-103.

Pandharipande, Rajeshwari. In Press. Experiencer (dative) Nps in Marathi. Experiencer subjects in South Asian languages, ed. by M. K. Verma and K. P. Mohanan. Stanford: Center for the Study of Language and Information.

COMPLEX PREDICATES AND LIGHT VERBS IN HINDI

Manindra K. Verma
University of Wisconsin

This article presents a unified account of several types of Hindi verbal constructions which could be regarded as involving 'complex predicates'.[1] What is presented here will be partially schematic for various reasons, but one of the reasons is that it raises more questions than it provides answers for. Certain things are clear, though. In more recent literature, 'complex predicate' is an appellation which has, for all practical purposes, been applied to Noun + Verb constructions in which the verb is what is called a 'light' verb. There is probably no doubt that this particular variety raises most of the interesting questions, but I will use the term 'complex predicate' to provide for the larger structural unity of the various categories of V_1V_2 type predicates, too, at least for Hindi. That will include, of course, the familiar 'compound verb' with an UNINFLECTED V_1 as in **[1a]** ***khaa liyaa*** 'ate up', but also the one with the INFLECTED V_1 as in **[1b]** ***khaane lagaa*** 'started eating', as well as the V_1V_2 construction in which the V_2 is recognized as a modal, such as ***saknaa*** 'to be able to', ***cuknaa*** 'to be done with', and ***paanaa*** 'to manage to', as exemplified in **[1c]**. In fact, I will go even further and consider even the '***jaa***-passive' of Hindi as part of the same phenomenon. I am tempted to go a step further still and consider what I have called the '***ho***-passive' in Hindi all as part of this general phenomenon, as in **[2a]** and **[2b]**.

[1] a. ***khaa liyaa***
ate took
ate up

b. ***khaane lagaa***
eat engaged
started eating

c. ***khaa cukaa***
eat done
done eating

[2] a. ***yah qaanuun sarkaar ke dwaaraa lagaa-yaa gayaa hai***
this ordinance government by promulgate - jaa-passive
This ordinance has been promulagated by the government

b. ***yah qaanuun sarkaar kaa lagaa-yaa huaa hai***
this ordinance government's promulgate - ho-passive
This ordinance is promulagated by the government

What makes me think that there is any justification in all this? Leaving out the passives for the time being, I would like to treat all cases of V_2 as instances of a modal. The *sak-*, *cuk-*, *paa-* type V_2's are readily accepted as modals. The V_2's of the complex verbs in which the V_1's occur in an inflected form, as in ***khaane lagnaa***, ***khaayaa karnaa***, etc., as illustrated in **[1b]**, are also clearly modal in nature, expressing modalities of 'initiation', 'habitual action', 'permission', 'compulsion', 'continuation', etc., etc. As regards the V_2's of the so-called 'compound verb' in Hindi, I have argued elsewhere[2] that they also indicate various kinds of modality, and, in fact, in some cases, even comprise neat classes of members which all indicate a given modality, and are in strucurally conditioned complementary distribution. I am thinking, for example, of the V_2's ***lenaa / denaa*** and ***jaanaa / aanaa***, which all express the modality of 'transition to a state or phase of the action', and are in complementary distribution relative to the verb subclassifications.

At any rate, these complex verbs with a bare stem V_1 are the ones for which the appellation 'compound verb' is reserved in Hindi. I do not see any reason why the ones with the inflected V_1, as in ***khaane lagnaa***, should not also be classified as members of compound verbs, in view of the common nature of the function of the V_2 in both cases. If much is sought to be made of the apparent difference between the form of their V_1's in terms of their being inflected or not being inflected, it may be pointed out that the V_1 counterparts of these compound verbs of Hindi are all inflected in the sister languages of Hindi, as seen in **[3a]**, **[3b]**, and **[3c]**, as in Nepali ***sunaa-i diyo*** 'let hear' (cf. Hindi ***sunaa-Ø diyaa***), ***khaa-i sakyo*** 'could eat' (cf. Hindi ***khaa-Ø sakaa***), or in Awadhi or in Northern Bhojpuri (Gorakhpur and Eastern U.P.) ***sut-i gail*** 'fell asleep' (cf. Hindi ***so-Ø gayaa***). As such, I do not see any essential structural difference between the three types usually sought to be distinguished, because they all fall together in the same complex predicate schema. They all involve a V_2 which is in the nature of a 'light' verb.

[3] a. *sunaa-i diyo* (cf. Hindi *sunaa-Ø diyaa*),
hear give
let hear

b. *khaa-i sakyo* (cf. Hindi *khaa-Ø sakaa*),
eat was able to
could eat

c. *sut-i gail* (cf. Hindi *so-Ø gayaa*)
sleep went
fell asleep

What is a 'light verb'? Let's say that a 'light verb' is a verb with lower calories, thematically speaking. (Maybe, the class should be renamed 'lite' verbs!) In that sense, then the passives -- both the *jaa*-passive and the *ho*-passive -- can be seen as employing light verbs, passive auxiliaries ***jaa***- and ***ho***-, to express the modality of 'transition to a state' and 'being in a state', respectively. The end result in both cases is a complex verb of the second type referred to above, namely, the type in which the V_1 appears in a frozen inflected form followed by V_2 (**V**-***aa jaa*** and **V**-***aa ho***) as in **[2a]** and **[2b]** given above.

After having briefly touched upon the various subtypes of what I would like to characterize as 'compound' verbs more generally, I would now like to turn to those complex predicates which are popularly called 'conjunct' verbs. This, as most of us agree, has two subcategories, namely, the Adjective+Verb and the Noun+Verb constructions. I intend to discuss certain aspects of the latter in some detail because that is the one that presents various kinds of analytical problems. Again, without going into any details, I will simply observe that the Adjective+Verb type as in ***saaf karnaa*** 'to clean (something)', ***saaf honaa*** 'to be clean' seems to be amenable to the complex predicates characterization a little more easily than does the Noun+Verb type. One characteristic it shares with the other complex predicate types listed above is that all of them could be considered to be LEXICAL in nature, their complex predicate derivation accomplished in the Lexicon.

Let's look at some of the obvious facts. In the Adjective+Verb type, the verb selection is rather straightforward, just ***karnaa*** 'do' for the transitive complex predicate and ***honaa*** 'be / become' for the intransitive complex predicate. The verb according to its valency then specifies the argument structure. It is very tempting to consider this simply a case of a grammaticalizing process for obtaining these verbal forms and treat these verbs essentially as affixal in nature. This would also lend support to the general feeling of such complex predicates as being lexical in nature, resulting from a process of 'lexical affixation' as opposed to 'syntactic affixation' à la Mark Baker 1985.[3] But, one may ask, what motivates such a temptation? Looking at the subcategorization frames of these two verbs, we find that ***honaa*** is a monadic verb whereas ***karnaa*** is a diadic verb with two arguments, one internal and the other external, the latter of which turns up as the subject. In a sentence like **[4]**

[4] ***mãĩ ne kamraa saaf kiyaa***
I-Nom room clean did
I cleaned the room

the lexical head ***karnaa*** 'do' (with the perfective tense in ***kiyaa***) has two theta-roles to assign, one AGENT and the other THEME. This 'lexical function'[4] is appropriately 'saturated' by the two arguments ***mãĩ*** and ***kamraa***. But, then, ***saaf*** is a left-over elemment. Where does it go? This certainly leads to a structural temptation to associate it with the verb in some way. The best way to accomplish this is to consider it a part of the verbal complex at the lexical level.

Incidentally, the standard way of looking at 'saturation' has been slightly different, though. The projection principle requires that the complements of heads (e.g. objects) must be represented at each syntactic level. This thus says nothing about subjects. The extended projection principle of Chomsky 1981 requires the external argument as the subject of predication. These two things can be combined in the 'saturation principle' of Rothstein 1983, which says that the lexical head can be regarded as a 'lexical function' which will be saturated by arguments fulfilling the theta-roles assigned by the lexical head (in its complement structure). Similarly, a non-NP or a non-clause maximal XP, that is, a predicate, could be regarded as a 'syntactic function' which will be appropriately saturated by a subject of which it is predicated.

Another way of looking at this structure, therefore, could be the following: ***saaf*** as an adjective is a 'predicate'. Following Rothstein (1983), a predicate is any XP which is not assigned a theta-role at D-structure. Such a structure then must be linked to an argument at S-structure (through mutual immediate c-commanding), i.e., it must have a subject. An adjective like ***saaf*** does not have an internal argument but may have an external argument. In that case in the sequence ***kamraa saaf kiyaa***, ***kamraa saaf*** is a 'small clause' in which ***kamraa*** is the subject of ***saaf***. It is to be noted that in such a construction, then, the position occupied by ***kamraa*** receives a theta-role by predication rather than as a complement of a head, since the structure would be as in **[5]**:

[5] ***mãĩ ne*** [$_s$ ***kamraa saaf***] ***kiyaa***
I-Nom room clean did
I cleaned the room

In this, then, the verb ***karnaa*** s-selects a proposition. The NP ***kamraa*** 'room', then, is not the object of the verb ***karnaa*** 'to do'. It is not s-selected by ***karnaa***. It ends up getting the accusative case, however. We have two options then. We could simply say that it is a case of exceptional case marking, or recognize the fact that in certain interesting respects, ***kamraa*** in this construction behaves like a main clause object. This latter tack might be accommodated by assuming that the main verb ***karnaa*** s-selects the proposition and that the main verb ***karnaa*** 'to do' and the predicate of the small clause, namely, ***saaf*** 'clean', jointly s-select the NP ***kamraa*** as the object with the theta role of THEME. In either of these solutions, then, the status of this Adjective+Verb complex is syntactic, the latter, of course, being a case of 'syntactic affixation'.

The case of Adjective+Verb as in ***saaf honaa*** 'to be(come) clean', then, is simply a monadic version of the above picture, with just one less argument to deal with. The only interesting thing to add there would be to say that the inchoative verb ***honaa*** 'to become', in addition to being monadic, is also 'unaccusative' in this construction, which triggers the (direct object) THEME argument of a (rather abstract) subjectless structure to move to a subject position to get case.

The complex predicates involving the Noun+Verb sequence create more headaches, for a number of reasons. First of all, in Hindi or Urdu, unlike a language like English, there aren't many pairs of simple predicates and complex predicates to establish a paraphrase relationship and trigger the quest for such an analytical relationship. The few that one can readily think of are as given in **[6]**:

[6]	***saraahnaa***	:	***saraahnaa karnaa***	'to praise'
	puuchnaa	:	***praśn karnaa***[5]	'to ask'
	dhamkaanaa	:	***dhamkii denaa***	'to threaten'
	bakhaannaa	:	***bakhaan karnaa***	'to eulogize'
	swiikaarnaa	:	***swiikaar karnaa***	'to accept'

or the special Urdu usage

filmaanaa	:	***film banaanaa***	'to film'

or the slightly substandard

gussaanaa	:	***gussaa karnaa***	'to anger'

Therefore, it really becomes very difficult to decide which of the hundreds of Noun+Verb sequences could be considered simply SEQUENCES and which ones could be considered COMPLEXES. In fact, it was because of the absence of such simplex verbs in Hindi as translatable counterparts of the simplex verbs in English that led to the whole approach of positing a special category of 'conjunct verbs' by western scholars. Maybe, we could use the English translation as a test -- shall we say, as a minor sacrifice in the cause of linguistic universals as determined by English? In that case, it would, of course, be very comfortable to think of the verb as a grammaticalizing device for the morphological derivation of a verb from a noun. In that case, then, it will be a case of lexical affixation (as opposed to syntactic affixation) accomplished within the Lexicon and syntactically unanalyzable. The light verb ***karnaa*** 'to do' seems to be the grammaticalizing affix par excellence for such a derivation. However, the situation becomes exacerbated because of the fact that ***karnaa*** is but one of the many others which are selected by the noun. Two of them can readily be seen in the examples above: ***denaa*** 'to give' with ***dhamkii*** 'threat', and ***banaanaa*** 'to make' with ***film***. There are, of course, many more such examples. In that sense, the Adjective+Verb sequence, on the contrary, provides a more unified situation and so is more comfortably amenable to the complex verb analysis.

Before proceeding any further, I want to state my overall personal bias as a point of departure here, and then proceed to examine the various analytical options. I do believe that the Noun+Verb sequences of the type under consideration here represent three different constructions regardless of how they translate into English: (1) one which is a purely analytical sequence syntactically in which the verb is just the main verb of the clause which both selects and case marks its own arguments. That I will call Type I as seen in **[7a]**; (2) another in which the verb case marks the Noun of Noun+Verb, but it is the Noun that also assigns theta-roles and selects arguments. That I will call Type II (syntactically complex) as in **[7b]**; and finally, (3) the one in which a verb like ***karnaa*** affixes directly to the Noun, which is then fully amalgamated with the verb. That will be Type III (lexically complex) as in **[7c]**.

[7]	a.	***kaam karnaa***	'to work'	(Type I)
	b.	***madad karnaa***	'to help'	(TypeII)
	c.	***praNaam karnaa***	'to greet respectfully'	(Type III)

If what I presume here is right, then Type I is no longer relevant to the present discussion. I will, then, argue that Type II presents a case of syntactic affixation, and Type III presents a case of lexical affixation. That is, both Type II and Type III are cases of complex predicates, but of diffferent kinds. They should hopefully involve different structural behaviors (case markings, the argument vs. the nonargument status of the NP's, the possibility of the transitive-intransitive alternation, etc.). I also note in passing that the last one, namely, Type III, would then be more like the relatively amalgamated complex predicates involving adjectives, as discussed above, which are internally complex but externally unitary.

I also believe that it is the last one, namely, Type III, that is more productive in the creative use of the language (amenable to expressive lexical innovations), and probably also easier to identify as a complex predicate intuitively. Among other things, most often, though not always, the case marking is such that the PATIENT or the GOAL of the main clause has a clearcut accusative-dative[6] marking in the postposition ***-ko***, making it easier to identify it as an argument of the total verbal complex, as can be seen in **[8b]** as contrasted with **[8a]**:

[8] **a.** ***mãĩ ne rameś kii madad kii***
I-Nom Ramesh-Gen help did
I helped Ramesh

b. ***mãĩ ne rameś ko praNaam kiyaa***
I-Nom Ramesh-Acc-Dat greeting did
I greeted Ramesh (respectfully)

In terms of productivity, one can also see unusual but creative uses of this mechanism, as in Ghalib's:[7]

[9] ***muddat huii hai yaar ko mehmãã kiye hue***
long time happened lover-Acc guest did
It has been a long time since I 'guested' my lover

Another interesting example of such a creative use of this grammatical device stems from the very early days of the post-independence Congress Party rule. At that time, it became great fun to level all kinds of allegations of political nepotism, such as the following:

[10] ***jagjiivan se kar ke mãĩ puurii sifaariś***
By strongly recommending (an undeserving candidate) to Jagjivan (a political leader)

gadahe ko ghoRaa kiye jaa rahaa hũũ
an ass-Acc horse do Progressive Tense
I am 'horsing' an ass (transforming an ass into a horse)

There is no standard lexical entry such as ***ghoRaa karnaa*** 'to transform into a horse' in a dictionary. Such complex verb constructions almost have the status of idioms or semi-idioms. This observation very neatly ties in with the subject-object asymmetry in natural languages. Idioms generally involve verbs and their internal argumnents and hardly ever the subject.

The closer the relationship, the more idiomatic the expression, which is what we find in the case of truly lexicalized complex predicates in Hindi. Though it will be generally true of both Type II and Type III of N+V complex predicates that I have tried to identify in this article, it is more true in respect of Type III that even though a relationship of object and verb can be perceived in these N+V sequences, there is no possibility of assigning a case marker even optionally, as seen in **[11a]** and **[11b]**:

[11] **a.** *dhyaan karnaa*
mental attention do
to meditate / contemplate

**dhyaan* <u>*ko*</u> *karnaa*
Acc

b. *laRkii dekhnaa*
girl see
bride hunting

**laRkii* <u>*ko*</u> *dekhnaa*
Acc

Part of the reason is that an idiomatic object is an object that does not bear a conventional thematic role but has a specialized dependency on its governor. There will, thus, be no postposition in the language that can assign that kind of thematic role.

While it seems clear that complex predicates of this type are a result of lexical incorporation, such as given in the diagram below, it is not so clear as to how exactly it will be triggered, or entered in the Lexicon. At any rate, the end result will be as in **[12]**:

[12]

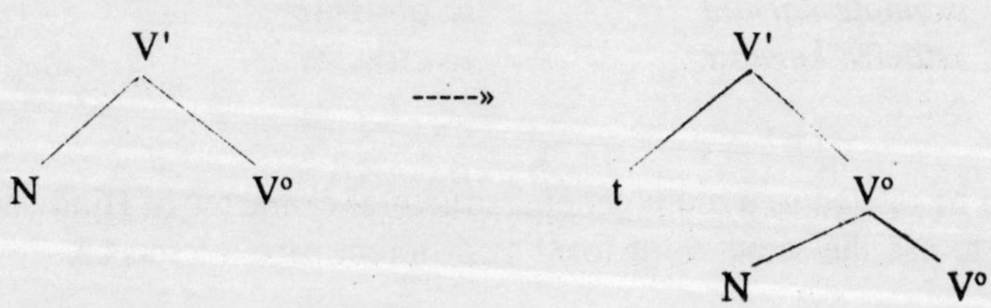

Perhaps this can be done by means of lexical redundancy rules, which are triggered by lexical features attached to nominals, which specify the light verbs with which they may combine. Some other examples of this kind would be as in **[13]**:

[13] *dhataa bataanaa* 'to tell off'
saamnaa karnaa 'to confront'
piichaa karnaa 'to chase'

The question of case marking will be taken up later. Suffice it to say here that even though in a sentence like

[14] ***mãĩ ne cor kaa piichaa kiyaa***
I-Nom thief-Gen back side did
I chased the thief

cor kaa piichaa ('the thief's back side'?) looks like an NP unit, separate from and as a whole an argument of the verb ***karnaa*** 'do', I have difficulty identifying or visualizing an NP entity like the ***piichaa*** of a ***cor***. Besides, in some cases, the postpositions could also alternate, as in **[15]**:

[15] a. *mãĩ ne us-ko qatl kiyaa*
I-Nom him-Acc murder did
I killed him

b. ***mãĩ ne us-kaa qatl kiyaa***
I-Nom him-Gen murder did
I killed him

The fact that the language uses this as a very productive lexical device of verbal derivation is, of course, amply demonstrated in the use of loan words, whereby it is generally a noun that is borrowed, or simply that the borrowed word regardless of its status in the original language is treated as a noun, and then treated as a verb through such a derivation. Some examples are in **[16]**:

[16]	*telephone karnaa*	'to telephone'
	love karnaa	'to love'
	join karnaa	'to join'
	promote karnaa	'to promote'
	criticize karnaa	'to criticize'
	etc.	

This may also be related to a more general structural character of Hindi, which, unlike English, does not like to use the same word form as different parts of speech.

Now, taking up the more knotty type of complex predicates, namely, Type II, let's quickly take note of some salient facts and then see what kind of analytical explanation is possible.

(A) As regards the nominals involved in this contruction, it turns out that it is not just any nominal that can be a candidate for this. Deverbals would be ideal, and Hindi does have some of them which neatly provide the kind of simplex and complex alternations in paraphrase relationship that could be helpful. But they are not numerous. Some examples are, as in **[17]**:

[17] *paRhnaa* : *paRhaaii karnaa*
to study — to do studying

caRhnaa : *caRhaaii karnaa*
to climb — to do climbing, to mount (an attack)

But if we look at the others, such as the ones in **[18]**

[18] ***madad karnaa***
help do
to help, to render help

intizaar karnaa
awaiting do
to await

pyaar karnaa
love do
to love

it seems that the nouns that occur here are at least abstract type nouns. Even intuitively we can see that of the two N+V sequences given below in **[19]** only the first one has any chance of being considered a complex predicate:

[19] **a.** ***aaśwaasan diyaa***
assurance gave
assured

b. ***xat diyaa***
letter gave
gave a letter

(B) The Noun in such a construction assumes the role of a predicate, that is, the functional equivalent of a verb. Of course, the Noun has to be of a type which is capable of assuming this role, as can be deduced from the contrast in the examples above, and of having an argument structure. A lexical item like ***pramaaN*** 'proof' in any morphological form will take an S-complement, regardless of the argument structure of the 'light verb', as seen in **[20]**:

[20] **a.** ***is baat kaa <u>pramaaN</u> <u>miltaa</u> hai ki*** [$_S$ ...
this matter-Gen <u>proof</u> <u>found</u> is that [$_S$ ...
The proof is available to the effect that [$_S$ ...

b. *is baat ko* ***pramaaNit*** ***kartaa*** *hai ki* [$_S$ ...
this matter-Acc prove-Pcpl do is that [$_S$ ...
This proves that [$_S$ ...

c. *yah baat* ***pramaaNit*** ***hoti*** *hai ki* [$_S$ ...
this matter prove-Pcpl be is that [$_S$ ...
It is proved that [$_S$ ...

(C) Even though the Noun in construction with a diadic verb like ***karnaa*** 'do', or any other non-monadic verb, looks like an honest-to-goodness argument of the verb as an object with the possible theta-role of THEME, it resists all attempts at case marking, even optionally, as exemplified above in **[11]**.

(D) As can also be seen in Examples **[18]** and **[19]**, it is the noun in this Noun+Verb construction that seems to select the light verb. This may have to be marked in the Lexicon. Presumably, some principle of congruence in the thematic structures of this 'nominal predicate' and the light verb is involved in this selection. For example, if the noun is of the type which has a theta-role like GOAL to assign, as in ***aaśwaasan*** 'assurance', then choosing a light verb like ***denaa*** 'give' will avoid incongruity and preserve the theta-roles as far as possible.

(E) Ideally, a light verb should really be 'light', that is, it should be a verb with no thematic calories. It should be there just to be a 'host' verb, and, maybe, just assign cases and carry inflection. Maybe, there are languages like that, but Hindi does not seem to be one of them. (Shall we say, Hindi cannot stand the "unbearable lightness of verbs"?) For Hindi, the light verb also theta-marks the arguments -- some of them, not all of them. It is a 'demoted' verb but not totally vacuous. As a matter of fact, this is what makes me think of them as modals. In other words, they are not the main predicates, this function having been taken over by the nominals. This is in consonance with what I have suggested above for the entire class of various complex predicate types. Certain verbs are more readily available than others as host verbs, such as, DO, HAPPEN, GIVE, HAVE, etc.

Once we have somehow identified an N+V type complex predicate, the important questions that arise are:

1. What is the motivation or the triggering mechanism for this amalgamation or incorporation?

2. Which of the two elements determine the argument structure and the theta-assignment, and if both do, then how is this task shared between them?

3. What arguments form constituents, if they do so at all? In other words, what are their D-structure and S-structure?

4. How is case marking determined?

What is presented below is in the nature of relevant considerations rather than a definitive proposal.

As regards theta-roles and arguments, the general picture seems to be something like this. There seems to be no doubt that the 'nominal predicate' has theta-roles to assign. For example, a nominal like ***madad*** 'help' will have the theta-roles GOAL and AGENT, a nominal like ***śikaayat*** 'complaint' will have the theta-roles PATIENT, PROPOSITION, and AGENT, and a nominal like ***intizaar*** 'awaiting' may have the theta-roles THEME, AGENT, etc. But the problem is that a nominal has no internal arguments of its own to assign them to. So it needs to team up with the verb.

Also, a noun in itself is not a case marker. So it cannot assign case to any internal arguments it might possibly have. So those internal arguments, even if present, are not 'visible' for theta-role assignment since they cannot be case-marked (à la Aoun 1985 and Chomsky 1986).[8] Combining with the verb will allow such arguments to be case marked and then to be theta-assigned.

Let's take a convenient example which has both the simplex and the complex versions, as in **[21]** to see how these considerations might apply.

[21] **a.** ***raam śyaam ko saraahtaa hai***
Ram Shyam-Acc commends
Ram commends Shyam

b. ***raam śyaam kii saraahnaa kartaa hai***
Ram Shyam-Gen commendation does
Ram commends Shyam

The first one is straight-forward, with two arguments for the verb ***saraahnaa*** 'to commend', one internal (***śyaam***) as the object and the other external (***raam***) as the subject. But in the second sentence, while the deverbal predicate ***saraahnaa*** could still be interpreted to have two theta-roles to assign, namely, PATIENT and AGENT, the Agent ***raam*** is now the subject of ***karnaa*** and an argument outside the deverbal NP headed by ***saraahnaa***. What about ***śyaam***? That looks like part of and within the NP headed by ***saraahnaa***. There is a problem, though; normally the head of a phrase theta-marks only its complements. In that case, ***saraahnaa*** could perhaps theta-mark ***śyaam*** somehow, but could not theta-mark ***raam***. At any rate, the phrase ***śyaam kii saraahnaa*** 'Shyam's commendation' looks like a composite single argument NP of the verb ***karnaa***, but this may be misleading. The fact that the NP-Genitive within the NP can be moved around -- a subpart of the NP moved around -- is probably evidence to the effect that they are two separate arguments.[9]

Let's take some other similar examples. Those in **[22]** present parallel sentences involving complex predicates, but one has a noun and the other an infinitival as part of an apparent composite noun phrase:

[22] a. ***mãĩ ne raam kii madad kii***
I-Nom Ram-Gen help (N) did
I helped Ram

b. ***mãĩ ne jaane kii aagyaa dii***
I-Nom to go-Gen permission gave
I allowed (someone) to go

Again, it is tempting to consider *jaane kii aagyaa* 'lit., going's permission, permission to go' as a composite NP argument in the clause because of the genitive postposition on the first nominal -- a canonical form of an NP. This is problematic and I may not have satisfactory solutions. But I will present various points for consideration. The genitive postposition may be misleading for various reasons. The genitive is an all purpose postposition in many languages (Remember Panini's **sasthi śese** 'the sixth case (the genitive) for the remaining', which is the grammatical counterpart of the American football expression: "When in doubt punt"). Hindi particularly is very fond of this postposition. Whereas in its noun phrases, English can use any of the various prepositions, as in **[23]**,

[23] a. the man <u>from</u> New York
b. the book <u>on</u> the table

Hindi has to use the genitive *-kaa* (or, maybe, an adjectivizer like *waalaa*), as seen in **[24]**.

[24] a. *nyu York <u>kaa</u> aadmii*
New York-<u>Gen</u> man
the man from New York

b. *mez par <u>kaa</u> phuuldaan*
table on <u>Gen</u> flower vase
the flower vase on the table

In sentence **[25]**

[25] *mãĩ ne jaane kii aagyaa dii*
I-Nom to go-Gen permission gave
I allowed (someone) to go

jaanaa 'to go' is a proposition, a complement of *aagyaa* 'permission', in which case a separate argument. The head *aagyaa* ought to assign a case to it as one of its internal arguments, whereby it can get a theta-role. Since the noun itself cannot assign case, the genitive *-kaa* seems to be the dummy postposition just for the purpose of assigning case. This is very much like what happens in English itself where in phrases such as those in **[26]**:

[26] **a.** destruction of the city
b. proud of John

the complements of nouns and adjectives have to take a dummy preposition.

-kaa is really a funny postposition in Hindi. As a complement in the sentences of **[27]**, *jaanaa* 'to go' occurs in two ways, one without a postposition, the other with the postposition *-kaa*. **[27c]** is unacceptable.

[27] **a.** *mãĩ jaanaa caahtaa hũũ*
I to go want
I want to go

b. *mãĩ jaane kii soctaa hũũ*
I to go-Gen think
I want to go

c. **mãĩ jaanaa soctaa hũũ*

Since in both cases, *jaanaa* is an infinitival complement in the theta-role THEME, the latter is an example of how an argument of a verb may be unusually marked. This simply means that an idiosyncratic feature like this will have to be indicated as necessary lexical entries for verbs. Probably the same will apply to all those nouns which have the potential of occuring in predicate function. On the other hand, semantic roles do get encoded via prepositions or postpositions and may not come directly from the head noun, as seen in **[28]** with some examples from Baker 1985.[10]

[28]	**a.**	destroy the city	:	destruction of the city
	b.	command the troops	:	command to the troops
	c.	fled the city	:	flight from the city

Similarly, in the Hindi sentences in **[29]**

[29] **a.** *raam ne siitaa se śaadii kii*
Ram-Nom Sita-Instr marriage did[11]
Ram married Sita

b. *raam ne siitaa kii śaadii kii*
Ram-Nom Sita-Gen marriage did
Ram married Sita off

siitaa has to be analyzed as having parallel functions as a complement in both sentences, but with different thematic roles (of GOAL? and THEME?). That is to say, *siitaa* is a separate argument in both cases and not simply part of a composite NP argument in **[29b]** just because it is in the genitive and superficially a part of a viable looking NP. At any rate, it is clear that ***siitaa kii*** is a separate independent argument on its own just as, very clearly, ***siitaa se*** is an independent argument with which it contrasts. In that case, then, ***kii*** here does not have to be treated as a dummy postposition.

Finally, since an N+V sequence might well be treated as separate elements in a clause, one may ask, what motivates the need to treat them as complex predicates in some cases. Two lines of argumentation suggest themselves to me as briefly outlined below. If in a sentence like **[30]**

[30] ***mãĩ ne raam kii madad kii***
I-Nom Ram-Gen help (N) did
I helped Ram

only ***kii*** 'did' is to be treated as the main verb, then the entire phrase ***raam kii madad*** needs to be treated as a small clause with two arguments in which the theta-role of the first NP ***raam*** is being determined by the second NP ***madad*** 'help', and it is the entire small clause that is the complement of the verb 'do'. In that case, then, ***madad*** alone is not available for theta marking by the verb and cannot be its ARGUMENT. If it is a PREDICATE, then it remains unsaturated, not provided with appropriate arguments fulfilling the theta roles it assigns, namely, AGENT and PATIENT (Agent as external for VP, not for NP).[12] The dilemma is that the NP is both an argument (at D-structure) and also a predicate (at S-structure). The solution lies in making it a predicate at S-structure through syntactic incorporation.

Another way to look at this could be as follows. A verb like ***denaa*** 'give' is subcategorized only for THREE arguments, as seen in **[31a]**:

[31]	**a.**	***mãĩ ne***	***raam ko***	***paise***	***diye***	
		I-Nom	Ram-Dat	money-Acc	gave	
		Agent	Goal	Theme		
		I gave Ram some money				
	b.	***mãĩ ne***	***raam ko***	***jaane kii***	***aagyaa***	***dii***
		I-Nom	Ram-Dat	to go-Gen	permission	gave
		Agent	Goal	Theme??	Theme	
		I permitted Ram to go				

but in **[31b]** the theta-frame of ***denaa*** 'give' is saturated and still ***jaane kii*** (which we have already argued for and established as a separate argument) is left over. It looks like THEME but then there will be two Themes. Even sentences with an intransitive verb like ***honaa*** 'be' can bring up this problem: ***honaa*** is supposed to have only two arguments, POSSESSOR and THEME, in the sentence in **[32]:**

[32] *raam ko siitaa se pyaar hai*
Ram-Dat Sita-Instr love is[13]
Poss ?Goal Theme
Ram loves Sita

So it cannot theta-mark *siitaa se*. The same situation obtains in **[33]**:

[33] *raam kii siitaa se śaadii huii*
Ram-Gen Sita-Instr marriage happened[14]
?Patient ?Goal Theme
Ram got married to Sita

It may be noted that *siitaa se śaadii* 'marriage with Sita' in **[33]** does not even represent a canonical form for a composite NP in Hindi.[15] It seems that the various problems described above can be alleviated at S-structure through syntactic incorporation, which may be considered the structural motivation for the treatment of some N+V sequences as complex predicates. The tree structures in that case would look like the ones given in **[34]**:

[34] a. D-structure:

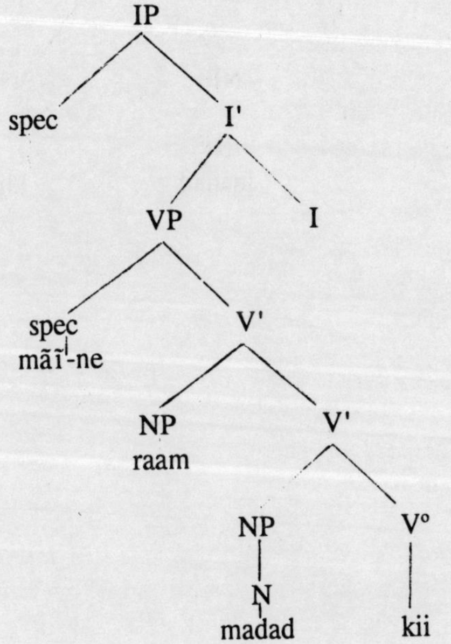

[34] b. S-structure:

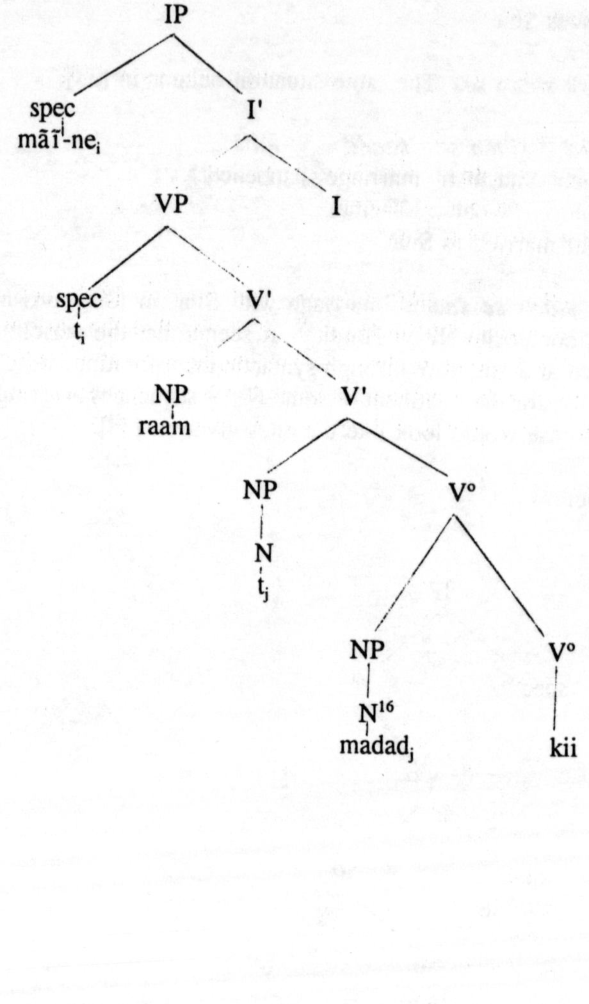

NOTES

1. I have benefited from the suggestions and comments on an earlier draft by my colleagues Kyle Johnson and Peter Schreiber. It is needless to state that the responsibility for any omissions and errors rests entirely on my head.

2. Verma 1980.

3. See Mark Baker 1985 for a discussion of this distinction.

4. See Chomsky 1986:116.

5. The complex prediacte of ***puuchnaa*** has only the Sanskritized ***praśna karnaa***. The stem itself may occur in the more idiomatic longer version ***puuch-taach karnaa***.

6. The postposition *-ko* in Hindi marks both the accusative (with definite NP's) and the dative.

7. Ghalib was an extremely prolific and the best known 19th. century literary figure in Urdu.

8. See Aoun 1985:55 for a discussion of 'Visibility Convention' and Chomsky 1986:94 for the inter-relationship of visibility, theta-marking, and case.

9. There have been various proposals in the literature about how to assign genitive case. Interestingly, however, this is one case which is conveniently put aside in all introductory discussions of case-marking in English NP's. It is a nice paradox since this is one overt case marking for non-pronominal NP's in English. See Comsky 1981 and Stowell 1980 for some thinking in this regard.

10. It is to be noted that the direct object or the accusative case may represent various theta-roles. See Baker 1985:4-5 for some discussion in this regard.

11. The Hindi postposition *-se* is a versatile postposition used to encode a variety of roles. The particular role here is one of 'reciprocity' (or 'accompaniment' in a stretched sense) as in an English sentence like *I conversed WITH him.* Since there is no standard designation for such a case, I have used 'Instrumental' in the morphological gloss in the sentence, which is one of the other uses of this postposition.

12. See Chomsky 1986:116 for supporting discussion.

13. See Note 11. Here again the postposition *-se* is more like a postposition of reciprocity than a postposition denoting instrumental case.

14. See Notes 11 and 14.

15. As has already been discussed above, the canonical form of the NP in Hindi is N-Gen-N. Unlike English, it does not allow postpositions denoting other cases.

16. The lowering of the N may look suspicious as it leaves the trace outside of the c-command domain of the moved N. However, if the verbal complex moves to I eventually then the resulting structure would be one where the incorporated noun does c-command its trace.

REFERENCES

Aoun, Joseph. 1985. A grammar of anaphora. Cambridge: MIT Press.

Baker, Mark. 1985. Syntactic affixation and English gerunds. Proceedings of the West Coast Conference on Formal Linguistics, ed. by Jeffrey Goldberg, et al., 4.1-11. Stanford: The Stanford Linguistics Association.

Chomsky, N. 1981. Lectures on government and binding. Dordrecht: Foris Publications.

Chomsky, N. 1986. Knowledge of language. New York: Praeger Publishers.

Jayaseelan, K. A. 1988. Complex predicates and θ-theory. Syntax and Semantics, Volume 21: Thematic Relations, 91-111.

Rothstein, S. 1983. The syntactic form of predication. Cambridge: MIT Ph.D. dissertation.

Stowell, T. 1980. Origins of phrase structure. Cambridge: MIT Ph.D. dissertation.

Verma, Manindra K. 1980. Typological aspects of the stative in some Indic languages. Revue Roumaine de Linguistique 24.2.185-193, Romania.

